Cathleen Kantner has offered a remarkably conceptually rich and empirically rigorous examination of sense and identity making in humanitarian interventions in the post-Cold War world. This book is a major contribution to the international relations constructivist corpus. Yet beyond this important contribution, Kantner's book should be read by political communication scholars who are interested in war, media, and global affairs.

    Steven Livingston, *The George Washington University, USA*

Conventional wisdom has it that Europe does not constitute a community of communication with regard to wars and humanitarian interventions. Yet, Cathleen Kantner demonstrates that transnational European public spheres exist even with regard to war and peace. The book is based on the largest database on transnational communication so far and employs new methodological tools such as corpus-linguistic quantitative content analysis. A must-read for anybody interested in transnational communication!

    Thomas Risse, *Freie Universität Berlin, Germany*

An excellent addition to comparative political communication. Kantner contributes significant theoretical concepts, methodological innovations and empirical evidence on debates in Europe and the U.S. on war and humanitarian intervention. The provocative analysis of "transnational political communication" and "European identity-formation," is very useful for any future research in these areas.

    Eytan Gilboa, *Bar-Ilan University, Israel*

War and Intervention in the Transnational Public Sphere

The post-Cold War era saw an unexpected increase in intra-state violence against ethnic and religious groups, brutal civil wars and asymmetric conflicts. Those crises posed fundamental questions for the European Union and its member states, to which Europe has so far proved unable to develop satisfactory answers.

This book contends that public debates over wars and humanitarian military interventions after the Cold War represent an evolving process of comprehension and collective interpretation of new realities. Employing innovative computer-linguistic methods, it examines the dynamics of this debate across Europe and compares it with that of the United States. In doing so, it argues that transnational political communication has shaped European identity-formation in significant ways and that, in trying to come to terms with important crises and institutional events, shared understandings of Europe have emerged. Looking at evidence from a wide range of countries, including Austria, France, Germany, Ireland, the Netherlands and the United Kingdom, and spanning a continuous period of 16 years, this book empirically analyses these shared understandings of the EU as a problem-solving and ethical community.

This book will be of interest to students and scholars of international relations, EU politics, security studies, comparative politics, political communication and European integration.

Cathleen Kantner is Professor of International Relations and European Studies at the Institute of Social Sciences of Stuttgart University, Germany.

Routledge/UACES Contemporary European Studies
Edited by Federica Bicchi, London School of Economics and Political Science, Tanja Börzel, Free University of Berlin, and Mark Pollack, Temple University, on behalf of the University Association for Contemporary European Studies

Editorial Board: Grainne De Búrca, European University Institute and Columbia University; Andreas Føllesdal, Norwegian Centre for Human Rights, University of Oslo; Peter Holmes, University of Sussex; Liesbet Hooghe, University of North Carolina at Chapel Hill, and Vrije Universiteit Amsterdam; David Phinnemore, Queen's University Belfast; Ben Rosamond, University of Warwick; Vivien Ann Schmidt, University of Boston; Jo Shaw, University of Edinburgh; Mike Smith, University of Loughborough and Loukas Tsoukalis, ELIAMEP, University of Athens and European University Institute.

The primary objective of the new Contemporary European Studies series is to provide a research outlet for scholars of European Studies from all disciplines. The series publishes important scholarly works and aims to forge for itself an international reputation.

1. The EU and Conflict Resolution
Promoting peace in the backyard
Nathalie Tocci

2. Central Banking Governance in the European Union
A comparative analysis
Lucia Quaglia

3. New Security Issues in Northern Europe
The Nordic and Baltic states and the ESDP
Edited by Clive Archer

4. The European Union and International Development
The politics of foreign aid
Maurizio Carbone

5. The End of European Integration
Anti-Europeanism examined
Paul Taylor

6. The European Union and the Asia-Pacific
Media, public and elite perceptions of the EU
Edited by Natalia Chaban and Martin Holland

7. **The History of the European Union**
Origins of a trans- and supranational polity 1950–72
Edited by Wolfram Kaiser, Brigitte Leucht and Morten Rasmussen

8. **International Actors, Democratization and the Rule of Law**
Anchoring democracy?
Edited by Amichai Magen and Leonardo Morlino

9. **Minority Nationalist Parties and European Integration**
A comparative study
Anwen Elias

10. **European Union Intergovernmental Conferences**
Domestic preference formation, transgovernmental networks and the dynamics of compromise
Paul W. Thurner and Franz Urban Pappi

11. **The Political Economy of State-Business Relations in Europe**
Interest mediation, capitalism and EU policy making
Rainer Eising

12. **Governing Financial Services in the European Union**
Banking, securities and post-trading
Lucia Quaglia

13. **European Union Governance**
Efficiency and legitimacy in European commission committees
Karen Heard-Lauréote

14. **European Governmentality**
The liberal drift of multilevel governance
Richard Münch

15. **The European Union as a Leader in International Climate Change Politics**
Edited by Rüdiger K. W. Wurzel and James Connelly

16. **Diversity in Europe**
Dilemmas of differential treatment in theory and practice
Edited by Gideon Calder and Emanuela Ceva

17. **EU Conflict Prevention and Crisis Management**
Roles, institutions and policies
Edited by Eva Gross and Ana E. Juncos

18. **The European Parliament's Committees**
National party influence and legislative empowerment
Richard Whitaker

19. **The European Union, Civil Society and Conflict**
Nathalie Tocci

20. **European Foreign Policy and the Challenges of Balkan Accession**
Sovereignty contested
Gergana Noutcheva

21. **The European Union and South East Europe**
The Dynamics of Europeanization and Multilevel Governance
Andrew Taylor, Andrew Geddes and Charles Lees

22. Bureaucrats as Law-Makers
Committee decision-making in the
EU Council of Ministers
Frank M. Häge

**23. Europeanization and the
European Economic Area**
Iceland's participation in the EU's
policy process
Johanna Jonsdottir

24. The Cultural Politics of Europe
European capitals of culture and the
European Union since 1980
Kiran Klaus Patel

**25. European Integration and
Transformation in the
Western Balkans**
Europeanization or business
as usual?
Arolda Elbasani

**26. European Union
Constitutionalism in Crisis**
Nicole Scicluna

**27. Transnationalization and
Regulatory Change in the EU's
Eastern Neighbourhood**
Julia Langbein

**28. Lobbying in EU Foreign
Policy-making**
The case of the
Israeli–Palestinian conflict
Benedetta Voltolini

**29. War and Intervention in the
Transnational Public Sphere**
Problem-solving and European
identity-formation
Cathleen Kantner

**30. The European Union's Foreign
Policy in Comparative Perspective**
Evaluating and generating
hypotheses on 'actorness and power'
Edited by Ingo Peters

**31. The Formulation of EU
Foreign Policy**
Socialization, negotiations and
disaggregation of the state
Nicola Chelotti

War and Intervention in the Transnational Public Sphere
Problem-solving and European identity-formation

Cathleen Kantner

LONDON AND NEW YORK

First published 2016
by Routledge
2 Park Square, Milton Park, Abingdon, Oxon OX14 4RN

and by Routledge
711 Third Avenue, New York, NY 10017

Routledge is an imprint of the Taylor & Francis Group, an informa business

© 2016 Cathleen Kantner

The right of Cathleen Kantner to be identified as author of this work has been asserted by her in accordance with sections 77 and 78 of the Copyright, Designs and Patents Act 1988.

All rights reserved. No part of this book may be reprinted or reproduced or utilised in any form or by any electronic, mechanical, or other means, now known or hereafter invented, including photocopying and recording, or in any information storage or retrieval system, without permission in writing from the publishers.

Trademark notice: Product or corporate names may be trademarks or registered trademarks, and are used only for identification and explanation without intent to infringe.

British Library Cataloguing in Publication Data
A catalogue record for this book is available from the British Library

Library of Congress Cataloging in Publication Data
A catalog record for this book has been requested

ISBN: 978-0-415-73814-9 (hbk)
ISBN: 978-1-315-66853-6 (ebk)

Typeset in Times New Roman
by Taylor & Francis Books

Contents

List of illustrations   x
List of abbreviations   xii
Acknowledgement   xiv

1 Introduction: Transnational political communication and European identity-formation   1

2 The theoretical building blocks: Transnational identity discourses on wars and humanitarian military interventions   9

3 Media and media analysis in Europe   50

4 Comparing debates on wars and humanitarian military interventions across nations   82

5 Reality and identities 'under construction'   146

Technical Appendix   158
References   164
Index   184

List of illustrations

Figures

2.1	Numerical and qualitative identification	26
2.2	Uses of the personal pronoun 'we'	29
3.1	Example of a WordSmith concordance	74
3.2	Time series to be compared (Jan. 1990–Mar. 2006, 195 months)	77
4.1	Issue cycles on 'wars and interventions' (absolute numbers)	84
4.2	σ-convergence of the issue-cycles coverage on 'wars and interventions'	98
4.3	Issue cycles on 'humanitarian military interventions' (absolute numbers)	102
4.4	σ-convergence of the issue-cycles on 'humanitarian military interventions'	109
4.5	Sequence chart of 'EU identity' in the overall sample (absolute numbers)	121
4.6	Sequence chart of 'EU identity' in the intervention sub-sample (absolute numbers)	122

Tables

3.1	Absolute frequencies of articles retrieved by the applied indicators	76
4.1	Descriptives of the issue-cycles on 'wars and interventions'	85
4.2	Bivariate correlations of the issue-cycles on 'wars and interventions' (Pearson's coefficients)	87
4.3	Bivariate correlations between coverage on 'wars and interventions' and aggregated event-data (Pearson's coefficients)	89
4.4	ARIMA models for 'wars and interventions'	96
4.5	Descriptives of the issue-cycles on 'humanitarian military interventions'	101
4.6	Bivariate correlations of the issue-cycles on 'humanitarian military interventions' (Pearson's coefficients)	103

List of illustrations xi

4.7	Bivariate correlations between the issue-cycles of 'humanitarian military interventions' and aggregated event-data (Pearson's coefficients)	105
4.8	ARIMA models for 'humanitarian military interventions'	108
4.9	Share of articles mentioning 'Europe' in the two samples	113
4.10	Share of articles mentioning 'EU institutions' in the two samples	116
4.11	Share of articles mentioning 'EU identity' in the two samples	118
4.12	Share of 'Europe' articles that mention 'EU identity' in the two samples (in %)	119
4.13	Descriptives of 'EU identity' in the overall sample	123
4.14	Descriptives of 'EU identity' in the intervention sub-sample	124
4.15	Bivariate correlations of 'EU identity' in the overall sample (Pearson's coefficients)	126
4.16	Bivariate correlations of 'EU identity' in the intervention sub-sample (Pearson's coefficients)	126
4.17	Bivariate correlations of 'EU identity' in the intervention sub-sample (Pearson's coefficients)	127
4.18	Bivariate correlations between 'EU identity' in the intervention sub-sample and aggregated event-data (Pearson's coefficients)	128
4.19	ARIMA models for 'EU identity' in the overall sample	131
4.20	ARIMA models for 'EU identity' in the intervention sub-sample	131
4.21	Share of articles that mention the EU as a *communio* or *commercium* (%)	135
4.22	Share of 'EU identity' articles that mention the EU as a *communio* and/or as a *commercium* in the overall sample (%)	137
4.23	Share of 'EU identity' articles that mention the EU as a *communio* and/or a *commercium* in the intervention sub-sample (%)	139
4.24	The EU as *commercium* and/or *communio* in relation to different crises	141
A.1	Sample characteristics	158
A.2	Overview for the results: 'wars and interventions', 'humanitarian military interventions', 'Europe'	160
A.3	Overview of the results: 'EU and its institutions', 'EU identity'	162

List of abbreviations

AU	Austria
ARIMA	autoregressive integrated moving-average
ASEAN	Association of Southeast Asian Nations
CFSP	Common Foreign and Security Policy
CSCE	Conference on Security and Cooperation in Europe
EC	European Community
ECSC	European Coal and Steel Community
ECOWAS	Economic Community of West African States
EDC	European Defence Community
EPC	European Political Cooperation
ESDI	European Security and Defence Identity
ESDP	European Security and Defence Policy
ESS	European Security Strategy
EU	European Union
FPÖ	Freiheitliche Partei Österreichs (Freedom Party of Austria)
FR	France
GER	Germany
ICFY	International Conference on the Former Yugoslavia
IR	Ireland
ISAF	International Security Assistance Force (NATO-led multinational force in Afghanistan)
KFOR	Kosovo Force (NATO-led multinational force in Kosovo)
MS	Member States
NATO	North Atlantic Treaty Organization
NL	The Netherlands
OSCE	Organization for Security and Cooperation in Europe
ÖVP	Österreichische Volkspartei (Austrian People's Party)
PRIO	Peace Research Institute Oslo
SFOR	Stabilisation Force (NATO-led multinational force in Bosnia and Herzegovina)
UCDP	Uppsala Conflict Data Project
UK	United Kingdom
UN	United Nations

UNMIK	United Nations Interim Administration Mission in Kosovo
UNSC	United Nations Security Council
US, USA	United States of America
USSR	Union of Soviet Socialist Republics
WEU	Western European Union

Acknowledgement

An extensive empirical study such as the one conducted for this book involves complex technical processes, data-searching, coding and analysis, often possible only through a wide division of labour among the members of a strong team. It also requires the generous comments of additional readers who are experts in the diverse disciplines addressed in the course of the investigation – each deserving of a lifetime's reading. As such, this book was possible only thanks to the substantial research grants received from a number of institutions. The data used here represent results of a unique, large-scale, comparative, quantitative–qualitative media content analysis carried out at Freie Universität Berlin and directed by myself and Thomas Risse. For the generous funding of this project, we are grateful to the German Research Foundation[1] and the European Commission's Sixth Framework Programme, within which our study was supported as part of RECON.[2] This funding allowed for the labour-intensive preparation of the text corpus, its qualitative–quantitative analysis, and the development of significant methodological innovations to render our ambitions technically possible. In working on this study, I have also been supported by a Marie Curie Fellowship of the European Commission,[3] which allowed me to concentrate on writing in crucial phases of the empirical and theoretical work. The finalisation of the book project was subsidised by a research grant by the Bundesministerium für Bildung und Forschung within the framework of the eHumanities initiative for the 2012–15 period.[4]

This study could not have been conducted without the contributions and cooperation of the following people: my special thanks go to Swantje Renfordt and Amelie Kutter for their creative and careful project work. Swantje took responsibility for the sampling process and supervision of the human coding by the student assistants. Amelie specialised in the corpus-linguistic methods and their application. I also wish to thank Jana Katharina Grabowsky for providing the Dutch data. Our student assistants Dominika Biegoń, Andreas Hildebrandt, Mark Püttcher and David Seelbinder supported the technical implementation of the analysis with extraordinary engagement and creativity. Elena Rinklef's and Robin Schuhmacher's help was indispensable during the editing of this book. I also thank the other 20(!) student assistants working on the project for their meticulous sampling and qualitative text analysis, as well as manifold data-searching work which they provided with outstanding quality and passionate engagement, while showing a remarkable degree of stress resistance in the face of occasional technical catastrophes. Each team member contributed to the very friendly, constructive and mutually supportive working atmosphere, which made the five years of project work a very pleasant experience.

Brit Helle Aarskog was the first to make me aware of the potential of advanced computational linguistics for media content analysis. For further corpus-linguistic advice we found partners in Manfred Stede and Peter Kolb. Giancarlo Corsetti encouraged me to use time-series analysis for my data. For statistical advice on how to finally conduct and present the data to the reader, I am grateful to economists Andreas Kern and Saverio Simonelli, and information scientist Sven Banisch. The following people read the whole manuscript or parts thereof, and enriched it with their always very constructive and stimulating comments: André Bächtiger, Federica Bicchi, Tanja A. Börzel, Nicole Dörr, Eva Heidbreder, Stephanie Hofmann, Skadi Krause, Hanspeter Kriesi, Henry Krisch, Thomas Risse, Monica Sassatelli, Miranda Schroes, Helene Sjursen, Udo Tietz, Bruno Wüest and two anonymous reviewers for Routledge. Finally, my thanks also go to Joshua Rogers, Barty Begley and David McCourt, who contributed much more than 'pure' language editing at different stages of the manuscript. Any errors remaining are, of course, my own.

Notes

1 DFG, contract no. RI 798/8 (Risse, T. and Kantner, C., *Auf der Suche nach einer Rolle in der Weltpolitik. Die gemeinsame Außen- und Sicherheitspolitik der Europäischen Union (GASP/ESVP) im Lichte massenmedial ausgetragener kollektiver Selbstverständigungsdiskurse*, Berlin: Freie Universität Berlin, 2003).
2 RECON (Reconstituting Democracy in Europe), Integrated FP6-Project, contract no. CIT4-CT-2006–028698. Host institution: ARENA Oslo, Norway.
3 Marie Curie Fellowship, contract no. 515055 EIF, Robert Schuman Centre of Advanced Studies (RSCAS) of the European University Institute (EUI), Florence, Italy.
4 BMBF support code: 01UG1234A.

1 Introduction
Transnational political communication and European identity-formation

After the end of the Cold War, many observers hoped for the establishment of a new world order based on the rule of law (Beck 2007; Beck and Grande 2007; Habermas 2001b, 2006: Ch. 8; Zangl and Zürn 2003; Zürn 1998). Instead, the post-Cold War era saw an unexpected increase in intra-state violence against ethnic and religious groups, brutal civil wars and new, asymmetric conflicts (Howorth 2007: 6). These phenomena seemed utterly anachronous: simultaneously old – resembling what Europe had experienced in the Thirty Years' War before the institutionalisation of the European state system in 1648 – and new, such that, initially, observers lacked appropriate terms to describe observed events.

International crises in Somalia, Rwanda, Haiti, East Timor, Sierra Leone and the former Yugoslavia, to name only the most prominent, posed fundamental questions for the EU Member States and the European Union – questions to which Europe has so far proved unable to develop satisfactory answers. International responses have almost always suffered from insufficient resources, inadequate troop contingents and underfunded civilian restructuring efforts, and have led to dramatic failures such as in Rwanda (1994) and Srebrenica (1995), where UN troops became passive bystanders in the face of genocide. These crises, together with the manifest incapacity of the international community as well as Europe to cope with the novel situations, created deep uncertainties. They called into question well established views about international security and foreign policy actorness, as well as ethical views regarding international crisis management. Between hope and despair, European countries – perhaps more than others[1] – found themselves in the midst of intense national and transnational debates that sought to come to terms with these disturbing phenomena and their implications for an emerging post-Cold War world order.

In this book, I show that the debates over international security after the end of the Cold War can profitably be viewed as an evolving process of collective sense-making (Dewey 1927) that occurred in transnational political communication, was triggered by the same events, and affected transnational identity-formation. These emerging identities, and the event- and problem-driven media debate that shaped them, form the focus of this study. On the

2   Introduction

theoretical level I distinguish ideal-typically between two kinds of identity discourse: on one hand *pragmatic problem-solving debates*, in which *problem-solving communities* (*commercium*) may emerge; and on the other hand *ethical discourses*, in which the ethical foundations of collective problem-solving practices are reflected and a *shared ethical self-understanding* (*communio*) may be created. This distinction allows us to address the two central empirical research questions: whether transnational collective sense-making took place in the face of the international crises after the end of the Cold War, and which aspects of European identity were problematised.

In adopting this focus, this study situates itself within a constructivist framework in International Relations theory and European Studies. Constructivists hold that *political communication matters in foreign politics* (e.g. Adler 2002; Checkel 1998; Fearon and Wendt 2002; Risse 2003 and many others). The shared public understandings that emerge in the course of the transnational debates that this study investigates are – to say the least – a powerful constraining or enabling factor for institutional foreign policy actors (for different models of this interrelation see e.g. Gilboa 2002).[2] This study, moreover, assumes a pragmatist-hermeneutic perspective. Pragmatists would add to the constructivist toolbox that political communication is not an end in itself; rather, people engage in debates in the context of real-world problems. In the collective search for solutions, various relevant actors bring to the fore multiple perspectives, interest-based claims and ethical convictions. In the democratic political process, they contribute to piecemeal, incremental – with Dewey, one could say 'experimental' – and of course fallible problem-solving, institution-building and collective learning processes (Albert and Kopp-Malek 2002; Bohman 2002; Cochran 2002). In a pragmatist-constructivist framework, moreover, the possible extension of problem-solving communities corresponds to the range of political, legal and economic interdependence, rather than cultural or linguistic boundaries (Brunkhorst 2002; Kantner 2004b: Ch. 5; Zürn et al. 2007).

Within these problem-solving communities, this study assumes that the relevant communicative actions are not only diplomats' negotiations behind closed doors, but processes of collective sense-making that reach deep into *civil societies* and encompass mass communication in the *larger public*. Especially in situations of intense change and high uncertainty, elites are themselves highly involved in public reasoning – and not only as speakers. When everything is changing, uncertain and risky, policy actors may feel especially unsure about what problems to address and what policies to adopt. One place to which they turn to make sense of the world around them is the mass media. The different institutional arenas of the political system and the informal arenas of political mass communication are interlinked. Therefore this study is interested not in the structure of elite discourse, but in the amount of information and 'the pool of reasons' (Habermas 1996a: Chs 7, 8) available to ordinary citizens as the 'intended audience' (Krippendorff 2004: 31) of the quality media. However, this study does not posit the media as the only or the strongest driver of collective identity-formation. Rather, it assumes a pluralistic universe of public arenas (including face-to-face encounters and interpersonal networks, organisational publics within political parties or civil society organisations and their networks, and alternative counter-publics and different mass media) (Gerhards and Neidhardt 1991). Nonetheless, political communication in the quality press provides a very important and methodologically accessible arena for these processes.

The empirical investigation presented here compares discourses in six European countries, which either were or became EU Members during the period under investigation, and the United States (US) as a comparative case. The European countries were chosen to cover the range of diverse positions on foreign, security and defence policy preferences prevalent in the EU. Small and large countries, with both post-neutral and Atlanticist foreign policy traditions and pro-European and EU-sceptic policies were included. The cases included were Austria (AU), France (FR), Germany (GER), Ireland (IR), the Netherlands (NL) and the United Kingdom (UK). For each country under study[3], a centre-left and a centre-right national quality newspaper was included.[4] The data investigated comprise a cleaned full sample of all relevant newspaper articles ($N = 489,508$). These newspaper articles are examined by a *quantitative content-analytical approach* based on *corpus-linguistic methods*. The data generated are analysed with complex statistical methods including correlation analysis, autoregressive integrated moving-average (ARIMA) time-series models and sigma-convergence analysis.

The study comprises a *continuous* period of 16 years (January 1990–March 2006) of news coverage and commentary on ('ordinary') wars and humanitarian military interventions. It covers the formative years of collective sense-making of the new realities after the end of the Cold War; the emergence of new understandings of the multilaterally agreed-upon use of military force in the interest of a 'post-Westphalian' legalised world, and rapidly changing conceptions of international and military actorness including both irregular armed forces as well as international troops. The period of investigation, however, includes not only the initial scepticism regarding the changing international realities and the period of high-flying, sometimes perhaps even hubristic optimism and 'can-do' fervour regarding humanitarian military interventions, but also the rapid disillusionment after 9/11 and the second Iraq War 2003. Arguably, we remain in this phase of disappointment, perplexity and helplessness today.

1.1 Major findings and added value of this study

The results of this study provide a differentiated long-term picture of transnational public discourses on wars and humanitarian military interventions across Europe and the US.

Introduction

Pragmatic problem-solving debates

The first research question addresses transnational pragmatic problem-solving debates:

- The study finds that transnational transatlantic and European *problem-solving debates* occurred, and that they were triggered by the same chains of significant events. This resulted in transnationally synchronous shifts in the intensity of the debate on wars and humanitarian military interventions.
- Focusing on the ethically positively connoted part of the debate – that is, articles that discussed the use of force as 'humanitarian military interventions' as opposed to 'ordinary wars' – also revealed synchronous issue cycles in reaction to the same chains of crisis events and institutional reactions to them.
- Contrary to most current news value theories, which assume that media attention rises and falls with certain types of dramatic event, this study shows that newsworthiness is an additive effect of crisis events and the international reactions by international organisations (including the EU) that they engender. In other words, the more international crisis-solving activities are directed at a conflict, the more media attention the crisis receives. Conversely, this implies that forgotten conflicts – those on which the institutionalised international community remains silent – are largely also ignored by the media.

Ethical discourses

The second research question asks whether transnational European ethical discourses emerged in the face of significant conflict events:

- In the EU Member States, attention given to the European Union was remarkably high, especially in the normatively charged debate on humanitarian military intervention. Yet *European identity* was not a major aspect in the debate on wars and humanitarian military interventions. This is the 'bad news' from the point of view of the integration of defence and security policy. The Europeans did not mainly talk about themselves *instead* of the international problems at stake, as some critics alleged (Kagan 2003).
- The 'good news,' however, is that over the whole period of investigation questions of *European identity* were present, albeit in a changeable manner. In addition, the EU was addressed as both a problem-solving (*commercium*) as well as an ethical (*communio*) community in all countries. The conflicts in the former Yugoslavia as well as the Iraq War 2003 challenged the EU as both of dimensions of collective identity.
- The study revealed interesting differences between the relative intensity of references to *European identity* between countries. In the French media,

links to European identity were strongest. In the British and Irish papers, expressions of European identity were less frequent than in the other European countries. In the US press, references to a European identity were almost absent from the debate. Over time, there is no continuous upward trend in the intensity of expressions of European identity, nor is there a clear pattern of convergence or divergence between the countries. However, within those articles that referred in some way to Europe, the share of expressions of European identity was substantial and – if one looks at broader time periods – increased over time for most countries, rising from the early 1990s over the late 1990s to higher levels in the first half-decade of the new millennium.

This study provides surprising empirical evidence regarding the dynamics of transnational political communication on wars and humanitarian military interventions and the expression of European collective identities in this context. The debates studied provided at least important background conditions for the rapid development of the Common Foreign and Security Policy (CFSP) and the European Security and Defence Policy (ESDP)[5] after the end of the Cold War (for similar intuitions see constructivist authors but also, for example, Baumgartner and Mahoney 2008; Mansbridge et al. 2012).

By adopting a long-term, comparative and large-n design, the study also pursues a methodological meta-aim. It significantly contributes to overcoming the most significant methodological weakness of the constructivist research programme in International Relations to date (Herrmann 2002: 125): its inability to show convincingly (i.e. in large-n studies) how public convictions regarding the international change over time and in comparative perspective. This disappointing state of the art is to a large extent due to methodological weaknesses and technological deficits. This study demonstrates, however, that these methodological and technological difficulties are surmountable. Using appropriate methods, it is possible to handle a large-scale multilingual set of almost half a million newspaper articles. These methods include a *quantitative content-analytical approach* based on *corpus-linguistic methods*, which, as this study shows, may include extensive *qualitative* steps in the analysis to assure a high level of semantic validity for the generated indicators. This study thereby adds to a recent research trend that attempts to apply advanced computational-linguistic tools to political science.

As one of the first of its kind, this investigation provides a continuous longitudinal examination of the debate on wars and humanitarian military interventions as well as processes of European identity-formation therein. This continuous long-time approach makes short-term effects at the peaks of the debate distinguishable from more structural features of the dynamics of transnational political communication. Discursive sense-making of real-world challenges in the pressing context of international crisis events is not limited to the most intense moments of the debate around possible decisions concerning the use of force. By painting a continuous picture of the intensity of the debate in the different countries, as well as the level of attention paid to important elements in it – for example, humanitarian military interventions, Europe, EU and European identity – this study enters uncharted territory.

1.2 The study plan

This book is composed of four main parts. It begins with an elaboration of the theoretical framework in Chapter 2. Sections 2.1–2.4 provide a discussion of the core concepts of the study. Section 2.1 starts with a brief review of the discussion on the development of CFSP/ESDP after the Cold War, the widely bemoaned lack of broad public debates on ESDP, as well as the perceived functional need for a 'strong' and resilient European identity on the citizen level for this (and other) grand projects of European political integration. Section 2.2 explores the debates this study investigates. To do so, it introduces the concept of '*humanitarian military intervention*' – as opposed to '*ordinary wars*' of self-interest – as a normative concept with deep roots in the history of political thought. As we will see, debates on European identity cluster around this normatively laden concept.

In Cection 2.3 I explain the *hermeneutical-pragmatist framework* I use for the conceptualisation of collective identity and its formation, distinguishing between *numerical identification* or categorisation, on one hand; and *qualitative collective identities* that involve shared convictions people hold about their multiple group memberships, on the other. We will see that *qualitative collective identities* comprise three different types of we-groups: a universal we$_1$- and particularistic we$_2$-groups in the pragmatic sense of a *commercium* and in the ethical sense of a *communio*. The awareness of people of sharing *commercium* identities emerges and becomes articulated and contested in what I call *pragmatic public problem-solving debates*, while by *ethical discourses* I refer to those public discussions that contribute to the formation of a *communio*.

Section 2.4 adds a final piece to the theoretical toolkit to be assembled in Chapter 2. In public and scientific debates, it is frequently claimed that political mass communication cannot transcend national boundaries (see e.g. Gerhards 2001; Graf von Kielmansegg 1996; Greven 2000; Grimm 1995). In line with recent research on European public spheres, I argue that *transnational political mass communication* should be conceptualised as transnationally intertwined communication in the national media, which citizens can consume in their respective mother tongues. It takes place when the *same transnationally interdependent issues* are discussed at the *same time* and under similar *aspects of relevance* or framing – but of course not necessarily with the same opinions (Eder and Kantner 2000: 81; Kantner 2004b: 58, 130–133; Risse 2010: 109–120; 2015). It is an empirical question whether, and how intensely, transnationally intertwined political communication on issues of common interest takes place in different countries. The drivers of the public debates are significant chains of events – problematic situations but also the activities of our political institutions. For its investigation, we should use the same concepts and research strategies applied in the analysis of national political communication. Section 2.5 integrates the theoretical ideas developed and translates them into specific, empirically testable hypotheses and assumptions for the empirical part of this study.

Chapter 3 focuses on important methodological decisions concerning the period of investigation, country selection and choice of broadsheets. The epistemic foundations of media content analysis are outlined, and the decision to use quality newspapers as sources, the sampling procedure, and the methods applied for cleaning such a large number of articles are explained and justified (Section 3.3). This study uses event-data as independent variables in some of the statistical procedures. Section 3.4 describes how they were gathered. Most importantly, however, Chapter 3 describes the innovative corpus-linguistic tools developed for generation of semantic field lists as indicators for the dependent variables of this study (Section 3.5). After the general approach is outlined, the indicators chosen to operationalise the hypotheses developed in Chapter 2 are introduced: the issue cycle on 'wars and interventions'; the specific issue cycle on 'humanitarian military intervention'; the intensity of attention to 'Europe' in general and the 'EU and its institutions' in particular; European identity ('EU identity'); and even more specifically, the *commercium* and the *communio* aspects of European identity.

Chapter 4 presents the empirical research results in detail. Each section starts with a brief qualitative description of the contents recorded by each indicator. It then presents a basic quantitative overview of the attention paid by the media to the respective features. For a more thorough comparative statistical analysis of the data, I conduct two correlation analyses (one compares the different countries with each other, the other uses the event-type data as independent variables). In the next step, I estimate a set of ARIMA time-series models in order to specify the factors that result in greater or lesser media attention to issues of war and humanitarian military intervention, as well as to European identity in this context. In a final step, I conduct a convergence analysis to check whether media attention in the different countries becomes more or less similar over time and at which particular instances.

Chapter 5 summarises my findings, links them back to the theoretical questions of transnational political communication and identity-formation, and underlines their importance for international politics. It reviews the main empirical findings and outlines prospects for further research, before concluding with a clear specification of this study's threefold contribution to the field. On the theoretical level, it contributes to pragmatist-constructivist approaches in International Relations theory, which it provides with a hermeneutic-pragmatist model of transnational political communication and collective identity-formation beyond the nation state. On the empirical level, it generates new insights into the dynamics of transnational political communication and identity-formation with relevance for policy making in international relations. And on the methodological level, it demonstrates how constructivist

8 *Introduction*

scholarship can study national as well as transnational political debates using a large-*n*, long time-span, cross-national research design.

Notes

1 In a new, ongoing empirical research project at Stuttgart University we are currently investigating the interrelations of multiple identities (i.e. national, transatlantic, cosmopolitan, religious, etc. collective identities) in public debates on wars and interventions (Kantner and Tietz 2013).
2 However, one should not misunderstand the relationship between public opinion on foreign policy issues and foreign policy decisions as either a unidirectional 'bottom-up' or a mere 'top-down' process. In democracies, the influence of public opinion is filtered by complex domestic institutional structures: different members of governments and parliamentarians represent the views of diverse sections of the public, are frequently internally divided and therefore have to build complex compromises (Risse-Kappen 1991).
3 There is one exception: for Ireland only one paper was available.
4 Quality newspapers were chosen as an effective proxy for media debate because, even as readership of this medium has decreased, it is still the traditional broadsheets that 'operate' the public 'pool of reasons' that this study investigates. By inter-media agenda-setting, the arguments elaborated in the quality press trickle through other fora of public communication – even if often in rudimentary form. They therefore provide a good proxy for the structures of public discourse. I am interested in the debates as they unfold before the eyes of ordinary citizens. Questions as to how news on wars and interventions is generated are consequently beyond the scope of this study.
5 With the reforms of the Lisbon Treaty, the ESDP became the Common Security and Defence Policy (CSDP). Because these reforms became effective only after our period of investigation, I use the older expressions throughout this book.

2 The theoretical building blocks
Transnational identity discourses on wars and humanitarian military interventions

In order to conceptualise the wealth of empirical material presented in this book, it is essential to develop an integrative view on transnational communication and identity. My hermeneutic-pragmatist theory marries insights of *political philosophy* and *political science* regarding normative models of political communication, the public sphere, the construction of reality, collective identity, and democracy with modern approaches to *analytical philosophy of language*.

In a first step I lay out the relevance of transnational political communication and identity for transnational political integration with special attention to the development of the European Security and Defence Policy (ESDP) (Section 2.1). Many researchers consider the lack of a strong European identity as one of the major obstacles to further European political integration, an argument that has been most intensely debated with respect to the constitutional process (Gerhards 2001; Graf von Kielmansegg 1996; Grimm 1995; Moravcsik 2006). Since this study investigates public debates on wars and interventions as critical junctures in the process of collective identity-formation beyond the nation state, in a second step (Section 2.2) I introduce the normative conception of 'humanitarian military intervention' as opposed to 'ordinary wars' fought for economic, territorial or geopolitical interests.

Third, I develop a hermeneutic-pragmatist concept of transnational collective identity, based on theoretical insights from analytic philosophy of language (Section 2.3). This understanding does not try to find 'objective' classification criteria to determine political communities from the perspective of a neutral observer (I later call such approaches '*numerical identification*'). Instead, I start from the ways in which people refer to themselves as members of we-groups. This approach leads to a redefined and differentiated ideal-typical mapping of 'collective identity' that distinguishes between a universal we-community (we$_1$) and particularistic communities (we$_2$), which can be further divided into problem-solving communities (we$_{2/commercium}$) and communities sharing an ethical self-understanding (we$_{2/communio}$).

Fourth, I outline why these communicative processes can also be at work at the transnational level (Section 2.4). Transnational political communication takes place when people across national borders have the chance to make up their mind about the *same political issues* at the *same time* under *similar aspects of relevance*. This means they do not need to read the same articles or speak the same language(s). This implies that the concepts and methods – of course, in a context-sensitive way – used for the empirical investigation of (national) political mass communication can be applied for research on transnational political mass communication. Section 2.4.2 briefly introduces key concepts such as 'issue cycle' and 'news values' for readers who might not be familiar with political communication research. Finally, having collected these conceptual tools, the overall hypotheses can be outlined in detail (Section 2.5), preparing the ground for their empirical operationalisation in Chapter 3.

2.1 Transnational discourse and transnational political integration

2.1.1 The end of the Cold War and development of the ESDP

European integration began with defence (Howorth 2000: 1). However, past attempts in the history of the European integration process to coordinate the sovereignty-sensitive issues of common foreign, security and defence policy between Member States had failed or ended in stagnation.[1] With the end of the Cold War, European Union (EU) economic and political integration took on unprecedented speed, and even integration in the realm of foreign, security and defence policy became possible. Why could the ESDP be developed so comparatively quickly and successfully after the end of the Cold War? While this study does not attempt to provide a fully fledged causal explanation, it sheds light on the transnational public debate on wars and humanitarian military interventions after the end of the Cold War, which provides an important context for foreign policy making in Western democratic societies.

From the early 1990s on, extreme humanitarian crisis situations and civil wars challenged the EU and its Member States to respond. Some of these conflicts took place in the immediate neighbourhood of the EU. Ethnic tensions caused the dissolution of multi-ethic states such as the Union of Soviet Socialist Republics (USSR), the Czechoslovak Socialist Republic (ČSSR) and the Socialist Federal Republic of Yugoslavia, in Europe's 'backyard'. As bloody civil wars took place, not only in distant countries but on the European continent, the Europeans often were unable to react with appropriate common strategies.[2] In order to achieve better political coordination, the Common Foreign and Security Policy (CFSP) was established with the Maastricht Treaty in 1993. The ESDP, as part of the CFSP, developed in the late 1990s.

While the use of armed force is usually strongly contested, in liberal democracies, debates about the use of force are not limited to a political caste, but involve the broader public via modern mass communication. Many ordinary citizens in the West expected a period of peace and prosperity after the permanent threat of a nuclear world war between the superpowers of the

Cold War era had disappeared. However, dramatic humanitarian catastrophes and international crisis events could not be ignored for long, and demanded an effective response by the West. After 9/11, support for international terrorism (as in the case of Afghanistan 2001) or the illegal possession of weapons of mass destruction (as in the case of the Iraq War 2003) were discussed as additional threats to international security justifying military action – in some cases with, in others without, the approval of the United Nations (UN) Security Council.

The rapid changes in international relations after the collapse of the Eastern bloc and the emerging new security threats defined by the Petersberg Tasks called into question the existing cognitive frames and institutional settings of international security policy and challenged previous wisdom and practices on all levels. Was the nation state able to react adequately to the new problems and challenges? How much responsibility should one's own nation take with regard to the emerging conflicts? How much military (spending) was necessary for national defence and/or new tasks? Was the national military appropriately equipped? Could one nation alone make a difference, or should the international community act multilaterally to respond to new global challenges? What would be the best framework for such action? Could it be the United Nations – despite its shortcomings – that could serve as the centre of a new world order based on legal principles (Habermas 2006: Ch. 8)? How much would the UN have to be reformed to become this centre? Or should conflict management be provided by regional alliances or security communities such as the North Atlantic Treaty Organization (NATO), the African Union, or the Association of Southeast Asian Nations (ASEAN)?[3] How independently should Europe act in the emerging uni- or multipolar world order? Europe, the continent most affected by the disappearance of the Cold War corset that had restricted foreign policy options for 45 years, began to search for its own security institutions.

Since the creation of the second pillar of the EU with the Maastricht Treaty in 1993, a *Common Foreign and Security Policy* (CFSP) was institutionalised by the EU Member States.[4] After 1998 it was linked to important advances in the *European Security and Defence Policy* (ESDP). However, the development of these new policy projects was characterised by growing confrontations among the Member States concerning Europe's role in the world. Debates about new (and old) security challenges after the end of the Cold War, and how the EU and its Member States should respond to these challenges in order to provide security for EU citizens, the broader region and neighbouring countries, and to exert a positive influence on the development of a new multi-polar world order, were intensely and controversially discussed among elites and the broader public.

Such public debates are the 'metatopical space' (Taylor 1995) in which public reasoning about, reflection on and interpretation of real-world events takes place, and where attempts to collectively make sense of changing international conditions, and proposals of feasible and ethically appropriate solutions, are aired. Public debates are thus the metatopical space in which dissent regarding perceptions of, and possible collective reactions to, crisis events are articulated. Analysing these spaces enables us to reconstruct how people were torn between pacifism and humanitarian obligations, which might sometimes require the use of armed force, and how that changed collectively shared ethical convictions regarding the use of military force. Public debates on ethically sensitive issues – such as military interventions – therefore represent the arenas in which collective identities are developed.

However, the inner-European controversies concerning the Iraq War brought up again the quest for a coherent and well functioning common foreign, defence and security policy that would state a clear vision of Europe's desired role in the world and express the normative principles on which the EU would base its policy actions. This vision not only would have to address the aims and standards of a common security and defence policy; it also would have to outline the future of transatlantic relations and NATO. The lack of a problem-oriented and problem-adequate European strategy has already been criticised in the literature before the Iraq crisis (see e.g. Caygill 2001; Czempiel 1999, 2002; Dembinski and Wagner 2003; Eliassen 1998; Kohler-Koch 2000; Regelsberger 1993). With the adoption of the European Security Strategy (ESS) in 2003 on the institutional level, this debate was for the time being settled.

On a broader societal level, these issues were also intensely debated. The issue of humanitarian military interventions outside of NATO and EU borders after the end of the Cold War has regularly led to an intensification of the academic, and even more so the public, debate on Europe's particular role in the world. Humanitarian military interventions, peacekeeping missions, peace-enforcing and later peace-making operations[5] are certain to raise this question, because participating in the use of military force, even if it is for humanitarian reasons, carries with it severe risks: these include the possibility of civilian casualties in the crisis country, casualties among the intervening forces, incalculable costs for the intervention and the following nation- and/or state-building process. The aim to bring back internal peace to a war-torn society may not be achieved.

The requirements for public justification of such measures are extraordinarily high. Intervening countries need good reasons to justify the use of force for humanitarian and peacekeeping reasons. I see the debate on humanitarian military interventions as the tip of the iceberg in the collective sense-making process in the dramatically changing security environment since the end of the Cold War.

In doing so, I examine aspects of European foreign and security policies, which mark a desideratum in existing research. European Studies and International Relations research on the CFSP/ESDP is well established and has provided many well founded theoretical and empirical insights into the institutional dynamics of external security policy-process in the EU-multilevel system (see e.g. Carlsnaes and Smith 1994; Carlsnaes et al. 2004; Hill 1996;

Larsen 1998; Nuttall 2000; Peterson and Sjursen 1998; Regelsberger 1993; Regelsberger et al. 1997; White 1999). A series of studies on the redefinition of Europe's role in international relations are available (see e.g. Jopp et al. 1991; Kubbig 2003; Miall 1994; Schmidt 1996). However, research still focuses mainly on negotiation processes between national actors (see, among others, Jopp and Regelsberger 1998; Laursen 2006; Levy et al. 2005; Wagner 2002, 2003). This state of the art urgently calls for complementary research with an extended perspective, sensitive to the increasing public contestation over this policy field.

Work on the CFSP/ESDP inspired by social constructivist theories of International Relations is of great importance for this study (see e.g. Glarbo 2001; Jørgensen 1997; Larsen 1998; Mérand 2006). This literature regularly refers to debates as relevant factors, though they rarely deal explicitly with public debates (see e.g. Larsen 1997, 1999, 2000; Wessels and Jantz 1997). Yet the mass media discussion of these issues has not been empirically examined to a sufficient degree. It is often assumed that CFSP/ESDP are virtually missing in public debate (see e.g. Howorth 2007: 2, 58; Kaldor et al. 2008; Wallace 2005: 454). The public is seen as the laggard and a source of friction for, and obstacle to, institutional development. Governments are seen as behaving spinelessly in front of the public, but they 'know better' and would do the right thing if it did not cost them approval in polls or elections. Wallace calls the lack of transnational public communication on ESDP the 'greatest inhibitor' of supranational reform in foreign, security and defence policy:

> The absence of a European public space – of a shared public debate, communicating through shared media, think tanks, political parties, responding to and criticizing authoritative policy-makers – remains the greatest inhibitor of further subordination of sovereignty, national traditions, and national expenditure to common policy. A transnational expert community has gradually developed across the EU, communicating through specialist journals and think tanks ... National parliaments and mass media, however, were only intermittently interested.
>
> (Wallace 2005: 454)

However, up to now there have been very few *comparative media analyses* of debates on issues relevant to CFSP/ESDP such as wars and humanitarian military interventions. The existing studies qualitatively compare the debate in two or three countries on one major conflict: on the Kosovo War 1999 (Grundmann et al. 2000), or on the Iraq War 2003 (Dimitrova and Strömbäck 2005; Meyer and Zdrada 2006; Renfordt 2007a, 2007b). Very few studies have included more than one conflict, and – for pragmatic reasons – few could provide more than snapshots of the debate, sometimes investigating time periods spanning only a few weeks before and after the beginning of the conflict (Meyer 2006; Wessler et al. 2008).[6] Nonetheless, these studies provided valuable insights into the differences and similarities across nations with respect to the most important reasons articulated in support of, or in opposition to, particular military interventions at the peaks of the debate. With regard to the interpretative pattern in the debates, I cannot – through this study – challenge their findings. However, in assuming that discursive sense-making of real-world challenges in the pressing contexts of international crisis events is not limited to the moments right before and after the intervention, this study contributes a continual long-term investigation of coverage on wars and humanitarian military interventions that can elucidate transnational collective sense-making attempts and identity-formation processes in the long run, including debates prompted by the 'minor' crises usually left uninvestigated. Such sense-making processes (also) take place in the course of monitoring the developments after (non-)intervention decisions and earlier experiences may 'programme' later perceptions and debates. By presenting a continuous survey of the intensity of the debate in the different countries, as well as the level of attention paid to important elements (humanitarian military interventions, Europe, EU, European identity) in it, this study maps uncharted terrain.

2.1.2 *The perceived functional need for a European identity*

This is of particular interest as there is an extensive literature that states the need for strong collective identities as a precondition for legitimate governance in the national as well as the transnational European realm. This *leitmotif* is also common in public debates. Especially since the failure of the constitutional project, politicians, publicists and the media have outperformed each other with laments about the missing European identity. The lack of a 'strong' *European identity* – so goes the common diagnosis – is the main reason for the recent failure of the democratisation efforts and the narrow-minded disputes among the Member States that prevent the European Union from solving its – in principle well recognised – strategic problems. This diagnosis is shared by Euro-pessimists and optimists alike. Both draw – with different accentuations – on communitarian theoretical traditions.

The pessimists, inspired by communitarian ideas, hold that collective political identities beyond the scope of the nation state are impossible. With a Euro-pessimism that comes close to fatalism, they demand a pause in the political integration process or even a dismantling of the EU towards a free trade zone. Euro-pessimists felt confirmed that national identity is key after the failed constitutional referenda in 2005 and the Irish 'No' to the Lisbon Reform Treaty in 2008. They plead for identity politics and identity rhetoric within the borders of the nation state in order to save what is left of the communitarian resources that integrate at least our national societies and political systems.

The logic of the argument constitutes a vicious cycle (Kantner 2004b: 108): without a common transnational collective identity, transnational politics would not be accepted as legitimate (even if these politics were based on more democratic mechanisms of decision-making). However, a strong enough transnational (European) identity could not develop since its preconditions were lacking: a common *lingua franca*, which would allow for transnational debates. Without sharing a common language, the pessimists maintain, citizens will derive different interpretative perspectives from different national media and will not be able to exchange arguments and engage in discussions across national borders. Therefore audiences are unable to organise as a transnational civil society, which could form the basis for the emergence of a transnational political identity (see e.g. Gerhards 2001; Graf von Kielmansegg 1996; Grimm 1995).[7]

Optimists such as Føllesdal and Hix (2006) and Habermas (1995), on the other hand, hope that democratisation on the transnational level would soon stimulate the growth of a transnational public sphere with a collective identity.[8] Or they appeal for the completion of political unification in a *tour de force* despite all backlashes – this time, however, with 'more heart', in order to bring the citizens on board. A similar approach was adopted by the European Commission, which, lacking a plan B after the negative referenda on the Constitutional Treaty, advocated a plan 'D' for democracy[9] in the hope that more publicity would lead to more *European identity* and hence, quasi-automatically, to greater acceptance of the European project. Those who still favour a further deepening of the integration process often try to figure out how it might be possible to purposefully 'construct' or 'create' a *European identity*. Large-scale identity-political measures are favoured by both former advocates of direct democracy and conservatives. This plea for identity rhetoric is as much an overreaction as the fatalism of the pessimists. However, it rests on an – often implicit –conviction that it might be possible purposefully to create new identities, and that identity is not only something inherited that one can at best try to preserve, but something that can be built in a top-down manner. However, pessimists as well as optimists consider collective identity as a functional prerequisite for legitimate politics generally as well as in the new post-national realm.

Issues of humanitarian military interventions offer the opportunity to study these questions in detail. EU governance meanwhile includes policy fields formerly viewed as the core competencies of sovereign states, and increasingly touches policy issues that are highly value-laden. Some of these policy fields have been constitutive of the specific national paths to modernity and the evolution of national democratic institutions. National policies in ethically sensitive fields have a history of 'hot' conflicts, in which 'national identity' and the national political system coevolved. Due to such specific collective experiences in the nation-building process and during the establishment of the national political and welfare state systems – and not just out of nationalistic stubbornness – Europeans have different views on ethically sensitive policy fields.

If today policy areas such as constitutional policy, social policy, biotechnology, immigration, internal security, or security and defence come under EU-induced reform pressure, integration tends to become highly controversial. A European identity would make EU policies more acceptable, as Herrmann and Brewer summarise:

> Common identity and the idea of community are seen as providing diffuse support that can sustain institutions even when these institutions are not able to provide immediate utilitarian payoffs. Identification with a common community, such as Europe, is also seen as valuable for sustaining mass-based support when institutions at the international level make decisions that promote the European common good but may demand sacrifice from particular national communities.
>
> (Herrmann and Brewer 2004: 3)

The 'willingness to grant the EU authority requires some identification with Europe' (Risse 2004: 250), even if European identity does not come at the expense of national and other existing identities. Amitai Etzioni even identifies a general mismatch between the current state of policy integration – single market, free movement of people – and the low degree of 'normative-affective community building' (Etzioni 2007: 27). He also holds that normative-affective community building must precede democratisation since democracy requires a willingness to make sacrifices for one another as well as shared values (Etzioni 2007: 31). In short, many analysts maintain that diversity of national interests and identities undermines European ambitions and that shared values would be a necessary common ground for transnational consensus and solidarity.[10] Without shared values, they argue, European governance in these ethically sensitive policy fields is condemned to fail.

Yet strong collective identities are a rare thing in any modern society. In a transnational framework, moreover, any aspirations for a significant reduction of the complexity and heterogeneity of values will be disappointed. Why should this be different when 'hot'[11] political issues are discussed on a European scale? How then would it be possible to accommodate 27 different national experiences with regard to normatively sensitive policy issues such as constitutional policy, social policy, biotechnology, or internal and external security?[12] Given their overwhelming heterogeneity, how could EU citizens ever arrive at common normative standards for the evaluation of European policy action with regard to these delicate issues, even if we view an affirmation of diversity as part of the European identity (on the latter point see Delanty 1995; Eriksen and Fossum 2004; Fossum 2004; Fuchs 2011, 2013; Olsen 2005; Reif 1993; Wallace 1985; Zielonka and Mair 2002).

If these contradicting concerns are valid – (i) identity is presumed to be a functional precondition of democracy; and (ii) there is no stable substrate of common European values to draw on – the question of how it will be possible to find common solutions for complicated and ethically sensitive affairs becomes urgent. Without a 'collective identity' beyond the borders of the national communities as common ground for shared future projects – so goes the thrust of the argument – European efforts to institutionalise common political procedures, problem solutions or mutual commitments to solidarity might fail. Obviously there is much public, political and scientific interest in questions of European identity-formation. Yet what is this, presumably missing, 'collective identity?'

This study contributes to the theoretical debate on *collective identities*. It outlines a conceptual framework and the mechanisms of transnational processes of identity-formation. The pessimistic view that collective identities are endangered inherited resources, and the optimistic view that collective identities could simply be 'created',[13] 'constructed' or in more polemical terms 'manufactured', are both questioned. This study argues that a 'European identity' is emerging as ordinary citizens across Europe already share important pragmatic and even ethical convictions with regard to European policies. This is demonstrated by analysing a special policy field – foreign, security and defence policy – and its institutionalisation in the CFSP and the ESDP. This policy field was chosen as it constitutes a 'hard case' for the study of 'European identity'. A 'European identity' is least likely to be prevalent in this particular policy field because matters of foreign and security policy are at the core of national sovereignty. Moreover, these policies are regarded as being deeply rooted in national traditions.[14] In Europe, those national traditions also took shape in the numerous wars and hostilities that today's EU members fought *against* each other; they were coined in response to the experience of a long and dark history of wars of aggression, human rights abuses, totalitarianism, ethnic cleansing and genocide that culminated in the middle of the twentieth century. Evidently there is much doubt that the Europeans will trust each other enough to join their efforts with regard to questions of war and peace and the international order. All this leads to the expectation that these issue fields are especially resistant to European-wide identity-formation.

During the past 15 years, research on European identity has undergone a profound transition from normative-theoretical contributions to empirically founded examinations from various disciplines of the social sciences. The early belief that a European identity would (or would have to) replace other (national, regional or local) identities has been abandoned (Risse 2010, 2015). Instead, a consensus emerged in the research community that European and national identities interact in various ways, resulting in new hybrid forms of political identification (see e.g. Citrin and Sides 2004; Giesen and Eder 2000; Herrmann et al. 2004; Hooghe et al. 2002; Risse 2001). Foreign and defence policies are core parts of modern nation states and statehood. The analysis of mass media ethical discourses on humanitarian military interventions, in which collective ethical self-understandings are contested, make it possible to draw conclusions about the extent and the mechanisms and counter-mechanisms at work in the development of a common European identity.

A significant body of the literature on a 'European defence identity' searches for a 'European defence identity' in official documents. In fact, since the early 1990s the term became common in official documents and expert discourses under the label *European Security and Defence Identity* (ESDI) (for an overview and critique of the discussion see Bretherton and Vogler 1999; Howorth 2007: 8; Manners and Whitman 2003; Sedelmeier 2004: 125f.). In this study, I do not refer to ESDI when I talk about European identity, since 'identity' in that context was merely used metaphorically and had nothing to do with elites' or people's views towards the EU.

In order to investigate collective identities in the social scientific sense, we have to turn to citizens' convictions. Those convictions are – in the absence of direct experiences with international crisis events – to a large degree shaped by mass media communication. Especially when political communication refers to dramatic events and critical junctures, such as new wars and civil wars involving large-scale human rights abuses, security identities on the citizens' level may change (Risse and Kantner 2003). Such dramatic and morally unbearable events cry out for international reaction – in the most extreme cases, for humanitarian military interventions. This concept is clarified in the following section.

2.2 'Ordinary' war versus humanitarian military intervention

After the end of the Cold War, the fear of a third World War – probably fought on European territory and with nuclear weapons – faded away together with the communist bloc. However, Western democracies were soon confronted with new and unexpected security issues. It is intuitively plausible that the development of CFSP/ESDP after the end of the Cold War was a reaction to the bloody civil wars in the former Yugoslavia and other parts of the world, as well as the emerging 'new security threats' that began to dominate the foreign policy agenda in the 1990s. This study suspects that international crisis events such as wars and interventions trigger political debates and act as identity-challenging and identity-building events. It further maintains that developing common problem perceptions and ethical convictions is important for the institutionalisation of new policies – as for example transnationally integrated foreign and security policies of the EU.[15] Therefore I will spell out how the concepts 'war' and 'intervention' are used in this study.

Everyday language does not distinguish much between the many different forms of the use of military force. In everyday conversations we tend to call them all 'war', and usually we agree that this word refers to some of the worst aspects of human nature: aggression, extreme violence, cruelty and killing. For the purpose of this study, however, it is necessary to distinguish between different forms of collective violence. We will see in this section that 'humanitarian military intervention' is a normative concept. It is about the use of military force not for material gain, but with reference to a number of normative criteria that distinguish it from 'ordinary wars'.

'War' is usually defined as large-scale organised violence between sovereign states (Bull 1977: 184; Levy 2001: 351; Vasquez 1993: 21–29). In an anarchic international system that does not possess central institutions to powerfully enforce conflict solutions on the parties, conflicts about major security, power and economic interests may ultimately escalate into wars. Historically, wars therefore have been described using the metaphor of a large-scale duel between more or less equal enemies with egoistic interests (von Clausewitz 1984: 75). Despite its violent and archaic elements, this notion of 'ordinary war' already entails several elements of rationality and discipline that by definition make wars – in comparison with other forms of armed group conflict – much more calculable. The ideal-typical war is: (i) fought between states; (ii) over state interests; (iii) by well organised and disciplined armies. The elements of this ideal-typical definition and its explications, of course, derive from political and social theory and are not to be mistaken as empirical descriptions:

- Wars are waged for explicit, major security, power and/or economic state objectives that – as perceived by the actors involved – cannot be achieved by other political means. War implies the existence of states that successfully uphold the claim to a monopoly of the legitimate use of physical force in the enforcement of order (Weber 1978: 54). War could therefore be viewed as 'the continuation of policy by other means' (von Clausewitz 1984: 87). The outbreak of violence in war – in contrast to other forms of collective violence – is subsumed under political aims that can legitimately be stated only by authorised individuals (government, the head of government) in the name of a political community:

    > When whole communities go to war – whole peoples, and especially *civilized* peoples – the reason always lies in some political situation, and the occasion is always due to some political object. War, therefore, is an act of policy.
    >
    > (von Clausewitz 1984: 86f.)

    It follows that the violence can be authoritatively stopped by the representatives of the states involved.
- Other terms were created to grasp 'deviant' empirical instances of armed conflict. If one side of the conflict would fit the criteria of this definition and the other not, we would call it an 'asymmetrical conflict'. If non-state armed groups would be the agents on both sides, we would speak about a 'civil war' (Münkler 2003b).
- Wars are fought between states that command organised military forces. While pre-modern warriors, *condottieri* and militias, or today's non-state violent collective actors (insurgent groups, warlords and so on) usually fight for private or particularist reasons – be they personal gain and subsistence or individual and group grievances – 'regular' military forces are maintained by the state and are politically controlled. This is a demanding organisational task that requires considerable material and social resources and has so far been accomplished only by modern

bureaucratic states and their hierarchically structured standing armies (Weber 1978: 981). Without the military as an essential part of the bureaucratic apparatus, there is no 'monopoly of the legitimate use of physical force' of the state externally. And only because of this link to the politically responsible sovereign is it at all imaginable to systematically bind the exertion of violence in war to the rules of international law (*jus in bello*).[16]

Historically, this form of bureaucratically organised large-scale violence is a comparatively recent invention. Von Clausewitz was perhaps the first to notice this – at his time – historical novelty and stated that war is not a 'complete, untrammelled, absolute manifestation of violence' (von Clausewitz 1984: 87), but a disciplined exertion of violence, the calculated means to achieve rational political objectives, that can be allotted and is insofar 'tamed' (Münkler 2003a).

Yet to acknowledge the regulated character of inter-state wars is, of course, not yet to judge their moral justification. 'No political leader can send soldiers into battle, asking them to risk their lives and to kill other people, without assuring them that their cause is just – and that of their enemies unjust' (Walzer 1992: xii); however, 'just war theory', following Aristotle, Cicero and Augustine, Aquinas, de Vitoria, Grotius, Vattel and Mill, developed clear evaluative criteria for the justified use of armed force. In particular, two mutually independent sets of norms are identified – *jus ad bellum* and *jus in bello* (Walzer 1992: 21) – which differentiate the classical 'ordinary war' from 'just war'.

The first set of criteria concerns the reasons leading to the war: *jus ad bellum*. *Just reasons* exclude aggression and are restricted to defence – self-defence including defence of allies against unjust attack; self-protection of lives, liberty or property. These have to be coupled with *just intent* – that other motives for selfish gain are not dominant; and *reasonable prospect of success* – when defeat is inevitable all casualties are, by definition, in vain and therefore unnecessary, fighting further becomes unjust. Tensions can also arise between the principles of just intent and *proportionality*. The conduct of war that tacitly accepts disproportionate military and civilian victims compromises even the most legitimate aims such as national defence (Walzer 1992) – an issue also discussed with regard to 'collateral damage' in recent interventions.

The second set of criteria concerns the way a war is fought – *jus in bello*. War must be the *last resort*, that is, all reasonable diplomatic means must have been used first and the war must be officially declared. The principle of *discrimination* between combatants – military; and non-combatants – civilians must be respected and the latter held immune from attack and unnecessary harm. The use of military means must be *proportional* to the cause, and the rules of international and customary law must be respected.

All of these elements re-occur in the definition of 'humanitarian interventions'. However, it also adds a new essential element to the discussion of legitimate aims: a *neutral third party* intervenes in an ongoing armed conflict in order to prevent large-scale violation of *human rights*. Hence 'humanitarian interventions' share the *just cause* with ideal-typical 'just wars' because they are intended to stop grave violations of fundamental human rights of large numbers of civilians in a crisis country, but the action is not justified by self-defence. In consequence, massive human rights abuses within a country may even devaluate this country's right to self-determination:

> If the dominant forces within a state are engaged in massive violations of human rights, the appeal to self-determination ... [*which is at the root of the principle of non-interference into the internal affairs of a sovereign state, CK*] is not very attractive. That appeal has to do with the freedom of the community taken as a whole; it has no force when what is at stake is the bare survival or the minimal liberty of (some substantial number of) its members. Against the enslavement or massacre of political opponents, national minorities, and religious sects, there may well be no help unless help comes from outside.
>
> (Walzer 1992: 101)

A humanitarian intervention by definition is motivated not by self-interest, but by a concern for protecting a substantial number of civilians from massive and systematic human rights abuses. This sets extremely high moral standards for the legitimation and evaluation of any empirical action labelled as 'humanitarian intervention'.

Humanitarian interventions may have varying additional tasks, such as delivering aid, monitoring the situation, protecting civilians, enforcing ceasefires or peace agreements, pacification and stabilisation, disarming the conflict parties, or supporting state-building processes. According to these different tasks, humanitarian interventions can take on varying degrees of intensity: from the provision of lightly armed Blue Helmets to the deployment of heavily armed troops or aerial bombardment of the aggressor. For the purpose of this volume, I concentrate only on missions that are conducted by third-party soldiers. Purely civilian missions (e.g. of the Organization for Security and Cooperation in Europe, OSCE) for the provision of humanitarian aid, police missions, legal assistance or monitoring missions are not the focus of this study. I therefore use the term 'humanitarian military interventions' to refer to these missions (Münkler and Malowitz 2008).

In a '*humanitarian military intervention*' a foreign state or military alliance intervenes in an ongoing conflict or crisis from the outside. The intervening foreign troops are not a party to the conflict. While classical humanitarian (military) interventions in the past usually were undertaken with the consent of the target state, the new, more robust missions often are an 'incursion into what would ordinarily be the protected domain of state sovereignty, without the state's consent, chiefly for the sake of preventing the violation of human rights' (Buchanan and Golove 2002: 919f.).

22 Theoretical building blocks

Humanitarian military interventions occur on the territory of internationally recognised states or in a conflict area outside the international community, such as a failed or a failing state. That means that humanitarian military interventions may depart considerably from the definition of 'war' as inter-state war, inasmuch as the forces against which military means may be used in order to fulfil the aims of the mission may not be organised, state-controlled armies, but irregular forces. This may cause severe practical and normative problems with regard to the criteria of *jus in bello*, which to a large extend depends on clear distinctions between combatants and non-combatants.

Who should intervene? Walzer argues that there is no imperative obligation and there cannot be any legal duty for any state to intervene. However, in the face of major and large-scale violations of fundamental human rights '[a]ny state capable of stopping the slaughter has a right, at least, to try to do so' (Walzer 1992: 108). Hence it remains a matter of political judgement – within the UN institutions, between possibly intervening powers or alliances, and within the public of the possibly intervening states as well as the global public – to judge whether or not a humanitarian military intervention is an appropriate and proportional measure to take. The international community meanwhile tried to codify these criteria with the Responsibility to Protect in 2005 – almost at the end of our period of investigation (Bellamy 2009; Evans 2008).

'Humanitarian military intervention', in contrast to 'ordinary war', has hence developed as a highly normative concept with deep roots in the history of political thought. It refers to the use of military force by a foreign state or military alliance in an ongoing conflict or crisis for the protection or promotion of human rights, rather than for the pursuit of 'conventional' materialistic or ideological aims. The intervening foreign troops must not be party to the conflict. As a special form of just war, humanitarian military interventions have to be in accordance with two sets of moral principles: *jus ad bellum* (just reason, just intent, reasonable prospect of success) and *jus in bello* (last resort, discrimination between combatants and non-combatants, proportionality to the cause and the rules of international law). If conflicts are discussed as requiring 'humanitarian military interventions' in public debates, this implies a highly moral interpretation of dramatic large-scale human rights abuses in crisis countries and calls for strong moral responsibility. This can severely challenge collective self-understandings in the field of foreign and security policy. At this point we come closer to questions of collective identities.

2.3 Transnational collective identities

We have seen in the introduction to the problem tackled in this study that strong collective identities are perceived to be a functional prerequisite for legitimate politics on the national as well as on the transnational level. A 'strong' European identity is considered to be of crucial importance for the prospects of further political integration – especially in the highly contested field of CFSP/ESDP. However, it is much less clear in the literature what 'collective identities' actually are.[17]

In this section, the ways in which people refer to themselves as members of we-groups are clarified in order to contribute to an innovative model of the problem- and policy-related formation of collective identities. I introduce the concepts *'numerical identification'*, 'we$_{2/commercium}$' and 'we$_{2/communio}$', which provide the conceptual tools for the analyses provided in the rest of this study. These concepts are based on theoretical insights from analytic philosophy of language, which I introduce into the social scientific discourse on collective identity in order to redefine and differentiate the concept of 'collective identity' and to link it with empirical research investigating public ethical discourses.

2.3.1 What is collective identity?

Many scientific contributions on collective identity in the sub-national, national or transnational realm start with typologies of different group affiliations and/or their ordering into a hierarchy of preferences. Much has been written about the relations between different types of identities:

- They may be organised as nested, concentric circles. This is the way we are used to imagining the process of socialisation of an individual (Clausen 1968; Parsons and Bales 1956). In the beginning, a child identifies with their family as the relevant group in which they have to fulfil certain roles. Later the horizon (together with the tasks of the individual) broadens towards more abstract collectives such as a town, an ethnic or religious group, or a class. An adult person should have reached enough political maturity to be a conscious citizen of their country, and some individuals broaden their horizons even towards universal, cosmopolitan identifications. Functionalist socialisation theory tended to assume such an onion-like system of rings of identifications with broader and broader groups or – using more maternal imagery – it proposed thinking of various identities as a Russian doll.
- Identities may be mutually exclusive. In certain situations they represent a zero-sum game where the individual has to choose radically between two groups: they would have to be a fan of either soccer team A or B and not – at least not publicly – a fan of both. In the same way, especially in highly polarised or conflict situations, individuals may have to choose between conflicting ethnic or national loyalties, or between a national and a European identification.
- Yet things are often not that complicated. Different identities may also be imagined as cross-cutting or overlapping sets, as in the case of a person who inhabits different roles, identities and loyalties at the same time. One can be a father and a worker and a member of a collectivity such as a

24 *Theoretical building blocks*

>   rowing club without getting into identity conflicts or being considered 'schizophrenic' by others. Sometimes, however, expectations related to the diverse roles an individual inhabits can produce contradicting demands (Merton 1957: 111f.), resulting in 'role conflicts' or, seen from the perspective of the individual concerned, 'identity conflicts'.
>
> - Recently, a new way of thinking about the relations between different identities has been proposed: different identities can mutually define each other and become so entwined, meshed and blended that they are as inseparable as the brown and white parts of a marble cake (Risse 2001: 201; 2004: 252; Risse and Grabowsky 2008: 2). For instance, it became part of German political identity to be a reliable transatlantic and European partner in international affairs. This model also proves productive for research on transnational European identities, where it could be shown empirically that multiple identities reinforce – rather than exclude – each other (Bruter 2005).

In this section, however, I take one step back and start with a consideration of what collective identities are actually about, because the concept is often used very imprecisely. It is clear only that 'collective identity' refers to actors' deep convictions and that it includes all the features that other, 'harder' types of theory do not catch: properties such as values, traditions, culture, morality, religious beliefs and so on. 'Identity' became a catchall phrase for the ostensibly needed 'thick' moral underpinnings of social and political order. It is considered by many to be something that 'makes things easier'. Since everybody who belongs to the community is assumed to believe in the same set of values, a common identity is supposed to provide a foundation for bridging conflicts and accepting sacrifices in favour of the common good. Indeed, from this perspective, the existence of shared values, and thus agreement on at least some fundamental questions regarding the good life, provide a common evaluative ground – some conflicts then do not occur.

The strong common beliefs that make up these identities are often thought to be derived from certain substantial commonalities of the group members (e.g. ethnic, cultural, traditional, or religious uniformity, and so forth) and to translate into feelings of commonness. Collective identity is supposed to provide 'social glue'. It is seen as an inherited 'resource', and communitarians fear it is 'eaten up' in everyday politics and thus maintain it cannot be politically reproduced (Böckenförde 1991: 112).[18]

This communitarian understanding – a widespread, if rather simplistic, reading of the philosophical ideas underlying the original communitarian project – has been criticised. After decades of intense discussions about national, ethnic and European identities, the concept of 'collective identity' seems to have lost all clear-cut analytical contours (Niethammer 2000). Brubaker and Cooper (2000) even proposed completely giving up this term, replacing it with other more precise categories. Still, 'collective identity' is an indispensable concept of cultural and political sociology, necessary to theorise and conduct empirical research about value-oriented collective action. One can hardly deny that there are collectives that are involved in conflicts not simply because of material interests, but rather because of matters such as mutual recognition and normative dissent. Such disputes deal with the ethical question of 'what is good or better for us to do?'.

The terms Brubaker and Cooper recommend to replace 'identity' do not solve the conceptual problems, since neither purely descriptive terms,[19] nor 'emotional' terms such as 'feeling connectedness' (Brubaker and Cooper 2000: 19–21), provide the theoretical means to cope with strong normative convictions shared by the members of a community. Descriptive terms remain within the *perspective of the neutral observer*, which is blind to the socially relevant convictions of the individuals concerned. Affective terms only mythologise community membership and put it into a black box inaccessible to intersubjectively comprehensible social science. There are only a handful of authors who turned emotions and feelings into objects of theoretical thinking in the social sciences (as opposed to psychological or other accounts). These authors highlighted the intrinsic interconnection of emotions and value judgements (Nussbaum 2001: 4f.; Salomon 1993). If this holds true, we are again back to the analysis of a specific type of propositional beliefs – that means a special type of cognitive content: the normative convictions shared by the members of a community in the *participant's perspective*.

What we need are conceptual tools that enable us to handle the different types of convictions commonly held by the members of communities, and to grasp what precisely characterises those 'thick' (Walzer 1994) ethical convictions for which the members of a community sometimes fight passionately, and for which they might be willing to make sacrifices. Analytical philosophy has developed a way to come to terms with exactly these types of convictions (Tietz 2002: 64–72).

2.3.2 Counting similarities: the categorisation trap

In the effort to raise 'objective' criteria for the study of collective identities, one could be tempted to classify people according to certain criteria they meet. The descriptive terms Brubaker and Cooper suggested give examples of different ways of categorising objects – humans or anything else – by certain characteristics (Brubaker and Cooper 2000: 14ff.). Yet categorisation from the perspective of a neutral observer does not constitute personal or collective identities: stones, toys or dogs can be categorised, but they do not constitute social groups. Living on a certain territory, ethnic origin, culture, religion, language, history, lifestyle and the like are frequently used indicators to identify 'groups' – implying that the 'members' (must) have some sort of collective identity.

Yet what we can grasp from the standpoint of a neutral observer is only *numerical identification* (Tietz 2002: 215ff.). Even if a number of individuals share certain identifiable characteristics, this does not imply that these characteristics are meaningful for their individual or collective life. In fact, it does not predetermine at all whether these individuals perceive themselves as members of a group. Identifying individuals numerically is treating them like objects – we do not yet know whether the chosen characteristics are relevant to the individuals concerned. Following Tietz, I therefore propose to distinguish between *numerical identification* (or categorisation in Brubaker and Cooper's terms) and *qualitative identity* (Brubaker and Cooper 2000: 14ff.; Tietz 2002: 215ff.).

Any kind of object can be numerically identified in space and time and classified according to certain characteristics: material things, animals and humans. Yet humans are the *only* ones who are able to use the personal pronoun of the first-person singular or plural in a self-determined way. This is why 'speaking' toys such as the voice of your GPS system, as well as 'speaking' parrots or 'interactive' computers, perform something that sounds similar to a statement in the first-person singular, but do not have qualitative identities.

This in turn means that groups of persons are not identifiable in the same way as other observable 'objects'. Persons are the only kind of 'objects' who have an opinion about their being classified into one category or another (Tietz 2002: 217). Misidentification therefore may occur not only with regard to *numerical identification* in space and time, but also with regard to *qualitative identification*: each person can claim that he or she, or any other identified

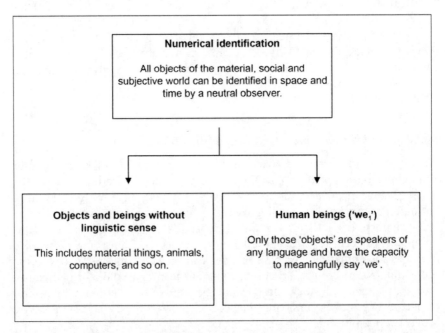

Figure 2.1 Numerical and qualitative identification
Source: Tietz (2002: 54–72), own depiction.

person, is not part of 'the group'. Even the existence of a numerically identified 'group' as a social group can be denied – for example because the classification criterion is irrelevant to the individuals concerned. This is the linguistic reason for the often-observed phenomenon that all collective identities and their respective identity markers are continually contested.

The distinction between *numerical* and *qualitative identity* resembles Durkheim's (1950 [1895]) fundamental insight that a 'social fact' in no way follows automatically from empirical facts. From the perspective of a neutral observer, nothing at all can be said about the self-understanding of the individuals concerned.

Nevertheless, numerical identification is not a trivial thing. If we can identify persons in space and time by certain criteria, it is logically implied that the pure existence of those objects is already out of question – 'no identity without entity' (Quine 1981: 102). Numerical identification – leaving open how the individuals concerned think of themselves – might be useful: for the purposes of social statistics or bureaucracies, or for legal uses, for example, these criteria are sufficient. We operate with them – even if they are inadequate indicators for deliberate or even active membership in a political community.

Substantialist conceptions of collective identity typically get trapped at this point: they suggest that primordial, cultural or linguistic similarities *per se* constitute social community. This means that they confuse the ontological dimension (*numerical identification*) with the hermeneutic dimension of the ethical self-understanding of the members of a community. Research on European identity has occasionally fallen into this trap. Different numerical identification strategies have been used to distinguish 'the Europeans' from the rest of mankind by geography, cultural heritage, religion, ethnicity, by reference to some sort of shared ancient, medieval or modern history, and so forth.[20] These strategies, however, have often paid little attention to the question as to whether at all, and if yes, to what degree (some of) these 'objective' features are considered relevant by the individuals concerned.

Some of those typical identification strategies are more plausible than others – however, pure categorisation of people according to some criteria does not yet constitute group membership, nor does it establish mutual obligations of any kind. None of the many attempts to define the limits of Europe by apparently pre-given criteria could give an answer to the question of European identity. Likewise, none could convincingly encompass all the small and large exceptions in history, the cross-connections, the flows of migrants and goods, and the cultural, economic, religious and political influences between the core of Europe, its peripheries, neighbouring regions and more distant parts of the world. None of these efforts could quiet the intense debates about who belongs to Europe and who does not.

There is, however, one formal criterion that has important practical implications. The single, most relevant political feature of the Europeans is EU citizenship status. It numerically identifies Europeans from the perspective of a neutral observer: everybody who holds citizenship status in any member state is an EU citizen. This 'group' has no essential features – its size changes with the borders of the Union. Every enlargement broadens it; a withdrawal of one member state would reduce it. Like any other *numerical identification*, it is ascribed regardless of the self-understanding of the individuals. Yet there is no ontological doubt: the described individuals exist and they are entitled to real rights and duties. This situation certainly creates real-world experiences – such as travelling without controls within Europe, enjoying increasing mobility within Europe regarding education and work, and being affected by EU governance. Those experiences in turn may become starting points for the development of *qualitative identities*, as will become clear in the following sections.

2.3.3 Sharing convictions about who we are: qualitative collective identities

In the previous section it was argued that 'collective identity' is not accessible from the perspective of the neutral observer. We need to take the perspective of the participants and ask for the self-understanding of the individuals concerned. When do persons refer to themselves as members of a community? How do they use the personal pronoun 'we'? What sorts of convictions do the members of a 'we-community' share with one another?

In the footsteps of new accounts of analytic philosophy (Austin 2009; Searle 1978, 2010), in the following I distinguish between three types of *qualitative identities*, proposing a simple way to overcome some of the typical aporias of sociological thinking on collective identities. Analytic philosophers used to clarify and logically analyse conceptual problems by scrutinising the use of natural language. They do not conduct empirical analysis as linguists or content analysts, but ask how certain terms can be meaningfully used in everyday language. This method proved to be especially fruitful because it released philosophical thought from several classical dichotomies (Davidson 1991). Recent accounts of analytic philosophy applied this methodology to the use of the personal pronoun 'we', which we use to refer to groups we are part of. As a result, three ideal-typical kinds of qualitative identity from the perspective of the speaking participant could be distinguished and marked by indexes (Tietz 2002: 54–72) – the community of all beings who have the capacity for language and action (we$_1$); and two kinds of groups smaller than humanity taken as a whole, which can be referred to as particularistic we-communities. Following Kant, members of groups who interact and cooperate for the purpose of different aims will be called we$_{2/commercium}$. Finally, there are also particularistic we-communities, who together pursue 'social goods' (Walzer 1983: 6–10) and developed a collective identity in the sense of a shared ethical self-understanding. They will be called we$_{2/communio}$ (see Figure 2.2).

Philosophers used to describe communities as groups of individuals who share certain beliefs (Rorty 1986). For the sake of systematic discussion, we

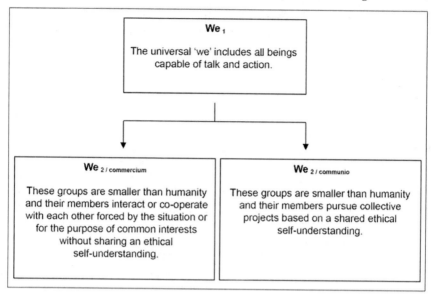

Figure 2.2 Uses of the personal pronoun 'we'
Source: Tietz (2002: 54–72), own depiction.

shall look at what can be said about the convictions that the members of the three ideal-typical 'we'-communities share with one another. While analytic philosophy proceeds by formal logical analysis or common-sense reasoning about the meaningful use of certain terms, the social sciences are today well equipped to study empirically the different uses of the personal pronoun 'we' and the convictions individuals share. Thus it is possible to transform these philosophical concepts into operational concepts for the social sciences. In the following sections, on one hand I further explain the different ways in which speakers express their conviction of being part of a community, and on the other I sketch in each instance what might follow from a language-analytic approach to collective identity for the study of European identity.

2.3.3.1 Humankind: the universal we₁

One meaningful use of the personal pronoun of the first-person plural refers to humanity in general – in contrast to animals, the dead material world, computers and so forth. When we use the term 'we' in this way, we express our membership in the *universal we₁*-community, which includes all beings capable of speech and action. This use is far from negligible: it is the expression of the fact that, by learning their first language, persons develop a linguistic sense, and they develop it together with the consciousness of sharing this sense with all humans and only with humans (Tietz 2002: 54–64). As children we learn concepts, verbs, personal pronouns and all other terms together with the relevant everyday knowledge about the things, social relations and feelings referred to. Hence knowing one language already includes a multitude of true convictions about the objective, social and subjective world: that the sun rises in the morning; that children need protection; or that people need to eat when they are hungry. By learning the system of personal pronouns of our language, we learn what it means to be a person, what it means to interact with a 'you', to be member of a group and so on. Countless of these convictions are shared across all boundaries of language and culture. 'Membership' in this universal community is the logical precondition of being a potential candidate for membership in any particularistic we_2-*community*.

What can be said about the identity of the Europeans in this sense? First, it is evident that the EU citizens are 'members' of the universal we_1. As such they can become members of particularistic we_2-groups: they know what it means to become and to be a member of a group. Like all humans, EU citizens are potentially able to cooperate with each other in order to accomplish their individual purposes and to make agreements or contracts with each other. Moreover, they are potentially able to create communities in an emphatic sense and strive for collective normative projects (see the following two sections). Whether they really do this – of course – remains an empirical question.

2.3.3.2 Sitting in the same boat: the $we_{2/commercium}$

Particularistic we_2-groups in the sense of a *commercium* consist of members of the universal we_1-community, and additionally draw on a collective identity in the sense of a shared interpretation of their situation or the awareness of being involved in a cooperative enterprise. This implies that they share the view that there is a collective problem, what it consists of, and that they themselves are the people who have to solve it. This is not given, but emerges, expresses itself and is reproduced in *pragmatic problem-solving debates*. The members of a *commercium* consider themselves as 'sitting in the same boat' – whether they like it or not. This shared conviction, however, does not include common ethical convictions: everybody follows only his or her own idiosyncratic desires and purposes. Various motives may be involved – but it is not a common, ethically motivated project that the members of the $we_{2/commercium}$ participate in. The members see the group as a club or neighbourhood, not as a family (Walzer 1983: 35–42).

In everyday life, political communities resemble the $we_{2/commercium}$: 'Egoistic' interests are negotiated against each other, mutual obligations are established, and contracts are agreed and upheld, but the participants primarily follow their own reasons without orientation towards any common good. The affiliation within a community in this minimalistic sense consists of the awareness of the individual participants to be – willingly or not – part of the 'game' and to be perhaps already equipped with certain rights within an institutionalised setting. In a classical liberal as well as in a procedural democratic view, the pragmatic identity of a we$_{2/commercium}$ is sufficient for the functioning of democracy (Habermas 1998b: Ch. 9).

2.3.3.3 Sharing ethical convictions: the we$_{2/communio}$

While in everyday political life our communities rather resemble the we$_{2/commercium}$ type, sometimes there are situations in which another kind of good is at stake: collective instead of individual interests. This may happen in the face of dramatic events, in situations of perceived crisis or sudden social change, or when people try to cope with traumatising collective experiences or striking injuries done to fundamental, ethical or moral convictions of the community members (Giesen 2004). Yet major positive changes, such as the defeat of a dictatorship, could also stimulate ethical discourses. It might be a major historical event (either catastrophic or fortunate), a proposal for the initiation of a grand collective project, or a major revision of it – in those situations, suddenly a certain nerve might be touched, and people begin to argue quite passionately for their normative convictions and values. In such rare historical situations, the political community appears, or has to prove itself, as a value-integrated we$_{2/communio}$.

A we$_{2/communio}$ consists of members of the universal we$_1$-community, but they do not necessarily possess shared 'objective' characteristics that the external observer could access. What characterises the members of a we$_{2/communio}$ is that they – beyond the universal linguistic sense and perhaps some practical interests – share values regarding a distinct common enterprise or a certain conception of what counts for them as a 'good life'. By *values* I understand predicates that are reified into 'goods'. Every attribute ('democratic', 'great', 'fit') can therefore become a value that is important for the ethical self-understanding of the members of a community who are proud of making these values essential for their shared life-form ('democracy' – for Germans today in contrast to their ancestors; 'greatness' – for the ancient Greeks; 'fitness' – for the community of body-builders). Only the group members as participating speakers can answer the question 'what is good or better for us to do?' (Tietz 2001: 113–124).

All kinds of different attributes might become values, but *communio*-identities in the political realm most often draw on one of three different 'identity codes': the *primordial*, the *cultural* and the *civic* (Eisenstadt and Giesen 1995). Bruter (2004) applied this distinction to European identity. It has been contested whether *constitutional patriotism* or civilian collective identities are comparable with the presumably 'stronger', 'deeper', more affective identities of the primordial and cultural type. In the perspective proposed in this study, and in line with authors such as Dewey, Apel and Habermas, the civilian code is a civil form of mutual recognition as fellow citizens and a form of solidarity (Apel 1988; Dewey 1927; Eriksen and Weigård 2003; Habermas 1996a; Kantner 2004b: Ch. 4.2; Sjursen 2007: 7; Tietz 2002). Civilian collective identity is not to be mistaken as mere respect of the laws for whatever instrumental reasons (including, for example, fear of sanctions). Civilian identity – or *constitutional patriotism* – is a 'hot', particularistic we$_{2/communio}$-identity. It consists in the fact that universalistic principles have been translated into values central to the self-understanding of the members of the collective.

In light of their specific conception of a 'good life', the members of a *communio* interpret their past and continue their traditions. Only collective identities in this normative sense consist of the widely shared ethical self-understanding of the individual members of a we$_{2/communio}$. This shared ethical self-understanding may be 'inherited' to a certain degree. Indeed, individuals are born as members of existing communities and are socialised into the basic ethical convictions of the group – later on, they deliberately share some of these beliefs and challenge others. Yet there is also another way to establish a *communio*: people might come together and create new we$_{2/communio}$ groups in order to pursue common ethical projects.

Especially in the latter case, the participants put emphasis on *present* problems and question how they want to live together in the *future*. Collective political identities in the sense of a *communio* develop, emerge, express and change through political debate and political conflict. Throughout this study, I refer to these debates on the ethical self-understanding of the members of a political community as '*ethical discourses*'. These debates are always action-related (Delanty and Rumford 2005: 51; Kantner 2004b: 186; Risse 2001: 201). This argument is put forward in another way by Etzioni (2007: 34, 36ff.), who calls identity discourses 'moral dialogues', as they touch the basic convictions of a political community. How the members of a community narrate their *past*, which events in which interpretation are considered to have the main importance, how events are ranked and so forth depends on how the members of the we$_{2/communio}$ see themselves today and which future they are striving for (compare also Stråth 2005).

Are such *communio*-identities a prerequisite for legitimate political decisions? With Habermas (1998b: Ch. 9)[21] I argue 'no' for ordinary politics and 'maybe' for coping with extraordinary challenges. For the establishment of far-reaching collective projects, a collective identity in the sense of a we$_{2/commercium}$ might *not* be sufficient. It may well be that a certain 'critical mass' of public support needs to be mobilised in order to institutionalise costly policies – such as establishing the welfare state or sending military troops into battle. Unlike communitarian positions would suggest, however, most public debates are *not* identity discourses – *ethical discourses* in our terms – that contribute to the redefinition of the ethical self-understanding of the community members. Only in the face of extraordinary problems and conflicts is the shared ethical self-understanding of the community members challenged. In those cases we are talking about 'hot' ethical convictions.

Yet these ethical core convictions can – much to the irritation of some identity entrepreneurs – never be fixed and defined too narrowly. Sharing ethical convictions does not mean that conflicts disappear or even diminish.

Identities in both particularistic senses are 'children' of conflicts. The ethical self-understanding of a group should be imagined as a *'corridor of normative convictions'* still large enough for intense dissent. This corridor of basic ethical convictions in fact demarcates the limits of what is ethically 'appropriate' within which further contention takes place (this adds to a better understanding of the 'logic of appropriateness'; March and Olsen 2004; Risse 2000).

2.3.4 Interim conclusions

This section has developed important conceptual tools regarding the debate on collective identities in general, as well as on European and other possible transnational identities in particular:

- In public debate and scientific discourse, it is quite common to try to answer the question of who might possibly belong to the European Union by identifying some 'objective' measures that would allow for a categorisation of a certain group of people as European or not. It was demonstrated that these strategies of *numerical identification* assume the *perspective of an uninvolved observer* and hence cannot access the convictions that the possible group members – assuming a *participant perspective* – may or may not share with each other. Therefore we concluded that the problem of a European identity cannot be solved by classification strategies. It might be that people who share identifiable characteristics in time and space fail to see themselves as group members. And it might be that people, despite not having 'European' geographical, ethnic, religious and historical features, do consider themselves as a – not yet recognised – part of the community. The poor, women and minorities claimed equal rights in national democracies' history in a similar fashion. If something is to be said about European identity in the qualitative sense, one has to evaluate how Europeans see themselves as Europeans.
- It can be further stated that Tönnies' (2001 [1887]) conceptual decision to put society (*commercium*) and community (*communio*) into radical opposition and, moreover, to romanticise the *communio* following a model of pre-modern rural or medieval guilds, led the tradition that followed him to rule out from analysis a whole universe of particularistic we-groups. This conceptual tradition often pushes empirical investigators who find shared convictions among the members of *commercium*-like groups into difficulties that can be solved only by stretching the concept of the community. In so doing, they contributed to the conceptual confusion criticised by Brubaker, Cooper, Niethammer and others (Brubaker and Cooper 2000; Niethammer 2000).
- In this section, three concepts have been introduced: for the remainder of this study I distinguish between *numerical identification* on one hand, and particularistic we-groups in the pragmatic sense of a we$_{2/\text{commercium}}$ and in

the ethical sense of a we$_{2/communio}$ on the other hand. *Numerical identification* proceeds from the perspective of non-involved observers who may classify objects according to chosen 'objective' features in space and time. However, these features are not necessarily relevant for the qualitative individual as well as collective identities of human beings. By contrast, we-groups in the pragmatic sense of a we$_{2/commercium}$ consist of members who *refer to themselves* as 'we'. They share at least certain beliefs about a common problematic situation in which they find themselves 'sitting in the same boat'. This may lead them to begin common undertakings. However, this does not depend on holding shared *ethical* convictions. The members may have very different motives and no sense of a common project. In everyday life, political communities tend to resemble a we$_{2/commercium}$. This has important virtues. As a matter of fact, it is a central civilising achievement of the liberal state, rule of law and modern representative democracy to organise political life by procedures for conflict resolution without pressure to reach consensus on values. Citizens in a democracy have the right to be different and distinct from each other. The pluralism of values and the search for political compromises is, in addition, an important mechanism for peaceful change and reform in modern democracies. We-groups in the sense of a we$_{2/communio}$ consist of members who – in addition to what has been said about we$_{2/commercium}$-groups – also share basic ethical convictions and values, and perceive themselves as having a common vision of what is, for them, a 'good life'. We called this a 'shared ethical self-understanding'.

These concepts are of course ideal-types. In reality, what the group members mean when they refer to themselves as members of the group by using the first personal plural pronoun – 'we' – oscillates between the two meanings. Democratic political communities, for example, appear most of the time in the *commercium*-sense (Habermas 1998b: Ch. 9). Only in extraordinary moments perceived as historical events or critical junctures, and with regard to especially sensitive matters, do they appear in the *communio*-sense. But if identity-formation is a communicative process, can it be conceived of beyond the nation state? The following section tackles this question.

2.4 Transnational political communication

2.4.1 Can we conceive of a transnational public sphere?

I have shown, then, that collective identities emerge, express themselves, and are transformed in *pragmatic problem-solving debates* – which may lead to shared problem-perceptions, a we$_{2/commercium}$ collective identity based on a sense of 'sitting in the same boat' – and *ethical discourses* about the shared ethical self-understanding of the community members in the context of the problem at hand. The latter may result in the establishment or reformulation of a we$_{2/communio}$ identity, a 'normative corridor of ethical convictions', which demarcates the limits within which further argument takes place. Yet are such political debates possible at all beyond the nation state?[22]

In the literature we find two opposing camps concerning this question. On one hand, scholars of globalisation processes and global public spheres are, in general, optimistic about the prospects of transnational political communication and the possibilities of transnational democracy (see e.g. Bohman 1998; Dryzek 1999: 44; Rabinder 1999; Stichweh 2003; Volkmer 2003). Paradoxically, the literature on European public spheres tends to hold that transnational European communication encounters almost insurmountable obstacles (see e.g. Gerhards 2001; Graf von Kielmansegg 1996; Grimm 1995). The sceptics object that on the transnational level, associative (*Vergesellschaftung*) and even more communal (*Vergemeinschaftung*) relationships in the sense of Max Weber (1978: 40–41) are – for the time being – almost impossible because of a lack of ability to communicate transnationally. In their view, the lack of a transnational European public sphere is at the root of the impossibility of democratising the European Union.

This is a crucial question also with regard to public debate on the use of military force – a former core issue of national interest and sovereignty, which has become transnationalised (or rather Europeanised) over time. The development of a transnational European public sphere is a precondition for overcoming the often criticised 'democratic deficit' with respect to CFSP/ESDP (Born and Hänggi 2004; Kantner and Liberatore 2006; Peters et al. 2014; Wagner 2006, 2007).

But what is a *public sphere*? We know much about the functions that the public sphere fulfils in democratic societies (Gerhards and Neidhardt 1991; Habermas 1989, 1998b: 239–252; Luhmann 1990: 181f.; Neidhardt 1994: 8–10). It has – in a classical liberal and in a system-theoretical view – a *transparency function*, in the sense of a fourth power that controls the political system and its actors, but also in the sense of providing a 'mirror' in which the political actors can compare how present they are, how strong their political camp is and how their positions are evaluated. The public sphere has – in a more discourse-theoretical view – a *heuristic validation function*. In discursive processes opinions are argumentatively formed, sharpened and verified. On the larger societal scale, public opinion formed in the public sphere has an *orientation function* in that it allows citizens to build informed opinions about the important political issues (Habermas 1989; Taylor 1995: 186). All these functions contribute decisively to *social integration* in highly differentiated, modern, heterogeneous societies via their systematic, constitutionally guaranteed and procedurally filtered input into the institutional political decision process (Habermas 1996b).[23]

Following Habermas and Taylor, as well the 'arena model of the public sphere' (Hilgartner and Bosk 1988), I conceptualise 'the public sphere' as a *metatopical common space* consisting of multiple arenas of political communication in which people discuss common interests and form their opinions about them. Taylor (1995: 190) uses the term *metatopical* space to differentiate between arenas where people physically come together at a certain place – topical spaces – and a 'larger space of non-assembly' – the non-local, abstract, imagined metatopical common space.

The different 'arenas' are formalised to different degrees, hierarchically structured and socially organised: everyday political encounters are unorganised and very open, encompassing only few people; organisational publics (e.g. associations, political parties, civil society organisations etc.) are more hierarchically structured and differentiated in active speaker and passive listener roles. The media represent, in modern societies, an arena that can include a very large audience; however, they are complex social organisations, and ordinary citizens are rarely present as active *speakers* in this arena (Gerhards and Neidhardt 1991). What links these different arenas together and gives the social practice of 'talking about politics' a meaning is the idea that the different arenas are inter-communicating and inter-referring, that what I say, criticise, demand, scandalise … can in principle be heard by other citizens and the political authorities:

> I say 'a common space,' because although the media are multiple, as well as the exchanges that take place in them, these are deemed to be in principle intercommunicating. The discussion we're watching on television now takes account of what was said in the newspaper this morning, which in turn reports on the radio debate yesterday, and so on. That's why we usually speak of the public sphere, in the singular.
> (Taylor 1995: 186)

This 'naïve' understanding of communicative practice is a constitutive presupposition that gives 'talking about politics' any sense at all. When we talk about politics, when we publish a newspaper article criticising a politician, when we burn flags or other political symbols at a protest event, we know that in fact few people listen to us, read what we wrote, or become angry about our protest gestures. However, we 'pretend' that the whole country or even the whole world sees us. Moreover, the assumed mutual observation of the actors in the diverse arenas of the public sphere is a fiction only on the individual level. On a systemic level, mutual observation is a practice that contributes to *inter-media agenda-setting* effects:

> Each institution is populated by a community of operatives who scrutinise the activities of their counterparts in other organizations and arenas. Journalists read each other's work in a constant search for story ideas. Television producers scan the symbolic landscape for fresh subjects for dramas. Legislators seek ideas from neighboring states. Activists 'network' to gather information, maintain contacts, and spread ideas. Nor is this attention only passive and reactive. Indeed, an active attempt to influence events in other arenas is the rule, rather than the exception. …

If we explore these complex linkages, we find a huge number of positive feedback loops, 'engines,' that drive the growth of particular problems.

(Hilgartner and Bosk 1988: 67)

The development of a *transnational (European) public sphere* has been at the centre of controversial scientific debates over the past 15 years. In the first stages of this debate, it seemed quite uncontroversial that meaningful political communication and deliberation was confined within national borders (see e.g. Gerhards 2001; Graf von Kielmansegg 1996; Grimm 1995). How could one conceive of transnational public discourses, given the diversity of languages, media systems and civic traditions? Meanwhile, there are strong theoretical arguments that transnational political communication can take place across language barriers and across national media systems:

- The homogeneous vision of 'the national public sphere', sketched by those who argue that a European public sphere would not be possible in the debate, is under-complex and idealised. Already, in national public spheres, people do not form a homogeneous group and they are not all exposed to exactly the same media content (Eder and Kantner 2000, 2002, 2004b; Risse 2010: 109–120; 2015). Any *political* discussion is about conflicting interests, contradictions and incompatible visions of the good life. We do not exchange compliments and reassure each other of our collective identity when we discuss political affairs. With the help of democratic procedures, we try to deal with our differences in a peaceful way. Citizens use media products selectively and receive only a small proportion of the available 'messages'. However, in the metatopical space of the public sphere, which consists of a myriad individual arenas in which various speakers compete for the audiences' attention and try to convince them of their interpretations and evaluations of events, as well as of their proposals for problem solutions, a 'national debate' emerges through the thematic intertwinement of these discourses.
- Elsewhere I have argued that the linguistic sense of the members of the *universal we$_1$* provides the theoretical and empirical basis for the conceptualisation of transnational communication. Since humans share a linguistic sense, they are potentially able to enter each other's language games by going through the *hermeneutic circle* and getting to know each other's convictions (Kantner 2003, 2004b: 111–130). Speakers of any natural language can mutually enter each other's language games in the discourse about subject matters they consider interesting and improve their mutual understanding step by step. Thus it is possible to overcome language barriers, cultural differences and the like. Indeed, this is only a more extreme version of what people do every day: any real discussion involves different perspectives on the problem in question as well as concepts in need of clarification (Kantner 2004b: Ch. 4; Tietz 2002). The language games constituted by different natural languages are not

incommensurable: we$_1$ can start to communicate with each other if we$_1$ want to. Whether we$_1$ do so, of course, remains an empirical question.

Why should debates on European or international issues not also be intertwined and interlinked –via common experiences of problematic situations, via press agencies, journalistic, policy and civil society networks – so that people in different countries can develop their opinions about the same events and issues? If it is true that the 'public consists of all those who are affected by the indirect consequences of transactions to such an extent that it is deemed necessary to have those consequences systematically cared for' (Dewey 1927: 15f.), local, national and transnational political communication develops according to the same problem-focused logic:

> At the other limit there are social groups so separated by rivers, seas and mountains, by strange languages and gods, that what one of them does – save in war – has no appreciable consequences for another. There is therefore no common interest, no public, and no need nor possibility of an inclusive state. The plurality of states is such a universal and notorious phenomenon that it is taken for granted. ... But it sets up ... a test difficult for some theories to meet. Except upon the basis of a freakish limitation in the common will and reason which is alleged to be the foundation of the state, the difficulty is insuperable. It is peculiar, to say the least, that universal reason should be unable to cross a mountain range and objective will be balked by a river current. The difficulty is not so great for many other theories. But only the theory which makes recognition of consequences the critical factor can find in the fact of many states a corroborating trait. Whatever is a barrier to the spread of the consequences of associated behavior by that very fact operates to set up political boundaries.
>
> (Dewey 1927: 42f.)

Since technological change has led to an extension of the range of economic, political and communicative interactions, it becomes even more likely that political communication is limited by the interaction radius of the problem at stake and less according to 'arbitrary' borders. The horizon of political communication on international issues also follows the same 'naïve' understanding of communicative practice as that outlined above. When we talk with friends and colleagues about shocking events in Rwanda; when we publish a newspaper article criticising George W. Bush for his administration's *à la carte* approach to international law; when people burn flags at demonstrations against the Iraq War, they 'pretend' that the whole world notices. Hence when we meet people from other countries, say on an aeroplane or in a beach bar during our holiday, and we happen to talk about political issues, we start the discussion as we would talk with somebody from our own country. Perhaps we listen more carefully at the beginning[24] until we have a feeling for the

Theoretical building blocks 39

political camp he or she tends towards, and then later seriously discuss facts, claims and appropriate policy solutions about the given issue. Hence we can speak of a *transnational public sphere* to the degree that:

- the same transnational issues are discussed;
- at the same time; and
- under similar aspects of relevance (Eder and Kantner 2000: 81; Kantner 2004b: 58),[25] that is, with a similar framing but not necessarily with the same opinions.[26]

In these debates, bilateral, transnational and international institutions and politicians are likely to be frequent objects of discussion: their *visibility* in the media corresponds to the degree of supra-nationalisation (della Porta and Caiani 2006; Gleissner and De Vreese 2005; Kevin 2003; Koopmans and Erbe 2004; Koopmans and Statham 2010; Machill et al. 2006; Semetko et al. 2000: 130). Especially in regard to this expectation, media debates on war and peace are a 'tough case' for the development of transnational European public communication. On one hand, 'Europe' here competes directly with Member States as traditional security actors who might insist on their national sovereignty; on the other hand, it rivals the Western-transatlantic security relationship with the USA and other NATO members.

Comparative media content analyses on EU-related political communication in general, as well as studies on particular European policy issues, came to the conclusion that many issues are debated cross-nationally. The media do cover a broad range of EU issues on a regular basis, and their share of coverage compared with national issues is much larger than thought by the sceptics (Kantner 2006b; Kevin 2003; Peter and de Vreese 2003; Trenz 2004). European integration is not only covered in relation to distinct EU issues, but has become an integral part of national political and economic coverage (Semetko et al. 2000: 129). Disagreement persists over the question whether the glass is half full or half empty and how intense inter-discursive relations between the national publics are needed.

Most studies on transnational European public communication come to the conclusion that – despite important differences – similar interpretations and structures of meaning prevail across national media arenas when EU-related subjects are reported. The interpretation or *framing* (though not necessarily the majority opinion) of European and Europeanised issues is astonishingly similar across national borders (see e.g. Eder and Kantner 2000; Kantner 2004b, 2006b; Risse 2010: Part III; Trenz 2004, 2005; van de Steeg 2000). Empirical studies could, moreover, demonstrate that transnational debates are not limited to the government positions on the international political level. The same *set of competing arguments* (not *one* frame or *one* opinion) dominates the discourse in different countries. Surprisingly, this also holds true with regard to ethical issues: instead of 27 different national frames of meaning on each topic, there are only a couple of normative positions that

40 Theoretical building blocks

are critically debated in all countries. This could be shown in a cross-national frame analysis of the Haider debate[27] concerning European sanctions against Austria, when the right-wing populist FPÖ came in second in the 1999 national elections and entered the government coalition in 2000. With regard to this scandal, one would have expected opposing interpretative frames and opinions across Europe. Instead, the same four frames dominated the debate in all countries studied by the authors (Risse 2002a, 2002b: 15; 2010; van de Steeg 2004, 2006; van de Steeg et al. 2003). A similar pattern was observed in the media discourse about the European constitution (Bärenreuter et al. 2005; Fossum and Trenz 2005; Kutter 2009). Discussions remained largely within a limited set of possible views on the topic – even across countries.

Hence the *same European issues* are being debated at the *same time*, with similar issue cycles, under *similar aspects of relevance* (i.e. interpretative frames) within Europe. If citizens want to inform themselves about European political issues, they can do so in their mother tongue through the national mass media (Eder and Kantner 2000, 2002; Kantner 2004b: 130–162; Risse 2010, 2015). These problem-oriented pragmatic debates and ethical discourses do not emerge as a result of central coordination or identity politics. Speakers in the public realm, editorial staff and journalists seem to perceive these ethically sensitive issues as common transnational problems of broad public interest. Fundamental questions such as 'how do we, as EU citizens, want to live together?' and 'what is good or better for us as Europeans to do?' are already intensively discussed in the European public sphere for many crucial policy fields.

2.4.2 Termini technici: *issue cycles and news values*

Having argued on a theoretical level and demonstrated at the empirical level – through reference to the research literature – that transnational political communication is possible, opens the way to applying the concepts and methods used in the analysis of national political communication beyond the nation state. For this study, the concepts '*issue cycle*' and '*news value*' used in political communication research are of central importance and must be briefly introduced.

In this study I am interested in comparing the intensity of media attention on wars and humanitarian military interventions cross-nationally in order to establish whether the debates in the national arenas are thematically intertwined. I refer to *issues* rather than 'the coverage of this and that event'. An *event* is a particular instance of something happening – such as an international crisis event or a NATO summit. It is not the same as an *issue*, a controversial social problem, which constitutes a broader topical structure, encompassing several events as belonging together. Issues compete with each other on the public agenda. The attention paid to issues has a kind of life cycle, the *issue attention cycle* or *issue cycle*:

public attention rarely remains ... focused upon any one ... issue for very long ... Instead, ... [e]ach of these problems suddenly leaps into prominence, remains there for a short time, and then gradually fades from the center of public attention.

(Downs 1972: 38)

The issue cycle conceptualises the intensity of attention paid to an issue over time – usually quantified in the form of article numbers. Downs discovered that public debates follow a typical cycle in which different stages can be identified. In the *pre-problem stage* an undesirable social condition already exists, but has not yet captured much public attention. However, some experts or interest groups may already be alarmed by it (Downs 1972: 39).[28] In the second stage, some dramatic series of events results in sudden public awareness and *alarmed discovery* of the problem together with *euphoric enthusiasm* about society's ability to 'solve this problem' effectively within a narrow time frame.[29] Pressure on political leaders is exerted 'to do something' (Downs 1972: 39). Solutions that are not institutionalised at this point have to wait until the issue returns – some time in the future – to the public agenda. At this peak in the issue cycle, ethical discourses, appeals to common values and common projects, are also likely to be most intense. In the third phase, attention has been raised and solutions are debated. This, however, ultimately leads to *realising the cost of significant progress* (Downs 1972: 40), which may lead in a fourth step to a *gradual decline of intense public interest*. People are discouraged, threatened – not by the issue, but by proposals for its solution – or they become bored. Disillusionment about the prospects for simple *ad hoc* solutions spreads. Attention to the issue wanes, and new issues may enter the scene.

Downs calls the last phase of a typical issue cycle the *post-problem stage*. It is characterised by less attention and spasmodic recurrences of interest. Yet, while interest was sharply focused on the problem (stage 2), the problem may have been institutionalised in the public consciousness and/or the policy agenda more or less successfully. New institutions, programmes, groups of experts and policies may have been created to help solve it. If that was the case, these institutions persist and work to handle the problem more or less successfully in a routinised, professionalised way. Important aspects of the problem may become connected to new problems – they turn into an established interpretative 'frame'. Interpretative frames that emerge in transnational debates may 'hit home'.[30] Problems that have undergone the issue-attention cycle completely from then on generally receive a higher average level of attention than they did before their career (Downs 1972: 40f.). We should be able to observe this phenomenon as an upwards level shift in the time-series data presented in this study.

Besides describing the issue cycles for wars and humanitarian military interventions, this study is also interested in contributing to an explanation of *how events 'drive' issue cycles*. The most influential theory that addresses this question is the theory of *news values*. In assuming an interrelationship between real-world events, the intensity of news coverage and public convictions, we can draw on the theory of news values as developed in political communication studies. News value theories assume that real-world events feature certain qualities that render them more or less 'newsworthy' and that this 'newsworthiness' determines how likely events and stories are to be selected for news coverage by journalists.

The 'newsworthiness' of an event is of course no 'objective' feature, but is attributed to events and stories according to journalists' conventionalised assumptions about newsworthiness – their 'hypotheses of the (relevance of) reality' (Schulz 1976: 30). Scholars (and journalists) agree that audiences apply similar criteria when selecting news stories for reading, listening or viewing (Eilders 2006; Galtung and Holmboe Ruge 1965: 64f.). Therefore '[t]he more newsworthy an event is considered to be by the journalists, the more likely it will be selected for publication, and the more likely it will be prominently placed' (Eilders 2006: 6). News values serve as journalistic news-selection criteria, and may not be problem adequate from an intellectual perspective. As Dewey himself noted:

> The catastrophic, namely, crime, accident, family rows, personal clashes and conflicts, are the most obvious forms of breaches of continuity; they supply the element of shock which is the strictest meaning of sensation; they are *new* par excellence, even though only the date of the newspaper could inform us whether they happened last year or this, so completely are they isolated from their connections.
> (Dewey 1927: 180)

Following seminal works by Lippmann (1922), Buckalew (1969/70), Galtung and Holmboe Ruge (1965), Östgaard (1965) and Schulz (1976), researchers scrutinised published news stories in order to identify the factors that were attributed news value by journalists. These journalistic selection criteria include the following (Galtung and Holmboe Ruge 1965: 65–71; Staab 1990: 424–427):

- The importance of events has to be beyond a certain threshold. Events must have significant or dramatic effects in terms of concern and consequence in order to be reported upon. There must be some controversy, conflict, success or failure. Negative news will be privileged over good news. Personalised events or stories – those where we see the persons who are acting, who is in conflict with whom – will be preferred because they can also be more easily dramatised and moralised.
- A clear and unambiguous message makes it into the news more easily. Complex processes will be under-reported, simple interpretations (good versus evil) are preferred (Hilgartner and Bosk 1988: 59).
- News that fits well with the journalistic routines and rhythms of news production will be privileged. Hence processes that develop slowly will be

under-reported; events that seem to have immediate effects will be preferred. Follow-up stories to issues that are already on the agenda, however, are selected even if they have otherwise relatively low news value.
- Events interpretable within the cultural framework of the audience, and events with relevant implications for the reader or listener, tend to be given prominence. Moreover, what fits into a certain horizon of expectations, has been predicted (or institutionally scheduled), or is wished for against the background of already established beliefs or prejudices will be preferred. However, among meaningful and resonant events, those that are 'unexpected' or rare will be privileged.
- Journalists try to present a 'balanced' selection of news. Hence news items of the same type compete against each other. This increases the threshold for new or additional items to be covered (Hilgartner and Bosk 1988: 55).
- Members of social elites in terms of status, power, prestige or popularity will be favoured. 'Elite nations' will be preferred. This term is not further elaborated by Galtung and Holmboe Ruge (1965: 68, 71). It is rather a metaphor that draws on the observation that more 'important' or 'prestigious' or powerful nations receive more attention than the 'peripheral' ones.

Galtung and Holmboe Ruge hold that '[t]he higher the total score of an event, the higher the probability that it will become news, and even make headlines' (Galtung and Holmboe Ruge 1965: 71). News factors add up to the final 'news value' of an event – this has been called the *'additivity hypothesis'* (Galtung and Holmboe Ruge 1965: 71; Rosengren 1974: 145). However, if a story scores low on one factor, this may be compensated for by high values on other dimensions – this has been called the *'complementary hypothesis'* (Galtung and Holmboe Ruge 1965: 72; Rosengren 1974: 145).

However, as Rosengren (1970; 1974) pointed out, the investigation of relevance criteria in media content and media content reception will not provide us with the full picture of the 'media reality' if we do not compare it with data external to the media and search for correlations. In this study I use media-external event-type data as independent variables. They have been constructed according to the following assumptions, drawing on news value theories.

According to these criteria, one can expect that *dramatic crisis events* – outbreaks of war, massacres, major terrorist attacks – will trigger most media coverage, since they involve many victims. These events show immediate results and are highly significant, unambiguously bad news. Their *per se* extremely high news value can even be heightened if such events take place in elite nations, such as 9/11 in the USA, or the civil wars on the European continent in the former Yugoslavia in the 1990s, and somewhat reduced if they happen in regions that are peripheral to the Western countries, such as small African countries.

Bureaucratic institutional events, in contrast, are considered boring: they involve complex, ambiguous messages about the negotiation positions of the

44 Theoretical building blocks

diverse actors involved and a broad range of competing arguments, and they develop slowly. When a decision is announced, it still takes time until it is implemented and longer still until we see results. For these reasons, it is argued that the EU is and will remain under-reported by the media, and this is considered one of the central obstacles for the development of a European public sphere (Gerhards 2001). The same argument would hold for NATO and the UN: summits and other institutional events of the EU (including CFSP/ESDP events), NATO, the UN and other international actors should tend to have a low news value, even if they are reported upon as significant routine events in which elite nations participate. Only if the use of force is concerned might these institutions receive major media attention. Therefore *humanitarian military interventions* conducted by the UN, NATO, EU and other actors may gain significant coverage. This high level of attention might even be increased if the use of military force is conducted without UN consent, since this should result in a higher score of unambiguous negativity.

The *involvement of the countries under study* in international diplomatic or military crisis-management activities can also be expected to result in varying news values. All the countries in this study are, in Galtung's and Holmboe Ruge's terms, 'elite nations'. However, the US would rank first as the last remaining global super-power, followed by the medium powers France and Great Britain, and then the other countries under study (Austria, Germany, Ireland, the Netherlands). Although Austria and Ireland have a long and successful tradition of participation in humanitarian military interventions, their crisis-management activities might – because of their status as non-participants in NATO – have a lower news value. In general, important *national events*, such as *parliamentary or presidential elections*, could decrease reporting on international crises and crisis management to a substantial degree. For all these features, monthly counts have been generated as independent variables for the empirical part of this study. Having the conceptual tools prepared, we can begin to formulate empirically testable hypotheses for this study.

2.5 The study: research questions and hypotheses

This study investigates the occurrence and the dynamics of *pragmatic problem-solving debates*, in which common *problem-perceptions* and a European *problem-solving community* (*commercium*-aspect) may have emerged, on one hand; and *ethical discourses,* in which the ethical foundations of collective problem-solving practices are debated and a *shared ethical self-understanding* (*communio*-aspect of a European identity) may have developed, on the other.

The first central research question of this study concerns collective sense-making in pragmatic problem-solving debates beyond the nation state. Did transnational European or transatlantic problem-solving debates on the use of military force – in 'ordinary wars' or in normatively positively connoted 'humanitarian military interventions' – take place? What accounts for whether and when public attention is directed to the problems at stake? Were wars and humanitarian military interventions discussed in all the countries under study at the same time? Are the issue cycles similar across countries? Do the peaks respond to the same crises and/or to the same types of crisis events? Are there intra-European and transatlantic differences? Three empirically testable hypotheses or assumptions guide the investigation.

Hypothesis 1

Based on the arguments developed with regard to transnational political communication and a European public sphere, I hypothesise that there is a transnational debate on wars and humanitarian military interventions. Rather than each country following its own idiosyncratic logic, I expect the *same issues* to be discussed at the *same times* across the countries under investigation. This would result in very similar issue cycles in the different countries. Moreover, I expect convergence processes that are unlikely to vary much across the Atlantic, since with regard to issues of wars and interventions, interdependence and therefore also problem-oriented debate is assumed to be global in scope.

Hypothesis 2

While many authors hold that political discourses in different countries are more or less incommensurable with each other with regard to the frames of interpretation (most explicitly Greven 2000), I expect that *similar aspects of relevance* will be discussed – the more so the higher the density of interdependence and interaction in the policy field. While NATO is the most relevant security organisation for the majority of the EU countries, they were affected by the wars in the former Yugoslavia more directly than the US. These wars' externalities – such as refugee streams – had a substantial impact on EU countries and prompted radical changes in their stance towards the use of military force. The European governments and militaries experienced insufficient military capabilities and their lack of influence in NATO decision making (Mérand 2003, 2008). From the Saint Malo Declaration onwards, they built up the ESDP, which increased their interaction density in security and defence policy (Howorth 2007: Chs 1–2). Hence I expect the part of the discourse that addresses the normative framing of the – possible – use of military force as 'humanitarian military intervention' to be more similar and to more strongly converge among the EU countries. Conversely, this implies that transatlantic differences are likely to be more pronounced in the normatively framed part of the debate.

Hypothesis 3

In accordance with the pragmatist and pragmatist-constructivist tradition, I assume that debate is focused on concrete problems. This problem-focus can be operationalised, first, according to the theory of news values. This theory holds that specific *event-types* with high news values receive a disproportionally large share of media attention and hence 'drive' the issue cycle (Buckalew 1969/70; Eilders 2006; Galtung and Holmboe Ruge 1965; Östgaard 1965; Schulz 1976; Staab 1990). Second, assuming there is no automatism between crisis events and their becoming perceived as a public problem (Dewey 1927; Hilgartner and Bosk 1988), problem-focus can be alternatively operationalised as *individual crisis events* and episodes that 'drive' the debate. Both variants can be tested by using event data external to the media as independent variables in the study (as proposed by Rosengren 1970, 1974).

The second central research question of this study is whether a European identity emerged with regard to security issues as a result of public debates on international crisis events and crisis-management attempts in the form of humanitarian military interventions. If the EU is not visible in the discourse on wars and interventions, and if such a European identity is not expressed in the public discourse, it would be very unlikely that it exists on the citizens' level, as one cannot have a collective identity without knowing it. Three empirically testable hypotheses or assumptions guide the investigation.

Hypothesis 4

Since interdependence and interaction is assumed to be higher among the EU countries than across the Atlantic, drawing on Dewey (1927), I expect Europe in general and the EU in particular to be much more visible in the European than in the US media.

Hypothesis 5

If a European identity emerges after the end of the Cold War, this should result in an increase of expressions of European identity over time in the EU countries and a convergence in attention paid to European identity.

Hypothesis 6

With Dewey (1927), I expect that new collective identities emerge as both a pragmatic problem-solving community (*commercium*) and an ethical community of values (*communio*). I expect to find a persistently stronger presence of the EU as a *commercium* than as a *communio* in the debate, since, drawing on Habermas (1998b: Ch. 9), I assume that political communities resemble a *commercium* most of the time and that this is sufficient for political integration. Alternatively, one can assume – also in accordance with Dewey – that the concrete context of the conflict at hand matters most. With regard to some conflicts, the EU might be addressed as a problem-solving community (*commercium*), while with regard to other conflicts, it might be addressed as a community of values (*communio*).

Chapter 3 describes how these hypotheses will been translated into measurable indicators. It explains the methods developed for the investigation of more than one-and-a-half decades of transnational public debates on wars and humanitarian military interventions in the media of seven countries.

Notes

1. The most important predecessors of the ESDP were the Western European Union (WEU) created in 1948 (Italy and Germany joined in 1954); the Pleven Plan for a European Defence Community (EDC) in 1950, which failed in its ambitions; and the emergence of European Political Cooperation (EPC) since 1970 (an intergovernmental mechanism of foreign policy cooperation, which became integrated in the EC framework with the Single European Act 1986). For a short overview of these developments in the context of international crises events, see Wallace 2005: 430–435).
2. An example of such policy failure is the uncoordinated recognition policy of the 1990s with regard to the secession states in the Balkans, which contributed to the region's descent into conflict.
3. The concept *'security community'* was initially introduced by Karl W. Deutsch with respect to the development of NATO after the Second World War (Deutsch 1954; Deutsch et al. 1957). It has been further developed and extended in its territorial scope by Adler and Barnett (Adler 2005; Adler and Barnett 1998).
4. Throughout this study I use 'Member States' to refer to the Member State governments as institutionalised collective actors on the international level. However, I use 'member states' when referring to the countries of the EU in the sense of geographical, political or cultural spaces.
5. One distinguishes between *peacekeeping* (e.g. help to implementing a peace process, assistance); *peace-enforcement* (e.g. as in peacekeeping missions the impartial monitoring of ceasefires and peace contracts between the former opponents, albeit with a mandate and the respective military equipment to use force against violations of that contract); and 'robust' *peace-making* (i.e. ending the conflict without the consent of the conflict partners by use of severe military force).
6. The EUROPUB project included the issue of 'troop deployment' in its comparison of the degrees of transnationalisation (which turned out to be exceptionally high) and Europeanisation (which was low but slightly increased over time) of a number of policy fields (Koopmans 2004; Koopmans and Statham 2010; Pfetsch 2004).
7. Another variant of the argument against the possibility of transnational political communication on the level of ordinary people therefore holds that transnational publics emerged, but remain restricted to the (multilingual) elites only (see e.g. Schlesinger 1999, 2007; Schlesinger and Kevin 2000).
8. For a critique of the assumption of an automatism from the installation of more possibilities of democratic participation to more collective identity and political trust, see also Moravcsik (2006).
9. See, for example, the communication and public relations strategy 'Plan D for Democracy, Dialogue and Debate' proposed by the European Commission after the failed referenda in 2005 (Commission of the European Communities 2005).
10. Vobruba (1999) has argued, for example, that redistributive social policies in Europe would require a 'reallocation permissive identity'.
11. The term 'hot' is widely used in the German politico-philosophical debate over collective identities to denote issues and beliefs about which we are passionate because they touch upon core normative convictions. They go to the heart of what it means to be 'we$_{2/communio}$'.

48 Theoretical building blocks

12 Many deeply rooted views on ethically sensitive issues result from traumatic (national) historical experiences. This is valid for groups of former victims as well as perpetrators (Elster 2004; Giesen 2004).
13 It is not long ago that attempts to create a new 'socialist human' failed miserably in the former communist regimes of Central Eastern Europe. Attempts to manufacture identities even contributed to regime unpopularity. In light of these attempts, significant doubts towards identity politics on the EU level are justified.
14 Such cognitive trajectories and policy traditions in the field of security and defence policy derive from peculiar national experiences, such as victories – or defeats – in wars; national traumas experienced as victims – or perpetrators; or ties to former colonies, which often are of crucial importance for national identity (see e.g. Alexander 2002; Elster 2004; Giesen 2004; Levy and Sznaider 2002).
15 The link with institutionalisation of the CFSP/ESDP cannot be further empirically tested in this study; however, further analysis of the data produced for this study in combination with external data on CFSP/ESDP institutionalisation processes could follow this trail in-depth.
16 Modern international law regulating armed conflict (The United Nations Charter, The Hague Convention, The Geneva Convention) could be viewed as legal codifications of the norms and principles developed by the 'just war theory' in practical philosophy.
17 This section draws on ideas published elsewhere (Kantner 2004a, 2006a, 2006b, 2006c, 2010). I am grateful to the publishers for their kind permission to reproduce it here.
18 Habermas (1998b: Ch. 4) disagreed with this view and argued that a civil form of solidarity has been, and can be, produced in the democratic process itself.
19 Brubaker and Cooper propose terms such as 'identification' and 'categorisation' by external observers or agencies such as the state, 'social location' or 'self-understanding'. But even 'self-understanding' is used in a descriptive sense: for the two authors it means 'counting oneself among a certain class of objects' and represents an ethically neutral manner of self-description (Brubaker and Cooper 2000: 17).
20 Some very good overviews have been published of the different strategies used to distinguish between Europe and the outside since the Middle Ages and in recent decades (see e.g. Cole and Cole 1997; Malmborg and Stråth 2002; Münkler 1996).
21 Lacroix (2003: 161f.; 2006: 38–39) reaches a similar conclusion with regard to the democratisation of the European Union.
22 This section draws on research that also appears in other publications (Eder and Kantner 2000; Kantner 1997, 2003, 2004b, 2015; Kantner and Liberatore 2006). I am grateful to the respective publishers for their kind permissions.
23 Public opinion formation at the transnational level can be seen as a 'weak' public in Fraser's terms (Fraser 1992: 25ff.). The organised input of these opinions into the political decision making process, their procedural transformation into 'strong' publics, is under-developed even with regard to the European Union, the most democratic supranational political system (Habermas 1998a, 2004; Kantner 2004b). 'Strong publics' endowed with decision power or legally guaranteed influence on decision-making are widely missing on a global level (Brunkhorst 2002). Legally institutionalised participation of societal interests, NGOs and other non-state actors in the processes of political will-formation on the level of European (or global governance) is what currently comes closest to Fraser's 'strong publics' beyond the nation state (Eriksen 2005).
24 In the case of multilingual face-to-face communication, this has been tested empirically by Nicole Dörr in the context of the World and European Social Forums (Dörr 2008, 2009, 2012).
25 The formula 'the same topics at the same time under similar aspects of relevance' goes back to Habermas (1998b: 160). However, Habermas demands the whole set

of 'ingredients' of a 'complete' transnational public sphere with strong civil society organisations and political parties organised on a European scale, a common political culture, and so on. Instead, I proposed to distinguish between transnational European *political communication* and a fully fledged *'European public sphere'* (Kantner 2004b).

26 Other authors added further criteria to the list as 'cross-national mutual citation' or 'mutual recognition as legitimate speakers' (Risse 2002a, 2002b, 2010; Tobler 2002; van de Steeg 2002a, 2002b). For a response to these proposals see Eder and Kantner (2002), where we argue that mutual citation and the publication of media content from abroad can hardly be studied because of hidden processes of transnational inter-media agenda setting (e.g. journalists 'sharing ideas' from other sources without citing; reliance on the same pre-produced content provided by political institutions, NGOs or news agencies) and for methodological reasons (e.g. archives' copyright rules). Mutual recognition as legitimate speakers is logically implied by arguing with and against each other.

27 In 2000, the right-wing populist Freedom Party of Austria (FPÖ), led by Jörg Haider, and the conservative Austrian People's Party (ÖVP), led by Wolfgang Schüssel, formed a new coalition government. The EU reacted with diplomatic sanctions in order to demonstrate that an extreme right-wing party in government was at odds with 'European identity'.

28 In contrast to Downs, and in line with Dewey, Hilgartner and Bosk have argued that the existence of a 'problem' is no inherent feature of some negative condition, but is socially constructed: 'The extent of the harm ... cannot, in itself, explain these differences, and it is not enough to say that some of these situations become problems because they are more "important." All these issues are important/or at least capable of being seen as such. Indeed, the idea of *importance* and the idea of *problem* must be regarded as "essentially contested" concepts ... Finally it is not helpful to claim simply that some problems are more "marketable" than others because that begs the central question: Why?' (Hilgartner and Bosk 1988: 54)

29 For Hilgartner and Bosk, *alarmed discovery* of the problem and *euphoric enthusiasm* are specific ways to present an issue, which contribute to the decline of issue attention: 'Drama is the source of energy that gives social problems life and sustains their growth ...' (Hilgartner and Bosk 1988: 62).

30 The analysis of the Haider debate provides a good example of such an 'interpretative spill-over' (Risse 2010; van de Steeg 2004, 2006; van de Steeg et al. 2003).

3 Media and media analysis in Europe

This study tackles two central research desiderata: first, there are barely any long-term analyses on transnational political communication; second, there is a lack of research on mass media communication in the field of security and defence policy. By drawing on a long-time and large-n dataset, this study aims to fill this gap, pioneering a large-scale comparative design and corpus-linguistic methods. In this chapter I present the methods with which the empirical results presented in Chapter 4 were generated. Sections 3.1–3.3 explain the operationalisation of the hypotheses presented above, then Section 3.4 introduces the independent event-data variables, and Section 3.5 introduces the dependent content-analytical variables. Because this study's use of corpus-linguistic methods for the analysis of an extensive dataset charts new territory, this chapter also goes into some detail explaining the corpus-linguistic methods used.

3.1 Time frame and time periods

In order to find out whether a transnational pragmatic debate on humanitarian military intervention and a related ethical identity discourse emerged, we examined newspaper debates on wars and humanitarian military interventions over a total time period of 16 years after the end of the Cold War (January 1990–March 2006). The beginning of this period marks a point at which a new series of intense armed conflicts forced many countries to reconsider their foreign and security policies and many people to rethink their collective identities in this context. March 2006 marks the end of the period under review, as this was the most recent month for which digital media data were available when we conducted the sampling.

This period includes the initial period of flux and thus the first years of collective comprehension of the new post-Cold War reality, as well as the height of the debate. It was marked by the emergence of new understandings of the multilaterally agreed-upon use of military force in the interest of a 'post-Westphalian' legalised world, and conceptions of international and military actorness including both irregular armed forces as well as international troops. Moreover, the period covered also encompasses the decline of the discourse in terms of intensity as well as conceptual clarity and partial normative consensus after 9/11 and the second Iraq War 2003. This latter phase of disillusionment, disappointment, perplexity and helplessness continues today.

The chosen time period is covered continuously and sampled in full. Media analysis is personnel-intensive work. Most other studies encompass only short time periods and investigate only a few hundred articles on selected events. They often analyse no more than a few weeks of newspaper coverage, sometimes based on a detailed investigation of only a few days' reporting and limited to specified pages of a newspaper. These sampling decisions are sometimes not sufficiently justified and often downright opaque.[1] Such work usually proceeds in a case-dependent way and samples only selected crises, such as the Kosovo or the Iraq War of 2003. The mainstream approach typically restricts itself to major international crises and to those events that led to interventions. As such, they are biased, depriving researchers of the whole picture, which might reveal hidden dynamics of intervention as well non-intervention, in addition to possible feedback between the two. In addition, the predominant approach is blind to framing and identity-changes between and after conflicts, which are important parts of the story from the pragmatist problem-solving approach to collective action. Because of these methodological shortcomings, existing studies can tell us little about how the debate on a whole issue – not just on an event – developed over time, and which traces it leaves.

This study in contrast draws on continuous media coverage that comprises not only 'big' but also minor crises and conflicts as well as the time between distinct crisis events. This methodological decision rests on the assumption that important framing, learning and identity-building processes may also be prompted by smaller crises and may happen in the aftermath of (non-)intervention decisions. By drawing on the continuous data, this study can trace shifts in levels of public attention and changes in dominant frames of meaning with regard to European identity over time. In this way it is possible to reconstruct the dynamics of the national and transnational political communication process on 'ordinary' wars and humanitarian military interventions in great detail. The data mostly have been aggregated on a monthly basis to allow for the distinction between short- and long-term changes.

Based on the assumption that 'news coverage changes quickly, when issues and agendas are concerned', while the 'underlying ideas, ideologies or worldviews' tend to change rather slowly (Baur and Lahusen 2004: 16), this study therefore combines the advantages of investigating both short- and long-term discourse cycles. This is important with regard to the particular research targets of this study. At least in theory, problem-solving debates change relatively rapidly, reacting strongly to events. To investigate them, a detailed short-term view may be appropriate. By contrast, ethical orientations change more slowly, so that a long-term perspective is likely to be most appropriate.

By tackling a sample of nearly 500,000 articles, this study contributes to reducing this severe and chronic research gap in the field. It avoids the limitations of the existing snapshot studies by presenting internally and externally valid, and hence generalisable, results.

For presentation of the findings regarding the relative shares of *communio*- and *commercium*-aspects of European identity in Section 4.2.2, I distinguish three distinct sub-periods within the period of investigation. These sub-periods are characterised by particular series of crisis events and Common Foreign and Security Policy (CFSP)/European Security and Defence Policy (ESDP) institutionalisation processes at the EU level.

First period 1990–95

It has become a truism that the years immediately after the end of the Cold War were characterised by a certain inward turn. Relieved by the sudden end of the atomic threat, citizens looked forward to a future characterised by democracy and peace, which would sooner or later become truly global. Defence budgets were cut. Slowly, however, Europeans came to recognise that new security problems had emerged and that something had to be done in response – perhaps even by the EC/EU. Americans, perhaps, reacted earlier to the newly emerging security challenges and tried to 'wake up' their European partners, demanding more political and military responsibility from them, at least on the European continent. This was not easy, as Jolyon Howorth remembers:

> In the immediate aftermath of the fall of the Berlin Wall, friends and colleagues occasionally chided me for my continuing interest in security and defence. At a time when the talk was of the 'end of history' and of 'peace dividends', was this not a subject with little future? The reverse rapidly proved to be the case as violent military conflict shattered the pacifistic illusions of the post-Cold War world. By the mid-1990s an entire cottage industry was developing around the new field of 'security studies'.
>
> (Howorth 2007: xv)

By the mid-1990s, the first Gulf War and the wars in the former Yugoslavia had brought to mind that, despite the end of the Cold War, violent conflicts could occur even on the European continent. The second pillar of the European Union, the CFSP, was established with the Maastricht Treaty (1993). However, a genuinely common security and defence policy was not forthcoming.

Second period 1996–2000

The late 1990s were characterised by a more proactive approach to international security policy by the EU Member States and EU institutions. The CFSP and, from 1998 onwards, also its security component, the ESDP, became increasingly institutionalised in reaction to ethnic wars in Bosnia, Rwanda and Kosovo. The Kosovo case in particular made it more than clear that the EU Member States did not have the means to conduct large-scale military operations. This led the British Prime Minister, Tony Blair, to give up Britain's 50-year-old tradition of opposition to European political integration in the field of security and defence policy (Howorth 2007: 30). The ESDP became possible and, at the policy level, the discussion about European military capabilities was central to the process of its institutionalisation. This, in turn, put transatlantic relations under stress. Would the development of the CFSP/ESDP come at the expense of NATO?

Third period 2001–05

The new century began with the terror attacks of 9/11 in New York and Washington, DC. For the first time in NATO history, Article 5 was invoked – which provides for collective defence in case of an attack on one Member State. With the parallel missions in Afghanistan (NATO) and the Balkans (EU), NATO and ESDP began to be widely seen as complementary: there were conflicts in so many places that both institutions were urgently needed. The ESDP became operational in 2003. The institutional discussion during this period was not only about capabilities as such, but about different profiles and – especially within ESDP – about a combined approach of civilian and military means for conflict resolution. The EU was soon engaged in a number of military and civilian missions. However, in the context of the Iraq War, deep conflicts between those European governments that joined the US-led coalition and those that opposed the Iraq War divided the EU Member States. Shortly after this major disagreement, the Member States attempted to codify the principles and aims of ESDP in an inaugural European Security Strategy (European Union 2003). Since many missions lasted much longer than expected and did not achieve the high-flying hopes of many regarding what (humanitarian) military interventions could achieve, the third period was characterised by increasing doubt, criticism, disappointment and disillusionment. This phase is ongoing. In the context of the missions in Afghanistan especially, one can observe that a positive view of humanitarian military intervention has given way to increasingly critical interpretations. Although I cannot back up this impression systematically, the following trends appear clear: first, that the line between different types of armed conflict – notably 'ordinary wars' and 'interventions' – that previously seemed well defined has become more blurred (Aday 2010; Daxner and Neumann 2012; Ringsmose and Børgesen 2011; Schüßler and Heng 2013); second, the issue of war and intervention has become less salient than in phase 2. The result seems to be a return to dynamics evident during the 1980s, when all armed conflict was understood as 'ordinary war' for selfish interests.

It can be assumed that these broadly sketched developments influenced the perception of the EU concerning external security issues and have provoked changes in European identity with regard to security and defence issues. In particular, the Yugoslav Wars and the subsequent institutionalisation of security and defence policy in the second period have promoted awareness of the desirability of ESDP problem-solving capacities and perhaps fostered EU identity-formation processes, while the Iraq War 2003 posed a first, and severe, 'identity crisis' for ESDP.

3.2 Country selection

In order to search for similarities and differences in the inter-European and transatlantic debates on war and military humanitarian intervention after the end of the Cold War, the analysis covers public debates in a number of European Union countries, namely Austria (AU), France (FR), Ireland (IR), Germany (GER), the Netherlands (NL), and the United Kingdom (UK), as well as in a non-European but Western country, the United States of America (US). The EU countries were selected in order to record as far as possible the wide spectrum of typical foreign policy positions that compete within the EU. This country selection includes several cross-cutting dimensions and aims at covering a range of factors often advanced as important for determining state behaviour in international conflicts, rather than constituting a 'most different cases design' in the strict sense (Baur and Lahusen 2004; Przeworski and Teune 1970). The choice covers the following dimensions: *international power*, the national position towards the *use of military force, relations to NATO*, and the country's attitude to *EU integration* in general and the *ESDP* in particular.

International power

The six selected EU countries include not only the three most powerful Member States of the European Union (FR, GER, UK), but also three smaller states (AU, IR, NL). Three of the chosen countries possess nuclear weapons and hold a permanent seat in the United Nations Security Council (FR, UK, US), and therefore count as 'great powers'. It was hoped that Poland, a new, Eastern European Member State, could be included, but the required newspaper articles were not available.

Positions toward the use of military force

The availability of armed forces in combination with political attitudes and restrictions on their use in different kinds of military operations – measured on a scale ranging from 1 to 10 – varies strongly between countries. Measures range from small militaries restricted to deployment for Petersberg tasks with low intensity (IR, level 2) to the high-intensity expeditionary warfare capability of the US (level 10) and – to a lower degree – the UK and France (level 8) (Howorth 2007: 116). Some of these military forces rested on conscription (AU, GER) (conscription in Germany was not yet suspended at the time), other states had professional armed forces (FR, IR, NL, UK, US) (Howorth 2007: 100f.). In the observed time period, all countries participated in humanitarian military missions, the US and France marking the most proactive pole of the spectrum and the (post-)neutrals the least interventionist pole. Missions were conducted mainly within multilateral settings; however, some states (US, FR and the UK) also used military force within 'coalitions of the willing' or even unilaterally.

Relations to NATO

The selected countries also cover different security orientations after the Second World War in terms of transatlantic orientation, national sovereignty and Europeanisation. With regard to the preferred position towards the transatlantic alliance, the countries chosen cover the three most frequently distinguished camps: 'Atlanticists' (NL, UK), 'Europeanists' (FR, GER), and (post-)'Neutrals' (AU, IR) (Stahl et al. 2004: 418).

Relations to the EU and to the ESDP

With regard to national sovereignty and Europeanisation, the selection includes 'Intergovernmentalists' (UK) that adhere to the primacy of interstate cooperation; 'Supranationalists' (FR, GER, NL) that are prepared to yield foreign policy authority to supranational institutions; and countries with a rather pro-European stand but strong reservations when it comes to political integration of security and defence (AU, IR). Austria became an EU Member only after the end of the Cold War. Ireland was for a long time the only neutral EU Member State. None of the selected EU Member States opted out of the ESDP, and they all participate in the EU battlegroups. However, there are some differences. While France was clearly the most forceful promoter of the ESDP, other countries later joined the group of active 'Promoters' (GER, UK);; others can be described as 'Supporters' (NL); and the (post-)neutral countries (AU, IR) may be qualified as 'Reluctant followers' of the ESDP (Stahl et al. 2004: 420f.). Over time, the post-neutral states shaped policy more actively, especially with regard to the civilian and civilian–military dimension of the ESDP.

Given the diversity of these selected cases, it would be all the more interesting and significant if one could observe the gradual evolution of common discourse and even a collective European security identity in its *commercium*- or even *communio*-aspects.

3.3 Studying news: epistemology, data collection and data management

After choosing a set of countries, the next decision concerned the types of data from those countries that should be gathered and analysed. This study investigates *mass media* content as a proxy for transnational problem-solving debates and ethical discourses on the level of ordinary people. While at first glance the country selection might suggest that this study subscribes to the view that states, as mega-subjects, could hold different 'attitudes' (towards NATO, the EU, CFSP/ESDP etc.) in the same way that individuals do, this is a view that cannot be upheld in a constructivist approach to International Relations research.[2] Indeed, media content analysis is a method that opens the 'black box' of the nation-state, thus making visible the spectrum of different voices therein. Recent constructivist data-searching on national foreign policy making confirms this view – even when investigating different arenas with different methods (see e.g. Katzenstein 1996; Larsen 1997; McCourt 2014; Mead 2001; Meyer 2006; Stahl and Harnisch 2009).

Within each country, international crisis events and political reactions towards them are highly contested. Even if governments are entitled to speak and act in the name of the nation, they present only one of the prevalent positions, or a compromise position that tries to accommodate the views of several influential camps. Opening the black box of 'nation' thus allows for the possibility of substantial cross-national overlap: pacifists in all countries may, for example, use very similar arguments, and pro-NATO voices within Austria may have more in common with 'Atlanticists' elsewhere than with many of their fellow citizens.

Moreover, the end of one conflict episode and the debate it engendered does not typically lead to a consensus in public opinion: Governments and other involved decision makers reach a consensus decision – in the general public the 'defeated' positions of the last debate seldom completely disappear. More frequently they re-occur (in more or less modified forms) in subsequent debates. Changes in public convictions therefore often consist in the gradual shift of the relative weight of the prevalent views or, less frequently, are the result of the creation of new views.

Changes in the conviction of citizens cannot be observed directly. Therefore empirical investigation into the central motivating assumption of this study, that collective views on issues of wars and humanitarian military interventions have been dramatically challenged and may have changed significantly since the end of the Cold War, is confronted with a serious problem: lack of data. In order to investigate changes in widespread convictions and collective identities, data are required from the time period under investigation, since *ex post* data, like retrospective interviews, may be distorted by contemporary views and the interests of the interviewees (Baur and Lahusen 2004: 2f.).

Survey data may be one way out of this difficulty. However, survey data often give only a momentary picture of citizens' opinions towards certain specific questions, which are often not asked repeatedly over long time periods. Other surveys, such as the Eurobarometer, provide long-term and transnationally comparable data, at the expense, however, of the degree of detail of the questions asked. Moreover, survey data do not give an insight into *why* citizens answer a question in one or the other preconfigured way. Survey questions are asked with other theories and research questions in mind than the ones driving my particular analysis.

For research confronted with this type of difficulty, Krippendorff suggests that '[c]ontent analysis is potentially one of the most important research techniques in the social sciences' (Krippendorff 2004: xiii). Content analysis investigates texts that were produced in broader social and political contexts and makes replicable and valid abductive inferences from these texts to the broader social and political contexts of their use (Krippendorff 2004: 18).[3]

In this study, media texts are analysed in order to determine whether there was a transnational discourse, what shaped it, which international crises it responded to, whether the EU was perceived as relevant, and whether European identity-formation took place. Media content tells us something about otherwise inaccessible phenomena: namely the collective coming-to-terms with 'the end of the world as we knew it' for almost 50 years. More specifically, media data give us access to texts produced *as part of* the very problem-solving debates in which pragmatic collective identities (*commercium*) emerge and the ethical discourses in which new ethical collective self-understandings (*communio*) may have emerged, and allows us to investigate changes in them over time.

Confidence that such far-reaching abductive inferences are possible rests on the conviction that media texts are written not for their scientific analysis (which would give leeway to manipulation of the research by the text producers), but in order to be read and understood by ordinary citizens in whom they intend to invoke certain feelings, interest and, last but not least, changes of opinion (Krippendorff 2004: 23, 31). Media texts have meaning only in political context. Newspaper articles are written for readers other than researchers (Krippendorff 2004: 30), and they contribute to an ongoing debate of interest for ordinary citizens in an imagined community of readers. Therefore one can understand them as '*process-generated data*':

> Process-generated data is data not produced for scientific research. Instead, it is the result or by-product of social processes. Examples are newspaper articles, contracts, laws, speeches, ... emails, letters, websites, ... tools, furniture, architecture, landscapes, photography, films, comics, paintings, sculptures, maps and so on.
>
> (Baur and Lahusen 2004: 3)

A central advantage of methods using process-generated data is that they are 'non-obtrusive methods' (Krippendorff 2004: 40f.): The researcher does not influence those who produced the respective media texts, or used them. The research questions influence only the selection of the relevant newspaper articles and the aspects that will be interpreted, not the content itself (Baur and Lahusen 2004: 3).

A 'media-centric' approach is justified for a second reason in light of the particular research interests of this study. In modern societies, political opinion formation on the macro-level takes place first of all in the mass media (Habermas 2001a: 119; McQuail 1992; Neidhardt 1994; Renfordt 2007b: 7; Taylor 1995: 185f.). In this study, the public sphere is seen as a 'metatopical common space' (Taylor 1995: 190), which consists of interrelated arenas of political communication. With respect to the general public, the mass media are the most important arena of political communication in large-scale, modern, differentiated societies. Most citizens have no first-hand information about most political issues (i.e. international crisis events for our study) and it is the media that serve as the most important agenda-setters and frame-providers.

This does not mean, however, that political communication in face-to-face encounters, interpersonal networks or organised public meetings, associations, 'dissident' counter-publics, and so on is unimportant. Such micro- and meso-level political communications are crucial for individual opinion formation. The metatopical public space connects multiple arenas of different degrees of organisation, institutionalisation and hierarchical structuration. Yet, in fulfilling their agenda-setting function, the mass media 'tell' citizens which problems to think about (Schenk and Rössler 1994). They let us encounter views different from those common in our close social environment and give us an impression of which positions seem to be most widespread. Via the mass media, the universe of relevant speakers (politicians, experts, intellectuals, journalists, citizens etc.), the important issues and the various interpretations of the problems at stake become perceptible within a society (Kantner 1995; Neidhardt 1994). It is precisely this universe of contributions about issues of war and humanitarian military intervention available to citizens at certain points of time in which I am interested for this study.

Quality newspapers as 'typical discourse'

This study rests on a systematic media content analysis of *quality newspapers*. One standard sceptical argument against the analysis of quality newspapers is that their discourse mirrors only an *elite* discourse. Contrary to this view, it is in fact possible to draw conclusions from the study of national newspapers for the political opinion- and will-formation process of a *broader public*. This is the case for three reasons, as follows.

First, it is true that the *speakers* in the media are mainly elites. With regard to transnational European political communication, this general tendency even seems to be slightly more pronounced than with regard to domestic news (Kantner 2006d; Koopmans 2007; Koopmans and Statham 2010; Neidhardt 2006; Trenz 2004). Some methods, such as claim analysis (Franzosi 1987; 1990; 1994; 2004; Koopmans and Statham 1999), use media content in order to reconstruct networks of political-institutional and movement actors. Here the term 'elite' refers to, on one hand, the highest ranks in professional politics, and on the other, a self-elected elite of the politically most active citizens in the classical republican sense – independently of their socio-economic status or education (Arendt 1965). However, in this study I do not use newspaper articles as a shortcut to the reconstruction of discourse among politically active speakers and what members of policy networks say to each other via the media. What I am interested in is the concert of various voices, opinions and interpretations unfolding in front of the ordinary reading public. All these voices, some of them over-reported, others under-reported, together make up the quantity of articles referring to issues of interest for this study and the visibility of the European Union in the context of these issues.

Is this a source of data production bias? The answer is equivocal. It is true that quality newspaper articles cover the mainstream political discourse, and have a tendency to put institutional actors at the centre. Journalists and editors also function as gatekeepers in the debate, and their own political views may bias the intensity of coverage on different kinds of international crisis events and the presented spectrum of positions and arguments.[4] However, this does not constitute a severe problem for my particular research questions, because I use media content analysis as a method for reconstructing the universe of arguments and reasons that were prevalent in the public sphere at a certain time (Baur and Lahusen 2004: 5). Analysis of broadsheets covers the mainstream reporting unfolding in front of ordinary newspaper readers – as biased as it may have been – between January 1990 and March 2006.

What might be lost by limiting an investigation to the quality newspapers are some *untypical* arguments, not the *typical*. The analysis of quality newspaper texts does not generate insights into the arguments on the issue emerging in specialist discussions, expert circles, activist groups, ethnic lobbies, pacifists, political extremists and counter-publics of all kinds, even if these voices are occasionally reported or explicitly heard.

The analysis of quality newspaper texts also provides no insight into the tabloids' simplified interpretations of these issues.[5] In addition, the spectrum of international crises covered in the tabloid press might be reduced, given the rather limited share of text material devoted to political (and especially foreign policy) issues in comparison with society news, crime and soft news. Thus we can assume that international crises and arguments *not* present in the quality papers are even less likely to occur in the tabloid press. The same argument holds in a more moderate version for TV news. Similarly, regional newspapers – which are often weak in reporting international issues, relying on the big news agencies – may under certain conditions report differently on international crises. We know, for example, that after some years of converging foreign policy views, East and West Germans perceived the Kosovo War very differently (Biehl 2001).[6] These differences remained after the Kosovo crisis and might be present in the (especially East German) local newspapers. In other countries, the presence or absence of strong migrant communities from crisis countries could make a difference too. Yet, for this transnational study, I am interested in the mainstream discourse. I therefore cut down on the dimension of media variety, but aimed at the maximum number of articles (full sample) and a very long time-span (1990–2006).

A second way to formulate the elite objection concerns the *readers* of quality newspapers. Are those papers read only by the elite and not by ordinary people? For this study, quality newspapers have been selected that have a very wide circulation of between about 120,000 (*The Irish Times*) and 1 million (*The New York Times*) copies a day. Certainly, politicians may read those newspapers – in conjunction with many other sources including the yellow press. However, most of the readers of broadsheets are 'middle class' in terms of their socio-economic status and education. This is the group that has the highest voting ratio and is therefore most relevant with regard to politics. This 'attentive public' (Neuman et al. 1992) is no elite in socio-economic or educational terms. The attentive public is neither in the top strata of the political, economic, military or educational spheres, nor is it made up of the most influential or powerful individuals. However, as informed citizens and as typical voters, they are important in democracies – also in the context of matters of war and peace, which sometimes can determine the (re-)election chances of politicians. Ordinary politically interested citizens, presumably mainly from the middle classes, are exactly the 'intended audience' (Krippendorff 2004: 31) of the journalists and other authors who write articles for quality newspapers.

Third, communication scientists sometimes refer to 'elite newspapers'. Yet they do so not to describe the readership in social or demographic terms as elite, but because these newspapers are the best ('the elite') in the universe of media formats. As such, they still assume a pivotal, opinion-building position in the inter-linkage of the diverse arenas of public political communication. Because of their high standards for research and argumentation, the quality newspapers assume a central position in the cooperative management of the 'pool of reasons' and arguments on which citizens draw in the process of political opinion- and will-formation (Habermas 1996a: Chs 7, 8). The metaphorical use of the attribute 'elite' here should therefore not concern us further. On the contrary, the presumed *high standard of journalism* will provide our study with enough text material containing explicit arguments. With regard to finding answers to my research question, this is an advantage, not a deficit. The greater argumentative explicitness of quality newspapers as compared with television news or tabloid formats entails a higher chance of finding in the texts manifest arguments concerning, for example, European identity.

Conversely, this means that if the searched-for utterances and expressions – such as those referring to European identity – do *not* occur in the quality press, it is also unlikely that they appear anywhere else. This is partially due to the agenda-setting influence of the quality newspapers. Via inter-media agenda-setting (Neidhardt 1994), their issues and interpretations diffuse into other media formats. At the same time, this is also the result of the opposite direction of influence (e.g. some scandals start in the tabloid press). There are manifold inter-linkages, which allow important issues and frames to disperse across the diverse arenas.

Newspaper selection, digital availability and sampling

In order to obtain a picture of the mainstream discourse of each country, two national, widely read quality newspapers – one centre-right, the other centre-left – were chosen for the analysis. Most of the newspapers chosen sold approximately 350,000 copies a day (*Der Standard, Die Presse, Le Monde, Le Figaro, De Volkskrant, The Guardian*). *The Irish Times* (120,000), *Les Echos* (140,000), *NRC Handelsblad* (250,000) sold less; the *Frankfurter Allgemeine Zeitung* (370,000), *Süddeutsche Zeitung* (460,000), *The Times* (620,000), *The Washington Post* (670,000) and *The New York Times* (1 million) sold significantly more copies a day,[7] even if the figures might have experienced a downward trend over the period of investigation.

Articles were sampled from publicly accessible electronic newspaper archives or CD-ROM. The conservative *Le Figaro* was available only from 1997. So as not to bias the first period after the Cold War for France, *Le Figaro* was replaced with *Les Echos* for the time period 1993–96. For Ireland, only one paper (*The Irish Times*) was available. However, some years (mainly in the early 1990s) and some months are missing for some of the papers, mainly because of missing periods in the electronic media archives.[8]

Even if electronic newspaper archives contain millions of articles, the quality of the available archives is a potential source of data selection bias (Baur and Lahusen 2004: 21). Some archives are highly reliable with regard to articles written by journalists employed by the respective newspapers. For copyright reasons, however, articles written by external authors are often not included. How each newspaper or its archive decided to treat which groups of articles is barely made transparent.

Our sampling procedure was broad and standardised. A complex keyword search was used for the politics and opinion sections, as well as on the features/culture pages of the selected newspapers. The search strategy included two sets of keywords. These two sets were linked with each other by the logical operator AND. Within each set, the truncated keywords were linked by the logical operator OR. The raw sample thus included the *overlap* of these two keyword searches:[9]

- The keyword search strategy included *first* a combination of truncated keywords from the subject field of humanitarian military interventions, which were translated into all languages used. For languages other than English, country-specific terms and particular expressions were added to ensure the thematic area was completely covered. For all non-English newspapers, terms such as 'peace-keeping' and 'peace-enforcement' were also included in English language. One important adjustment was made in the process of sampling: after intense pre-tests, we had succeeded in developing a reliable keyword strategy on the subject of 'humanitarian military interventions' that, however, resulted in a very uneven inclusion of the Iraq War 2003. The war was strongly present in the British and US samples, yet almost invisible in the French and German samples, where it was seen rather as an 'ordinary war' fought for self-seeking interests. Therefore the word 'war' and related terms describing military conflicts were included in the sampling strategy in order to keep open the possibility of exploring further divergent normative connotations of armed conflicts. The data interpretation in this study is consequently done twice: once for the overall sample including 'ordinary wars' and once for a smaller sub-section on 'humanitarian military interventions' (based on a refined corpus-linguistic retrieval procedure, described in Section 3.5).

- The search strategy encompassed a *second* group of keywords: a list of the countries in which wars, civil wars and secession conflicts and/or UN, NATO, EU, ECOWAS and African Union interventions took place between 1990 and 2006. Sometimes several spellings of the country names had to be included. In attaining this listing we drew on the scientific debate on war, violent conflict and interventions (Bjola 2005; Chesterman 2002; Rytter 2001), the *Arbeitsgemeinschaft Kriegsursachenforschung* at Hamburg University[10] and the *Arbeitsgemeinschaft Friedensforschung* at Kassel University.[11] Further information was acquired from Wikipedia listings and its links to specific events.[12] Additionally, information from different international organisations that might intervene was considered.[13] In this way, apart from cases of actual international intervention, similar crises that received no international response were also taken into account. Finally, besides the names of countries in which conflict occurred, sub-state conflict regions – whose names have become shorthand for the conflicts in them (e.g. Aceh, Darfur, Kosovo or Bosnia) – were also included.

Although the study is interested in the role of Europe in the world, terms such as 'Europe', 'CFSP' and 'ESDP' were *not* included in the keyword search strategy to avoid a positive bias on one important dependent variable. A sampling strategy *excluding* EU and CFSP/ESDP terms guarantees that our sample only contains those articles that problematise Europe's role in the world *explicitly* in reference to wars and humanitarian military interventions. That means also that news on CFSP/ESDP institutional events or debates regarding the European constitutional process that address foreign policy and security issues etc. had no chance of entering our sample if they did not at least refer to one concrete international crisis.

Missions of the Organization for Security and Cooperation in Europe (OSCE) were also not included because the organisation's activities in weapons inspection and combating terrorism do not qualify as humanitarian *military* interventions as defined in this study. The OSCE's focus is on violence prevention and peace-making as well as long-term stabilisation of transitional societies.

In the sampling procedure it was often not possible to truncate the names of countries, since too many truncations overstrain the search engine. Thus some relevant articles may not have been retrieved. However, country names are usually mentioned to indicate the location of a conflict and they are often used in word combinations. Furthermore, in many articles more than one country is mentioned. The chance that a great number of relevant articles have not been taken into account is thus very low.

Cleaning the data: obtaining the cleaned full sample

The production of a raw sample was only the beginning of the work. The data had to be managed and cleaned. The team constructed and programmed a MySQL database, which included the development of tailored software for text analysis and database connectivity as well as the development of a dynamic internet application for maintenance of the database and data management.

The sampled articles had to be imported into this database. In the course of data preparation it turned out that the sampled articles had different qualities. Encodings,[14] special characters or corruptions of characters needed to be standardised, substituted or repaired before the sets of articles concerned could be logged.

Since the output of different electronic archives is structured differently, small software applications (patches) had to be programmed to import the content into the appropriate fields of the database (author, headline, newspaper, country, date, section, text). Each document was assigned an identity number, which was the precondition not only for effective management of the database, but also for the 'interoperability' of the diverse text-analytical procedures using different software applications employed during the various stages of the analysis (SPSS Clementine[15], WordSmith[16] and Atlas.ti[17]).

The cleaned multilingual full sample on wars and interventions from January 1990 to March 2006 encompasses nearly half a million newspaper articles from the political reporting sections as well as the editorial sections ($N = 489{,}508$). This figure consists of the raw sample obtained with the keyword search in the electronic archives minus *doublets* and *sampling errors*. Given the size of the sample, the cleaning could not be done without the help of computational-linguistic methods, which are explained in the following two sections.

Removing doublets

Doublets are articles that occurred more than once in the raw sample. Their definition involves many explicit methodological decisions that will be made transparent in this sub-section. The reasons for doublets are manifold. Sometimes electronic archives contained redundancies. Some newspapers seem – in an inconsistent and non-transparent way – to store both the A (morning) and B (afternoon) version of their printed content in the archives. These versions sometimes contain slight differences (e.g. a name is given in full in one version and is abbreviated in the other; one version contains one more paragraph mark than the other), so they cannot be found by a simple doublet-check that tests for 100 per cent identical texts. Sometimes online content is also included in the archives. However, the research question also influences what counts as doublet for a particular study. Another group of doublets resulted from the sampling procedure. A large amount of doublets had entered the samples because some of the search engines did not allow the whole sampling strategy to be typed in, and we had to split it. This of course could result in doublets when, for example, more than one conflict country was mentioned in an article.

Doublets are often invisible for media content analysis. As soon as the sample exceeds a certain size, doublets are not identifiable manually. Readers simply cannot remember whether they already read a specific text, or whether it just seems familiar since it is on the same topic as an article read earlier. Therefore we applied methods of *automatic character string comparison* within (linguistically not specified) character strings for the identification of doublets. We created a *vector space model* comparing the 'features' of the text documents pair-wise. This procedure was conducted for each newspaper separately, since different newspapers of one language quite often publish the same or very similar articles on the same day. This is often the result of papers basing their articles substantially on the same news sources (e.g. communiqués of international actors) or reports of the same international news agencies (e.g. Reuters).

A *vector space* is a multidimensional space. Its dimensions are formed of certain 'features' of all documents in a set of documents. Each document can be displayed as a vector (a point) in the vector space. For each dimension, a document has either the value 0 (i.e. the document does not have the characteristic) or a value higher than 0 (i.e. the document has the characteristic to a certain 'intensity'). Defining a measure of similarity (see below for our definition), the similarity of two documents can be calculated. By normalising these values, one arrives at a value between 0 (i.e. the two documents are completely distinct with regard to the chosen characteristics, they have no common characteristic) and 1 (i.e. the documents are identical with regard to all chosen characteristics).

Our documents (articles) were reduced to a character string containing only the 15 least frequent characters of the whole dataset (the respective newspaper). This reduces the computer calculation effort significantly, since pair-wise comparisons increase in complexity exponentially. For 100 documents 4950 pair-wise comparisons have to be calculated, 200 documents already require 19,900 comparisons. We had up to 100,000 articles to compare for some papers. Reduction was therefore important. Moreover, reduction neutralised slight differences in spelling and punctuation. Reduced character strings were taken as the characteristic to be compared automatically. The comparison proceeded on the basis of small units of these strings (n-grams). One n-gram constituted one '*feature*' in our procedure ($n = 5$).[18] After that, the frequency of each feature in the document set was counted. All features occurring less than twice (single features cannot occur in two different documents) and more than 12 times (features that occur too frequently lack expressiveness) were discarded.

The residual features form the vector space's dimensions. All discarded features were deleted from the document representations, which further decreased the amount of storage space needed for the calculation. Up to this point, the value for each feature of each document had been just the number of the feature's occurrences in the document. However, a more sophisticated type of value was needed. The tf – idf measure [term frequency – inverted document frequency, tf – idf = tf*($|D|$/df)] assigns to each feature its relevance for the document with respect to the document set. This means that the more often the feature occurs in the document and the lower the number of documents sharing the feature, the higher the tf – idf value will be. All feature values were converted to tf – idf. The resulting document representations were compared pair-wise using the cosine of the angle between the position vectors as a *similarity measure* – the smaller the angle, the higher the similarity between the two compared documents. The cosine measure abstracts from the length of a document, using only the proportions of its features. Due to the reduced completeness rate of the data, the cosine measure itself was not sufficiently expressive to classify the documents. Therefore two further measures were adopted: the *publication date* and the *document length*. Using these additional features, the classification could be carried out. We did not count similar articles at different days and/or in different papers as doublets.

The method described so far is constrained to pair-wise document comparison. However, multiple documents could easily be each other's duplicates. Hence all pairs had to be compared with other pairs containing one of both documents. By this means, sets of duplicates ('similarity sets') were identified. For all similarity sets, one document (the 'original') had to be kept, whereas all others had to be discarded from the article set. For very *similar articles* published on the same day (in the same paper), a human reader had to decide upon the margin[19] where pairs of articles started showing increasing features of doublets, that is, less and less difference in content and structure of the text. Above this margin, pairs of articles were considered doublets. The longer article of the pair was kept to ensure the surplus of information was not lost – assuming that the shorter version was very likely to be a teaser or the online version of the text. As each newspaper revealed different patterns of doublets, this margin was defined for each newspaper separately. For a study interested in priming or a comparison between online and print content, the shorter versions might have been relevant; we decided to leave them out in order to establish definite rules across all sets of articles stemming from quite heterogeneous sources.

Removing sampling errors

Sampling errors are articles that occurred in the raw sample but did *not* deal with wars and humanitarian military interventions. Many articles contained at least one keyword from each of the two keyword groups of the sampling strategy but did not deal with wars and humanitarian military interventions. Examples included articles on:

- sports events (e.g. in a soccer game one player comes from *Somalia* and in the twentieth minute there is an *intervention* by the referee);
- recreation and touristic information on countries in which *civil wars* took place some time ago (e.g. *Croatia*); and
- advertisements, calendars of events, legal disputes containing *military metaphors* and book and movie reviews dealing with *international conflicts*.

Our central formal criterion stated that articles that are *not* part of political communication had to be excluded, even if they were interesting for the research questions.[20] Some kinds of sampling errors – such as book reviews, advertisements, calendars, legal disputes, and some of the articles containing touristic information – could have been easily identified and deleted because they occurred in the 'wrong' sections of a newspaper. Yet electronic newspaper archives rarely provide these metadata. Moreover, sports events, for example, are often covered on the first pages of the papers, which also cover the most relevant political events. And one cannot simply discard all articles containing terms from the field of sports, since reports on foreign missions may also refer to sporting activities (e.g. background stories on soldiers in multinational missions playing soccer with each other or 'the locals'; references to peacekeepers repairing sporting facilities in a war-torn village).

Given the large amount of data, the challenge was therefore to develop strategies of *character string comparison* within (linguistically unspecified) character strings that were sufficiently fine-grained to respond to the specific content to be filtered and sufficiently general to ensure a consistent methodology. Through a check of the raw sample and the experiences during the sampling pre-tests and the sampling procedure, we had an overview of typical sampling errors. Using automatic text extraction, we constructed a measure of the *relative density* of the erroneous *semantic fields* as compared with the semantic field of 'wars and humanitarian military intervention'.

A semantic field is a conceptual field of meaning of a natural language.[21] It consists of:

> basic key-words, which command an army of others. The semantic area may be regarded as a network of hundreds of associations, each word of which is capable of being the centre of a web of associations radiating in all directions. A word like man might have as many as fifty such associations – chap, fellow, guy, gentleman, etc.
>
> (Mackey 1965: 76)

A semantic field can be understood as 'a closely knit and articulated lexical sphere where the significance of each unit is determined by its neighbours'

(Ullmann 1951: 157). The units of a semantic field are words and collocations that are constitutive for the meaning of a concept (e.g. man). *Collocations* or *collocates* are typical combinations of two or more words which co-occur on a regular basis. They may carry new, specific meanings not entailed in the component terms. 'Peace mission' has a different meaning than 'mission'; 'we Europeans' is a stronger expression than 'the Europeans'. A *semantic field* includes much more than synonyms (e.g. male human, adolescent), more general categories (e.g. human), and sub-categories of the key concept (types of 'man' e.g. according to age: boy, adult; according to social role: father, worker, professor). It also encompasses all the words and collocations speakers typically use to describe and explain the key category in other words and in relation to other concepts (e.g. according to social functions: provider for family, defender of family; according to gender clichés: strong, successful, virile). Therefore a semantic field is more open and broader than a dictionary entry.

We intended to establish empirically the semantic field of 'war and intervention' as presented in our corpus as well as the erroneous semantic fields accidentally included. Since we did not have access to software that could do this job for us in a satisfactory way, we had to establish the most significant key semantic categories (Culpeper 2009) of the respective semantic fields in a hermeneutic process conducted by human readers.[22] In a first step, therefore, we created lists of key semantic categories for the respective semantic fields ('war and intervention', 'cultural events/reviews', 'travelling/tourism' and 'sports'). We proceeded paper-by-paper in order to account for possible differences in wording between left-liberal and conservative papers.

SEMANTIC FIELD OF 'WARS AND HUMANITARIAN MILITARY INTERVENTIONS'

In creating this listing, we started with the war and intervention keywords of the sampling strategy in all possible grammatical forms. These terms were supplemented by concepts from the semantic field 'war and intervention', which occurred disproportionately often in the news articles under examination. The keyword analysis used the 'concept extraction function' of SPSS Clementine.[23] This function produced a wordlist that ranks all words occurring in the corpus according to frequency. The most often-used words are usually terms such as 'and', 'this' and so on. Their display can be restricted. The displayed 'domain list' of meaningful terms then needs to be checked and classified by human readers, frequently looking again into the texts for the meanings actually expressed. We manually checked all those words used in at least 2 per cent of the articles in the respective papers. The most significant words were put on the list to cover the semantic field. Again, we proceeded paper-by-paper in order to account for possible differences in wording, but eventually merged these lists per country. This systematic inductive method ensured that the indicator operated with expressions actually used in the coverage. Drawing on additional knowledge (e.g. new information related to the initial sampling query, dictionary entries, our experiences with typical sampling errors), human readers decided whether to include a particular term in a term-list representing the respective semantic field.

To construct the term-list of the key semantic field on war and military intervention, we started with setting the keywords of the sampling query in all possible grammatical forms, as lemmatisation in SPSS Clementine was not reliable. These terms were supplemented by terms that occurred disproportionately often in the news articles under examination, as displayed by the 'concept extraction function' of SPSS Clementine. To give one example, the following concepts were – in the context of our very specific sample[24] – indicative of the semantic field 'war and intervention' in the British newspapers:

> armed force, army, attack, battle, ceasefire, danger, ethnic cleansing, enemy, enemies, force, fight, genocide, murder, missile, security, safety, soldier, terror, troop, victim, victory, violence, weapon, casualties, casualty, death, fear, massacre, civilian, bombardment, uno, nato, united nations, refugee, protection, world war, rebel, military, human rights, shooting

The overall indicator list for the semantic field 'war and intervention' was comprised of these words and the sampling keywords (first part of the sampling strategy). For the *semantic field 'sports'* we created lists encompassing all kinds of sports[25] and words often occurring in our specific corpus, such as:

> champions league, championship, test game, friendly game, friendly match, qualifying match, UEFA-cup, UI-cup, world cup

The same was done for the *semantic field 'travelling/tourism'*. The term 'travelling' itself, however, had to be excluded from the list, since it is widely used in coverage on political themes: 'Foreign secretary Rice is travelling to Lebanon tomorrow'. There was no encyclopaedic entry on *'cultural events/reviews'* so the list for this semantic field was developed solely inductively. We checked several times whether the terms indeed identified those sampling errors searched for. A slash was often used in articles listing different cultural events, and as a result '/' was also added to the list as a good indicator.

With the list comprised of keywords for the semantic field 'war and intervention' in all possible grammatical forms, SPSS Clementine was able to calculate the density with which the terms were used in an article. The frequency of words from the semantic field list was weighted in this calculation with respect to their position in the text: Three points were awarded if a term was used in the title, one point for all other occurrences. The formula used for density is:

> D = (frequency of term weighted by points for position / number of characters per article) * 10,000

For all articles from the sample for which the value of the quotient equalled zero, it could be assumed that the articles did not deal with war and intervention. They were deleted from the sample.

Second, all those articles were deleted that mentioned 'war and intervention' in the context of sports, travelling and cultural events. This was the case with articles on tourism in former war regions or on a sportsman's childhood during civil war, and with reviews of books on crises. However, toavoid erroneous deletion of articles, all articles with more than four points were retained.

Third, using the keywords from the four semantic fields, the density of each semantic field in each remaining article was calculated and depicted in a chart using **SPSS Clementine**. To identify the articles for deletion, the keyword density in the fields 'cultural events', 'travelling' and 'sports' was added together and compared with the density of keywords for 'war and intervention'. This method had the advantage of also identifying articles with a mixture of two fields, such as sports activities during the summer vacation. These articles might have displayed a low density for each semantic field individually. By adding together coverage of the 'erroneous' topics, these sampling errors were kept from slipping through the filter. Mathematically, the following function (F) was used:

$$F(D) = D_P \text{ (war)} / D_P \text{ (travelling + cultural events + sports)}[26]$$

With this formula, we arrived at a relative measure to decide whether an article dealt more with 'war and interventions' than with other topics. For all articles the quotient was sorted in ascending order to identify blocks of articles with similar characteristics. Looking at these blocks, certain groups of sampling errors could be eliminated. For example, longer French articles with a quotient between 0 and 1.5 were deleted. Articles in this interval dealt not with war and intervention, but with other issues. This was applicable to 10,201 articles from the initial total of 70,807 longer French articles.

The margins set were comparatively demanding. Checks confirmed that most sampling errors could be traced and deleted. Very short newsflashes and articles in which related policy issues (e.g. migration, asylum policy, developmental policy issues) were debated while humanitarian military intervention was just thematised as a side issue[27] may therefore occasionally have not survived the cleaning procedure.

All the corpus-linguistic procedures applied for the identification of doublets and sampling errors involved careful reading of many texts, especially of texts that were difficult to classify. Therefore the methods developed have a high internal validity. The method development required intense conceptual work in order to decide on the rules to apply. For example, when is a text a doublet, when a re-publication? How can we disambiguate words and collocations? Which grammatical forms can a word assume? Answering these questions required profound lexical and grammatical knowledge of the four languages involved. The rules decided upon had then to be implemented in automated processes that had to be programmed. The available software made this work easier and made the processing of such a large multi-lingual text-corpus possible. However, it had also some severe limitations.[28] Therefore the development of procedures for the (semi-)automatic creation of *concept-ontologies* (e.g. semantic fields such as 'wars and interventions' or 'EU politics and institutions', which were also needed as indicators for the further corpus-linguistic analysis of the texts) as well as the development of *automatic character string comparison* within linguistically unspecified character strings, remain research desiderata. Moreover, the inter-operability between different currently available software packages is problematic. We compensated for this problem largely with our tailored database as a platform.

3.4 The independent variables: event-data

An external dataset was created in order to operationalise the factors that may have impacted on the issue-cycle on wars and humanitarian military interventions, or on the fluctuations in the frequencies therein of European identity. This second dataset provides the independent variables used for the bivariate correlations. In the statistical time-series analysis, the event-data were used as independent variables: if we know how many events of a specific type took place in a particular month – can we predict the change in reporting for this month?

These event-data have been gathered independently from the newspaper content using freely accessible data collections[29] as well as official websites of the UN,[30] NATO[31] and the EU[32] in combination with the available research literature.[33] The information collected was aggregated on a monthly basis like the issue-cycle data. For each event-type, a time series over the period of investigation was created, which could be used as predictor (independent variable) for each 'national' issue-cycle. Using this method, the events can be identified that typically caused moral shocks, led to political pressure and triggered intensified media debate about the issues of interest for this study. For interpretation of the results, more detailed information on the conflicts was used,[34] since sometimes months in which – according to the event dataset – 'nothing happened' turned out to be important.

3.5 The dependent variables: corpus-linguistic analysis of newspaper debates

In order to measure the intensity of debate on wars and humanitarian military interventions, the attention paid to Europe and more specifically to the EU, and the intensity of communication about European identity, we again applied corpus-linguistic methods. This section describes the development of these methods.

Almost everything can be counted. Measurements such as counts and frequencies of categorisation (e.g. word frequencies) cannot be 'false'. They cannot be falsified by independent evidence. One can only repeat them. This is a basic problem for all content analyses, making it all the more important to show that the counted terms actually tell us something about the question being investigated (Benoit et al. 2009; Krippendorff 2004: 32). Text analysis has to justify what the counting means with regard to the social world for which the researcher takes the counted 'word' as an indicator. Content analysis as a social science methodology tries to infer abductively the social *context*, an interesting but unobservable social phenomenon (e.g. the change of problem perceptions and collective identities after the Cold War), from *texts* (e.g. newspaper articles from a certain time period on a certain issue).

This problem is further complicated by the fact that people in their everyday life do not speak or write in the analytical terms in which social scientists think. Media texts are process-generated data (Baur and Lahusen 2004: 3) and as such are not produced bearing in mind the scientific meta-discourse to which the content analyst wants to contribute. In the case of this study it is, for example, very unlikely that newspaper articles directly state 'the threats we perceive are ...', 'EU citizens are a problem-solving community ...' or 'the EU's ethical self-understanding rests on the following basic values ...'. (Only in very few, especially reflective articles, editorials, opinion pieces and the political *feuilleton*, do such direct statements addressing the research questions of this study occasionally occur.) Part of the problem is that speakers (elected officials, public intellectuals, journalists) may have avoided speaking directly on behalf of the EU since, for most of the period of investigation, CFSP/ESDP were not yet institutionalised. Speakers may not have felt entitled to speak 'in the name of Europe' in the way that elected national politicians speak 'in the name of their country'.

In order to allow for abductive inferences (Krippendorff 2004: 36) from our multilingual longitudinal set of newspaper articles to the 'unobservable phenomena' in which this study is interested, and about which I have stated several comparative and event-related hypotheses, quantitative indicators accessible using computer-aided tools had to be carefully operationalised. Only via the created indicators is the life-world discourse 'translated' to make the speakers 'appear to "speak" in the analytical terms that the ... analyst is familiar with and brings to the analyzed' text material (Krippendorff 2004: 34). For this purpose, we created *lists of keywords and collocations* covering, as unambiguously as possible, the *semantic fields* of the political-communicative phenomena of theoretical interest for this study.

The corpus-linguistic procedure

Given the availability of electronic newspaper data on one hand, and the development of computational-linguistic tools for the analysis of those data (text-mining, word frequency computation, etc.) on the other, corpus-linguistic methods are highly valuable for the analysis of media content. *Corpus-linguistics* is an evidence-based methodology used for the description of language and language-use. It draws on the lexical-semantic, syntactic and pragmatic patterns of language that occur in large electronic text *corpora* and that are identified inductively, with the help of computer-aided (quantitative) methods (Lenz 2000).[35] In corpus-linguistics, the statistically significant frequency of word occurrences and regularly co-occurring words (collocates) are considered to provide at least a preliminary assessment of the general linguistic, and even more so about the lexical characteristics of a specific text-corpus (Gabrielatos and Baker 2006).

Accordingly, we assumed that the analysis of the occurrences and contextual meanings of particular words (e.g. a word specifying an aspect of military intervention such as 'troops') would provide us with some preliminary information about the distribution of certain *semantic fields* (e.g. all the words related to the issue of 'intervention') in the overall corpus.[36] The frequency of words constituting a semantic field in media corpora, in turn, will reveal the degree of media attention attributed to the topic, concept or actor described by this semantic field.

The 'cleaned full sample' and – for some parts of the analysis – also smaller sub-sets (only texts on 'humanitarian military interventions'; or only texts thematising the 'EU and its institutions') – were subjected to an extensive *corpus-linguistic analysis*. In order to efficiently identify the relevant articles in a newspaper corpus as large as the one used in this study, we specified a list of keywords and collocations for each concept of interest. However, we wanted the analysis to be much more sensitive to the contextual meaning of the counted features than classical keyword-based tools. Hence we generated our lists semi-automatically. The operationalisation of this idea encompassed six steps (Kutter and Kantner 2012).

Step 1

First we deductively made a list of all the possible paraphrases and related words of the concept to measure. For 'humanitarian military intervention' these were, for example, words such as 'peacekeeping', 'foreign mission', etc. For the EU these were, for example, 'EU', 'EC', 'Europe', 'Europe's', 'European', 'Europeans', etc. This had to be done for all seven countries. An analysis based on simple word counts would stop at this point and just count all of the words possibly related to the concept of interest (or rather all the words the researchers thought of when they made their list). Even with this simple procedure, the resulting figures would provide rough information about the concept or the actors most frequently mentioned. However, with such a procedure one cannot control for uses of the keywords that do *not* indicate the phenomenon of interest (Antaki et al. 2002; Billig 1988; Wilson 1993).[37]

Step 2

A more sophisticated approach is required, one that takes into account the context of the words, as it is the context that defines specific meanings. Accordingly, we had to 'mine' the semantic field of the concepts of interest (e.g. 'humanitarian military intervention') and inductively retrieve all those words and co-occurring words from the overall corpus that were typically used and were unambiguously related to the concept of interest. In the second step, we therefore generated wordlists. WordSmith sorts all words/lemmas of a corpus in alphabetical order, displaying information about the frequency of occurrence and the statistical significance of this frequency in relation to the total amount of words of the corpus. By evaluating these lists, we could verify whether the deductively defined keywords were indeed relevant in our corpus in quantitative terms. Many had some 'keyness', others not. The wordlists, moreover, revealed other, less abstract, but frequently used words related to intervention, such as 'troops', 'forces' etc.

We then displayed *concordances* to identify the contextual meaning of the inductively identified keywords. A concordance is the formatted display of all the occurrences of a particular word (i.e. a search item) in the corpus and the words regularly co-occurring (statistically significant 'collocates') with the search item as well as whole clusters of words of which the search-word is a part on a regular basis. This allows for a first look at the semantic relations within the corpus (Kennedy 1998: 247, 256).

Step 3

In a third step, we used a WordSmith-based concordance analysis to assess whether and in what uses these words were related to the semantic field of interest. WordSmith provides several ways to gain information that helps to judge the semantic relations of a search word in that corpus. The words co-occurring with a search word can be displayed with regard to particular features of regularity, e.g. overall frequency of co-occurrence ('collocates' view); the syntactical position in which they co-occur most frequently with the search word ('patterns' display); or, according to 'adjacency', displaying those words that are most frequently adjacent to the search word ('n-grams'; 'clusters' view) (Kutter and Kantner 2012).

Figure 3.1 shows an example of a concordance. Checking how the collocations were used and what they referred to required reading many texts. Through this work-intensive procedure, a high internal validity of our indicators was guaranteed. The supervised scanning of the displayed 'collocates' by native-speaking human readers allowed us to determine which word clusters were unambiguously used in the sense of our analytical concepts.[38] In the case of 'humanitarian military interventions' these were, for example, particular specifications of 'troops' (e.g. 'UN troops', 'blue helmet'), 'force' (e.g. 'monitoring force'), 'forces' (e.g. 'contribute forces', KFOR,

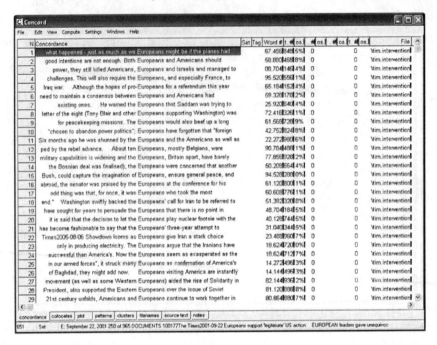

Figure 3.1 Example of a WordSmith concordance
Note: For the keyword 'Europeans' within the British intervention sub-sample.

ISAF), 'missions' (e.g. 'military mission', 'peace-keeping'), 'strikes' (e.g. 'NATO air strikes'), 'operation', 'action', etc. Similarly, in order to establish an indicator for the EU, all collocations encompassing 'Europe', 'European', 'Europeans' and 'Brussels' had to be disambiguated by excluding those that refer to the larger political or geographical context, or to the Belgian capital.

Step 4

Additionally, the corpus was subjected to an analysis in DISCO, an application developed by Peter Kolb (2008) for the representation of semantic spaces. The tool counts both the frequency of lexical collocates of a search word and of those words occurring in similar syntactic positions to the search word. It thereby facilitates the identification of words that are used in similar ways and may be part of a semantic cluster, but cannot be identified using the concordance analysis function in WordSmith. In this way we could further complete our lists and enhance the semantic validity of our indicators (Kutter and Kantner 2012).

The indicative words, names, abbreviations, collocations, phrases and paraphrases identified by these qualitative analytical procedures were checked and double-checked manually by our team, until the set included only those with no ambivalences and 'false friends' – expressions that were partly identical with the searched-for word cluster, but signified something else. The resulting indicators are therefore rather conservative, although highly valid, measures. This study thus assured that the measures developed indeed refer to the socio-political context the analysis attempts to study (Krippendorff 2004: 23). As a result of this procedure, we could compile large lists of word-clusters that entail unambiguous expressions from the respective semantic fields and that mirror almost the entire empirically observed universe of the analytical concepts operationalised – for our historical period and our theoretical background.[39]

Step 5

All the steps described so far had to be conducted separately for every country's text-corpus. The final set of keywords and collocations for each indicator was, in a fifth step, subjected to a cross-language comparison in order to secure a comparable list used for all the languages. This was necessary because all lists should also include expressions that are less important in one country but central in another. In this way we ensured that we actually used *one* instrument *for all* countries in the subsequent text-mining procedure. Each additional expression adopted as a result of this procedure was scanned and disambiguated again by human readers before entering the final lists.

Step 6

The extensive *final lists*, consisting of all possible grammatical forms of the initial keywords that survived the tests, unambiguous further keywords and disambiguated collocations, were then applied to a text-mining procedure that automatically retrieved all those articles that contained at least one of these phrases, word-clusters and collocations.[40] The retrieved article counts were aggregated on a monthly basis. The time-series analyses, sequence charts, correlation analysis and calculation of σ-convergence among the national curves used in this study work with the data generated by this corpus-linguistic procedure.

The indicators: semantic field lists

In this section I describe what each of the semantic field lists measures, and how each measure contributes to answering my research questions. This study uses seven different indicators: the overall sample including all articles on '*wars and interventions*'; an intervention sub-sample encompassing all articles referring to or debating '*humanitarian military interventions*'; the number of articles referring to '*Europe*' in a broad sense, including geographical uses; the number of articles addressing the 'EU and its institutions'; the number of articles using expressions of '*EU identity*' in the sense of an EU-specific European identity; and the number of articles more specifically speaking of the 'EU as a *commercium*' or the 'EU as a *communio*'. The latter completely separate indicators identify two sub-sets of '*EU identity*' and a residual group. Since many articles contain expressions for both types of identity, the summed article counts of *commercium* and *communio* do not equal the counts for '*EU identity*'. More in-depth information about the collocations included in the semantic field lists for each indicator is given in the respective sections in Chapter 4. The Europe-related indicators were applied for the full sample as well as the sub-sample. Table 3.1 shows the number of articles retrieved with the help of each indicator.

Each new indicator is more specific than the previous one. Therefore the number of articles identified decreases from the more general to the more detailed indicators. While 'wars and interventions' (the overall sample) encompasses all articles of the cleaned full sample, all other indicators identify sub-sets. For example, the intervention sub-sample excludes 'ordinary wars' and encompasses only articles that discuss humanitarian military intervention in the sense of our definition.

The data generated have been statistically analysed with descriptive statistics, correlation analysis, ARIMA time-series models and sigma-convergence analysis. For better readability, I describe the statistical procedures in conjunction with the analysis for which they are used. In the context of a concrete data interpretation, the reasons behind the choice of the different techniques can be more readily illustrated. Figure 3.2 illustrates the kinds of data included as dependent and independent variables in the statistical analysis.

Table 3.1 Absolute frequencies of articles retrieved by the applied indicators

Indicator	Overall sample	Intervention sub-sample
Wars and interventions	489,508	
Humanitarian military interventions		108,677
Europe	144,945	40,059
EU and its institutions	74,488	24,878
EU identity	11,844	3,633
EU identity as a *commercium*	4,524	1,736
EU identity as a *communio*	8,556	2,293

Notes: This table is based entirely on the author's own data. The table displays absolute article numbers for all countries together over the period of investigation January 1990–March 2006 (195 months). Because of missing data, three countries include fewer months: AU 163, IR 166, GER 182.

Media and media analysis in Europe 77

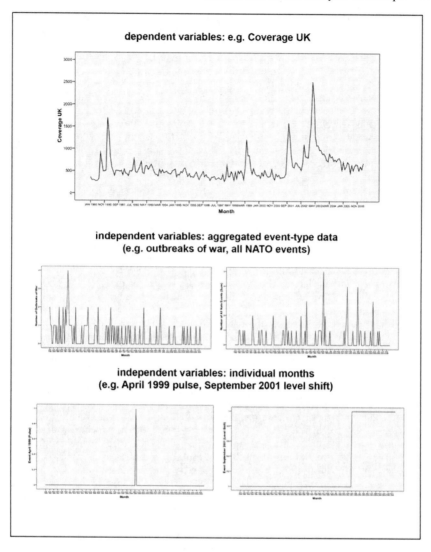

Figure 3.2 Time series to be compared (Jan. 1990–Mar. 2006, 195 months)
Note: Figures based entirely on the author's own data.

Notes

1 Some studies rely on 'constructed weeks' as a sampling method (see e.g. Knorr 2006; Wessler et al. 2008). This method stratifies the sample according to days of a week: data for one Monday of the first month, one Tuesday of the following month and so on are sampled. Other studies sample one (or more) random Monday, Tuesday and so on per year of the study. In each case, the aim is to cover longer time periods without biases of within-week fluctuation. While this method works well for themes evenly covered over long periods (as in comparisons of

advertisement frequencies and other standard media content) (Riffe et al. 1993), for extremely volatile issues and extraordinary events this method is inappropriate. Other studies choose – often without reference to the criteria applied – the 'most appropriate' articles from an initial raw sample (Wessler et al. 2008).

2 At first, constructivists in International Relations treated states as unitary actors – as realists do. They were interested in understanding how states 'perceive' international constellations, how they 'communicate with each other' and how national identities or security cultures programme state interests and behaviour on the international level (see e.g. Katzenstein 1996; Wendt 1999). With Herrmann (2002: 130), however, one should rather understand the treatment of states as unitary actors as a heuristic abstraction or a metaphor, subsuming the actions of statesmen, diplomats, representatives of international organisations, etc. who do something *in the name of* their country as an action of that state.

3 For the distinction between different logics of inference, Krippendorff gives the following definitions. *Deductive* inferences rest on the drawing of conclusions from generalisations to particulars. *Inductive* inferences rest on the drawing of conclusions from particulars to generalisations. *Abductive* inferences, in contrast, proceed across logically distinct domains, from particulars of one kind to particulars of another kind (in the case of content analysis, from texts to answers to a research question about a social and political context) (Krippendorff 2004: 36).

4 'Process-generated data is almost always biased. This means that the target population and the frame population differ. The frame population over-covers some types of cases of the target population, other types of cases are under-covered or even completely absent from the data' (Baur and Lahusen 2004: 7)

5 Media content analyses that included tabloid formats found – against initial expectations – the same frames as in the broadsheets; however, in a simplified version (see e.g. Risse 2010; van de Steeg 2004, 2006; van de Steeg et al. 2003).

6 Framing analysis of editorials found that in the five leading West German quality newspapers, unconditional or limited support for the war – despite the lacking UN mandate – was consensual with the exception of the left-wing *taz* (Eilders and Lüter 2000). A left–right cleavage occurred with respect to the function of the use of military force in the Kosovo intervention: conservative papers favoured robust military action, while liberal papers called for crisis diplomacy and directed attention to the humanitarian problems resulting from the crisis (ibid.).

7 Source: Wikipedia in the respective languages for up-to-date circulation figures.

8 See Table A1 in the Appendix for the missing years and sample sizes. In the tables and interpretation of results of the time-series estimations, significant peaks or level shifts at points in time when a formerly missing paper sets in have been excluded.

9 Sampling keywords (! denotes truncation): (war OR war on terror! OR foreign mission OR human! intervention OR human! invasion OR human! mission OR human! operation OR milit! action OR milit! force OR milit! intervention OR milit! invasion OR milit! operation OR military mission OR peaceenforc! OR peace-enforc! OR peace-enforcing OR peacekeep! OR peacekeep! OR peace-keep!) AND (Aceh OR Afghanistan OR Albania OR Algeria OR Angola OR Armenia OR Azerbaijan OR Bosnia OR Burkina Faso OR Burma OR Burundi OR Cambodia OR Central African Republic OR Chad OR Chechenia OR Chechnya OR Congo OR Cost Rica OR Croatia OR Cyprus OR East Timor OR Ecuador OR El Salvador OR Eritrea OR Ethiopia OR Georgia OR Georgian Republic OR Gibraltar OR Guatemala OR Haiti OR Honduras OR India OR Indonesia OR Iran OR Iraq OR Israel OR Ivory Coast OR Karabakh OR Kosovo OR Kuwait OR Lebanon OR Liberia OR Libya OR Macedonia OR Mali OR Mauritania OR Moldova OR Mozambique OR Myanmar OR Nagorno-Karabakh OR Namibia OR Nicaragua OR Niger OR North Korea OR Pakistan OR Palestine

OR Panama OR Peru OR Philippines OR Rwanda OR Senegal OR Serbia OR Sierra Leone OR Slovenia OR Somalia OR South Korea OR Sri Lanka OR Sudan OR Syria OR Tadzhikistan OR Tajikistan OR Uganda OR Western Sahara OR Yemen OR Yugoslavia OR Zaire).
10 Source: www.wiso.uni-hamburg.de/fachbereiche/sozialwissenschaften/forschung/akuf/akuf (28/01/2015).
11 Source: www.ag-friedensforschung.de (28/01/2015).
12 Sources at original access date: http://en.wikipedia.org/wiki/Invasion (28/07/2006), http://en.wikipedia.org/wiki/List_of_wars_1945%E2%80%931989 (28/07/2006), http://de.wikipedia.org/wiki/UN-Missionen (12/07/2006), http://de.wikipedia.org/wiki/Friedensmission (28/07/2006), http://en.wikipedia/wiki/Humanitarian_intervention (28/07/2006; original content no longer available online), https://en.wikipedia.org/wiki/Peacekeeping (28/07/2006; original content no longer available online). Where available, the versions used can be accessed through Wikipedia's 'View History' function.
13 Sources at original access date: www.un.org/Depts/dpko/dpko/index.asp (24/05/2006; no longer available) [today at www.un.org/en/peacekeeping/about/dpko (28/01/2015)], www.aseansec.org (12/05/2006; no longer available) [today at www.asean.org/asean/asean-secretariat (28/01/2015)], www.consilium.europa.eu/cms3_fo/showPage.asp?id=268&lang=en&mode=g (26/04/2006; no longer available) [today at www.consilium.europa.eu/en/home (29/01/2015)].
14 Some media texts were encoded in 'Latin1', others in 'UTF-8' and entailed corrupted characters.
15 See www.spss.com/de/clementine/ (10/11/2008; no longer available). Alternative software is now provided as the IBM SPSS Modeler at www-03.ibm.com/software/products/de/spss-modeler (28/01/2015).
16 For the version used for this study see www.lexically.net/wordsmith/version4 (28/01/2015). For the current version see www.lexically.net/wordsmith/version6 (28/01/2015).
17 Atlas.ti was used for qualitative sub-studies, see www.atlasti.com (28/01/2015).
18 $N = 5$ proved to be practicable and provided the best results.
19 The value of the similarity measure ranged between 0 = different and 1 = identical.
20 This decision was difficult, because cultural communication is often an important field for political communication too. We also discussed an article from the sports section which narrated the biography of a famous African marathon runner who fled from his country during the civil war and lost large parts of his family. Such articles are certainly extraordinarily important for raising ordinary people's attention to 'forgotten conflicts.' However, since we were not able to include the broader cultural discourse systematically into our study, we excluded it so as not to place in question the comparability of the data for different newspapers.
21 For a detailed history of the concept of 'semantic field' and the distinction of three distinct language-philosophical approaches to this concept, see Nerlich and Clarke (2000).
22 The logic behind our procedure is similar to – and inspired by – modern corpus-linguistic tools (see e.g. Rayson 2008). However, the available tools are not specific and transparent enough to be employed for the specific concepts we wanted to cover. So we used our software – especially SPSS Clementine – only for the preparatory steps of this procedure and then again for text extraction. The meaning-related part of the procedure was conducted by trained human readers.
23 For some papers, such as the French ones, the concept extraction was conducted with all articles. For others, like the US newspapers, only every third article was included, otherwise the calculation would not have been possible due to the amount of data.
24 It should be noted that in other contexts, such as a sample on migration, a sample of the complete content of a newspaper, or for different types of text (e.g. official

80   Media and media analysis in Europe

documents), these terms might not be appropriate – they make sense before the theoretical background of this particular study and do not apply universally.

25 In the absence of electronic dictionaries available in all the languages, Wikipedia lists had to suffice; see e.g. the source for Germany at http://de.wikipedia.org/wiki/Liste_der_Sportarten (03/11/2006).

26 D_P = density quotient of one article with regard to the specified semantic field (in brackets) weighted according to the point system.

27 In former research on transnational political communication, we found that newspaper articles which deal with the issues of interest as a side issue or just as reference without further in-depth discussion can still be an important indicator of the presence of a certain issue in public communication (Kantner 2006; Trenz 2004).

28 SPSS Clementine, for example, offered a tool for the automatic recognition of concepts (in lemmatised form). However, this tool was very general (it differentiates between categories as 'currency', 'location' or 'name', which are useful in commercial applications) and was not transparent enough in its workings to be adapted to our particular research questions.

29 For the crisis events, this was the Uppsala Conflict Data Project (UCDP)/Peace Research Institute Oslo (PRIO) Armed Conflict Dataset (version v.4-2006, 1946–2005) provided by the UCDP, Uppsala Universitet, Department of Peace and Conflict Research. All versions available at: www.pcr.uu.se/research/ucdp/datasets/ucdp_prio_armed_conflict_dataset (28/01/2015).

30 For example, www.un.org/en/peacekeeping/about/dpko (28/01/2015).

31 For example, www.nato.int/cps/en/natolive/topics_52060.htm (28/01/2015).

32 For example, http://europa.eu/abc/history/index_en.htm (28/01/2015) and www.eurocorps.org (28/01/2015).

33 We placed the focus on the EU and the developing CFSP/ESDP (Barbato 2000; Chirac 2003; European Union 2003; Fleischhacker 1996; Howorth 2007; Pond 2005) and NATO (NATO Public Diplomacy Division 2006; Varwick 2008).

34 Important sources used were the historical dictionaries by Scarecrow Press relating to Afghanistan (Adamec 2003) and African conflicts (Adelman and Suhrke 1996; Arnold 2008a; 2008b; 2008c; 2008d; 2008e; 2008f; 2008g; 2008h; 2008i; Fyle 2006; James 2004; Mukhtar 2003; Twagilimana 2007). Detailed event-data were derived from sources documenting individual conflicts, especially the Yugoslavian wars (Annan 1999; Benson 2001; Burg and Shoup 1999; Central European & Eastern Adriatic Research Group 1999; Elsie 2004; Mays 2004; O'Connell 2000; Silber and Little 1997) and the wars in Iraq (Ghareeb and Dougherty 2004; Jacobs 1991).

35 A *corpus* is a collection of texts assumed to be representative of a given language or sub-set of language (e.g. spoken versus written texts, newspaper versus academic texts) or of a thematic focus (e.g. humanitarian military intervention).

36 We could use as a point of reference some existing studies by computational linguists who investigated public debates about asylum-seekers and refugees (Baker and McEnery 2005; Gabrielatos and Baker 2008). In the social sciences, computer-assisted qualitative coding has become a broadly accepted method. For larger text samples, an emerging interest in the use of computational-linguistic approaches can be noted (König 2006; Kriesi et al. 2005). Others, published by now, were not yet completed at the time (e.g. Bayley and Williams 2012; Kluver 2009).

37 Discourse analytical computer- and more specifically corpus-linguistics today involves much more 'than counting words' (Roberts 1989) and necessarily involves returning to the original texts and reading much of them to disambiguate the initial findings.

38 A study of discourse on corruption in British newspapers used a similar procedure and proved the discourse to be biased insofar as more negative wording was used for the same corruption problems occurring overseas compared with 'at home'

(Orpin 2005). The linguistic theoretical foundations for looking at phrases, word-clusters and collocations instead of word frequencies have been laid by Stubbs (2001; 2003).
39 Here one note of precaution has to be made: the sample used in this study is a very specific one, encompassing articles from a specific time period (1990–2006) and a specific issue area. Since language use on political issues may change rapidly if the social context changes, the lists generated by our team may not necessarily be applicable to discourses from the 1950s or the 1980s, when international crisis events were discussed in different ways and the EU was less institutionalised.
40 For this procedure we used the software package SPSS Clementine which, as noted above, is no longer available; the recent equivalent software is the IBM SPSS Modeler.

4 Comparing debates on wars and humanitarian military interventions across nations

This chapter presents the results of the study on the debates on wars and humanitarian military interventions in Austria, France, Germany, Ireland, the Netherlands, the United Kingdom and the USA. We have seen in the theoretical chapters that particularistic collective identities, in the pragmatic and the ethical sense, emerge and develop through communication. New groups can be created by people – even in the total absence of an inherited shared background – by reaching a common interpretation of their situation and by coming together for cooperative undertakings, either to secure their 'egoistic' interests or to further a common ethical project. For *political* identities to develop, political mass communication is the decisive process.

The theoretical ideas sketched above suggest that, within the EU, a collective foreign, security and defence identity – in the sense of an awareness that we are 'sitting in the same boat', or even in the sense of an ethical self-understanding of the Europeans as Europeans – might have developed in the course of recent debates about important international crisis events and our institutional reactions. These reactions were not framed solely in a traditional national or transatlantic way, but included the search for coordinated European responses and led to the creation of the Common Foreign and Security Policy (CFSP)/European Security and Defence Policy (ESDP) – a policy field that raises fundamental ethical questions about the future role of Europe in the world.

The discussion of research results is organised according to the leading research questions of this study. Firstly, can we observe transnational *pragmatic problem-solving debates* and *ethical discourses* about 'ordinary wars' and humanitarian military interventions after the end of the Cold War? What kind of problematic situations triggered common transnational debates? Secondly, was European identity in the sense of a *commercium* or a *communio* articulated?

4.1 Crisis events and transnational convergence of problem perceptions

This section provides an overview of the coverage given in the different countries to the issue of wars and interventions in the quality newspapers. I describe the sequence charts of 16 years of media coverage on wars and interventions in general as well as on humanitarian military interventions in a normatively demanding sense in particular. I analyse and compare the time-series data statistically with correlation analysis and time-series models in order to identify the factors and events that impact on the curves across nations. With this method, the events that caused moral shocks, led to political pressure and triggered intensified media debate can be identified. Finally, phases of convergence and divergence between countries are identified by analysing convergence across countries over time.[1]

The overall issue-cycle: wars and interventions

The problem of security identity cannot be solved from the perspective of the neutral observer (*numerical identification*). If something is to be said about Western or European identity in the *qualitative* sense, one has to identify the views of the members of the group in question. A central assumption of this study is that issues are not discussed out of context, only in relation to important events that elevate certain questions at the expense of others. Identities – such as a European identity – are therefore not issues on their own. People reflect upon them only when background understandings conflict with real-world experience and become problematic.

Is there a transnational discourse on wars and humanitarian military interventions? An answer to this question is an essential preliminary because without thematically intertwined communication on this issue, it would be useless to discuss converging problem perceptions. Shared problem perceptions are – as we have seen – at the root of emerging transnational communities in the sense of a we$_{2/commercium}$ and even more for the development of shared ethical convictions that constitute a we$_{2/communio}$. The intensity of the debate on armed conflicts is, moreover, indicative for similarly intense problem awareness. Figure 4.1 shows the issue-cycle of newspaper coverage on wars and interventions per country. Each country except Ireland includes two newspapers and is represented as one line.

To the naked eye it is difficult to compare the issue-cycles. However, some observations are possible. Figure 4.1 does not show a straight upward trend in reporting. We rather see volatile issue-cycles with some major and many minor peaks. We can also see that the quantity of reporting on wars and interventions varies among the countries. This is partly due to the fact that the amount of newspaper space dedicated to the coverage of international crisis events varies with the different newspapers' specific journalistic styles.[2] The daily numbers of newspaper pages, articles printed, the length of a typical article and so on vary among newspapers and countries.

US–American and British newspapers published the highest quantity of articles on wars and humanitarian military interventions (Table 4.1). On average, the two US papers together printed 886 articles on wars and interventions each month. The maximum number of articles was reached in

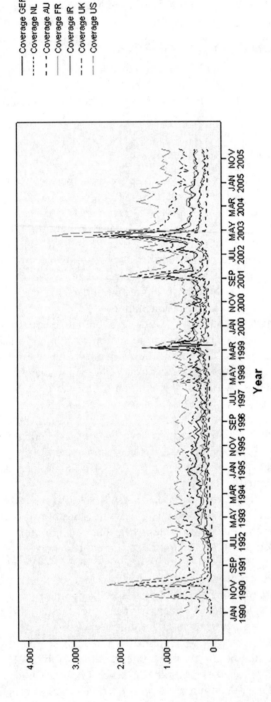

Figure 4.1 Issue cycles on 'wars and interventions' (absolute numbers)
Notes: Figures based entirely on the author's own data. $N = 489\,508$, cleaned overall sample, data aggregated on a monthly basis. Period of investigation: Jan. 1990–Mar. 2006 (195 months). Because of missing data, three countries include fewer months: AU 163, IR 166, GER 182.

Table 4.1 Descriptives of the issue-cycles on 'wars and interventions'

Coverage	Minimum	Maximum	Sum	Mean	Standard deviation
GER	1	2100	63,374	348.21	257.73
NL	16	1104	34,689	177.89	121.40
AU	2	559	12,691	77.86	70.34
FR	75	1545	63,712	326.73	210.20
IR	46	1003	28,313	170.56	109.39
UK	271	2517	114,057	584.91	307.13
US	497	3415	172,672	885.50	387.42

Notes: Table based entirely on author's own data. The table displays absolute articles numbers (min, max, sum) per country over the period of investigation (Jan. 1990–Mar. 2006, 195 months). Because of missing data, three countries include fewer months: AU 163, IR 166, GER 182.

March 2003 (3415 articles) and April 2003 (3050 articles). In the two British papers, approximately 585 articles on war and interventions were printed each month. With 2517 articles, the most extensive coverage was in March 2003. German, French and Irish papers also covered wars and interventions extensively, although with somewhat lower absolute numbers of articles. On average, 348 (GER), 327 (FR) and 171 (IR, only one paper) articles on wars and interventions were printed. On average, the two Dutch newspapers printed about 178 articles, while the two Austrian newspapers covered wars and interventions in only 78 articles per month.

Taking the peaks of intense media coverage as an indicator for public awareness of international crises and conflicts, I interpret the charts as a 'fever chart' of international crises that indicates when media attention was exceptionally high and when the countries under study paid less attention to a particular crisis. If one takes intense media coverage as an indicator for transnational attention to major international crises, four main shock events can be identified: the Iraq/Kuwait crisis in 1990–91; the 1999 Kosovo crisis; the intervention in Afghanistan in 2001; and the Iraq War of 2003. As seen in Figure 4.1, these peaks represent intense discussions on the deployment of military force. Yet the debate on wars and interventions does not disappear in between the major international events.[3]

March 2003 was the month with the maximum coverage. One can also see that there are simultaneous peaks in August 1990, the first three months of 1991, between April and June 1999, September/October 2001 and – as noted – March/April 2003.

These peaks can be unambiguously linked to distinct crisis events. The first clear common peak in August 1990 occurs at the beginning of the Iraqi invasion of Kuwait, followed in the next several days by international condemnation, including a Soviet–American joint statement on 3 August and Security Council Resolution 661, which imposed economic sanctions on Iraq.

These events were extensively covered in all countries under study. The next common peak coincides with the beginning of hostilities between the US-led coalition and Iraq in mid-January 1991 and continues to March 1991, when Kuwait's Crown Prince returned to Kuwait, Iraq brutally suppressed the Kurdish and Shi'a uprisings that had followed on the heels of the increasing disintegration of central authority, and the UN lifted its embargo on food shipments to Iraq (Ghareeb and Dougherty 2004: xxvi–xxviii; Jacobs 1991).

Early in 1999, when the Kosovo crisis led to intense institutional reactions, another peak is visible in the issue-cycles. After more than a year of international diplomacy, UN resolutions and negotiations, NATO started bombing the Federal Republic of Yugoslavia on 24 March – without a UN mandate.[4] Except Austria and Ireland, all countries under study participated more or less intensively in this operation.

In spring 1999 a number of important NATO events took place: Poland, the Czech Republic and Hungary became NATO members (March 1999), and at the NATO summit in Washington the fiftieth anniversary of the alliance was celebrated. Moreover, Member States agreed to create a European Security and Defence Identity (ESDI) within NATO (Central European & Eastern Adriatic Research Group 1999: 45–65; Elsie 2004: xlii–xliv).

In parallel, the young ESDP developed rapidly. In March and April 1999, Special European Council summits on Kosovo were held, and several EU Member States participated in sanctions against Belgrade and contributed to enforcement of the weapons embargo (Central European & Eastern Adriatic Research Group 1999: 45–65). EU foreign ministers supported the stationing of a peacekeeping force in Kosovo on 8 April 1999. On 1 May the Amsterdam Treaty came into effect, and with it the position of a High Representative of the CFSP was created.[5] On 11 May the Western European Union (WEU) Council of Ministers decided to make WEU capabilities available for the EU. On 3 June 1999 the EU Council in Cologne incorporated the WEU into the EU, and with the Cologne Declaration the participating Member States for the first time committed themselves to concrete steps for the establishment of military–political structures. Javier Solana was appointed as the High Representative of the CFSP (and took office in October). These decisions were important steps in the establishment of the ESDP.

When Slobodan Milošević accepted the conditions of the Rambouillet negotiations on 10 June 1999, the bombing of Serbia ended. Kosovo came under civilian UN administration (United Nations Interim Administration Mission in Kosovo, UNMIK).[6] A UN-mandated peacekeeping force led by NATO – the Kosovo Force (KFOR) – entered the country on 12 June. The aims were the return of the refugees and the security of ethnic Serbs in the province, the re-establishment of democracy and human rights, as well as nation-building efforts and economic reconstruction. On the initiative of the EU, the Stability Pact for South Eastern Europe was institutionalised to coordinate state aid of the participating countries as well as NGO activities, with a view to fostering peace, economic relations and free trade in the region (Central European & Eastern Adriatic Research Group 1999: 65).

The third big common peak in the coverage curves occurs between February and April 2003, when the disputes about the Iraq crisis were at their height. In January, EU Member States diverged over US plans for a 'pre-emptive war' against Iraq with the aim of ending Saddam Hussein's dictatorship. Some EU Members, especially France and Germany, doubted that Iraq had weapons of mass destruction or was cooperating with Islamist terrorists. They demanded more time for UN weapons inspectors and were against war – even with a UN mandate. beginning with the celebrations for the fiftieth anniversary of the Élysée Treaty between France and Germany, tensions between different groups of Member States and accession countries escalated. Diplomatic quarrel at the EU and UN levels continued throughout February. The EU did not find a common position at the Extraordinary European Council meeting on 17 February and remained divided when hostilities commenced. The UK, on one side, as well as France, Germany and Russia on the other, circulated proposals at the UN (Pond 2005: esp. 42–49).

On 19 March the US-led coalition attacked Iraq, with Baghdad falling on 9 April (Ghareeb and Dougherty 2004: xxxvii). In Somalia, a humanitarian catastrophe occurred during the same month (Mukhtar 2003). On 1 May the Iraq War appeared over, with President George W. Bush himself declaring it ended.

The observation of synchronous quantitative peaking of newspaper coverage on major international crisis events points to a shared cross-national interest in the same events in the countries under study. This impression can be further grounded empirically if we look at the correlations among the curves. All curves correlate strongly, with correlation coefficients ranging from 0.77 (US and GER) to 0.95 (AU and GER) (Table 4.2). These are very strong linear relations: if one curve goes up or down, the others do too.[7] This is a

Table 4.2 Bivariate correlations of the issue-cycles on 'wars and interventions' (Pearson's coefficients)

Coverage	Coverage						
	GER	NL	AU	FR	IR	UK	US
GER	1	0.900**	0.952**	0.857**	0.918**	0.812**	0.765**
NL	0.900**	1	0.916**	0.896**	0.921**	0.870**	0.827**
AU	0.952**	0.916**	1	0.885**	0.904**	0.850**	0.801**
FR	0.857**	0.896**	0.885**	1	0.885**	0.914**	0.891**
IR	0.918**	0.921**	0.904**	0.885**	1	0.936**	0.905**
UK	0.812**	0.870**	0.850**	0.914**	0.936**	1	0.954**
US	0.765**	0.827**	0.801**	0.891**	0.905**	0.954**	1

Notes: Table based entirely on author's own data. The table displays Pearson's correlation coefficients. Period of investigation: Jan. 1990–Mar. 2006 (195 months). Because of missing data, three countries include fewer months: AU 163, IR 166, GER 182.

preliminary indicator for a common – if not global – discourse on crisis events, and confirms our initial intuitions.

Did the coverage on war and intervention respond to the same type of events in the countries under study? Table 4.3 shows the correlations of the coverage and aggregated event-data our team collected. The figures indicate that the monthly numbers of certain types of events that would be strong candidates for news coverage on wars and interventions do not correlate significantly with the monthly number of articles. This holds true for the number of outbreaks of war, the number of massacres, instances of genocide or expulsion, for example, as well as major Islamist terror attacks.

UN institutional acts regarding wars and intervention also do not correlate with reporting on issues in any straightforward way. The numbers of UN resolutions adopted, of UN interventions and even of UN-mandated interventions correlate negatively (but insignificantly) with the quantity of reporting on wars and interventions. Conversely, it is extraordinary UN events and cases of the use of force without a UN mandate that correlate more strongly with the intensity of news coverage on our issue of interest. However, the observed correlation may be due only to the effect of the Kosovo intervention and the Iraq War, which caused such large peaks. Even the aggregated *number of all UN events* [8] does not correlate with the level of coverage.

A similar pattern can be detected with regard to NATO events. The number of NATO summits does not correlate significantly with the curves. Extraordinary NATO events, however, matter in the continental European countries under study, even if the correlation is weak. By contrast, the start of NATO interventions displays a stronger positive association in the EU member states (Pearson's coefficient higher than 0.30), but not in the US, where the association is also positive but remains weaker. All NATO events together are positively correlated to the quantity of reporting. This effect is again much weaker for the US and strongest for Austria.

In relation to EU activities, EU summits – that since the late 1990s have often brought with them important decisions on CFSP/ESDP – correlate moderately positively with the quantity of reporting on wars and interventions in all countries under study, albeit at a lower level in the English-speaking countries. The number of events explicitly dedicated to the CFSP/ESDP, and all of its predecessors such as the WEU, as well as the start of EU civilian missions, is not significantly associated with reporting levels on wars and interventions. The number of EU humanitarian military interventions, however, correlates quite positively with the number of newspaper articles on wars and interventions in all the countries under study. The US is no exception here (Pearson's coefficient 0.34); instead, it is the French quality press where this association is weaker (0.29). other EU events that might be relevant for our issue do not appear to matter. All EU events together are positively correlated to the quantity of reporting on wars and interventions on a moderate level.

Table 4.3 Bivariate correlations between coverage on 'wars and interventions' and aggregated event-data (Pearson's coefficients)

	\multicolumn{7}{c}{Coverage}
	GER	NL	AU	FR	IR	UK	US
Number of outbreaks of war	−0.109	−0.030	0.055	−0.051	0.066	0.017	0.027
Number of massacres	−0.034	−0.102	−0.133	−0.140	−0.045	−0.120	−0.145*
Number of Islamist terror attacks against Western countries	0.075	0.078	0.078	0.067	0.064	0.056	0.054
Number of UN Resolutions	−0.051	−0.005	−0.012	−0.050	−0.043	−0.030	−0.044
Number of beginning UN interventions	−0.109	−0.029	−0.130	−0.101	−0.131	−0.064	−0.043
Number of other UN events	0.267**	0.379**	0.279**	0.247**	0.277**	0.291**	0.280**
Number of all UN events	−0.031	0.092	−0.012	−0.017	−0.032	0.030	0.032
Number of use of force with UN mandate	−0.121	−0.044	−0.175*	−0.131	−0.150	−0.079	−0.072
Number of use of force without UN mandate	0.144	0.205**	0.355**	0.160*	0.337**	0.221**	0.221**
Number of NATO summits	0.062	0.003	0.071	0.005	−0.008	−0.026	−0.018
Number of beginning NATO interventions	0.345**	0.369**	0.381**	0.338**	0.317**	0.322**	0.249**
Number of other NATO events	0.186*	0.166*	0.241**	0.206**	0.116	0.110	0.073
Number of all NATO events	0.295**	0.277**	0.349**	0.287**	0.220**	0.211**	0.157*
Number of EU summits	0.205**	0.223**	0.218**	0.208**	0.177*	0.179*	0.195**
Number of WEU/CFSP/ESDP events	0.081	0.093	0.103	0.149*	0.047	0.080	0.088
Number of beginning EU civilian missions	0.060	−0.012	0.030	0.057	0.032	0.072	0.103

90   Comparing debates across nations

	\multicolumn{7}{c}{Coverage}
	GER	NL	AU	FR	IR	UK	US
Number of beginning EU interventions	0.340**	0.365**	0.311**	0.290**	0.377**	0.323**	0.335**
Number of other EU events	0.027	0.119	0.155*	0.134	0.119	0.075	0.092
Number of all EU events	0.199**	0.235**	0.249**	0.280**	0.193*	0.207**	0.233**
Number of other summits	0.349**	0.263**	0.390**	0.284**	0.361**	0.229**	0.254**
Number of beginning other interventions	0.026	0.022	0.052	–0.031	0.081	0.024	0.058
Number of other Agreements	0.086	0.047	0.091	0.003	0.091	0.047	0.106
Number of all crisis events	–0.078	–0.047	–0.005	–0.087	0.046	–0.026	–0.031
Number of all interventions	0.181*	0.252**	0.206**	0.144*	0.198*	0.196**	0.191**
Number of all crisis events and all EU, NATO and UN events	0.205**	0.281**	0.309**	0.249**	0.230**	0.219**	0.213**
Involvement Austria	0.300**	0.347**	0.311**	0.343**	0.211**	0.257**	0.270**
Involvement Germany	0.324**	0.342**	0.405**	0.349**	0.285**	0.272**	0.268**
Involvement France	0.272**	0.328**	0.347**	0.317**	0.237**	0.244**	0.245**
Involvement Ireland	0.206**	0.247**	0.249**	0.261**	0.164*	0.190**	0.220**
Involvement Netherlands	0.325**	0.354**	0.381**	0.352**	0.276**	0.264**	0.278**
Involvement UK	0.324**	0.364**	0.396**	0.354**	0.302**	0.287**	0.299**
Involvement US	0.250**	0.291**	0.308**	0.237**	0.214**	0.224**	0.203**
Number of parliamentary and pre-sidential elections	–0.065	–0.115	–0.082	–0.064	–0.110	–0.074	–0.050
Europe affected	0.186*	0.246**	0.275**	0.195**	0.156*	0.134	0.139
Middle East affected	0.179*	0.297**	0.251**	0.255**	0.315**	0.309**	0.360**
Asia affected	–0.061	–0.110	–0.031	–0.128	0.002	–0.079	–0.080

	Coverage						
	GER	NL	AU	FR	IR	UK	US
Africa affected	−0.036	−0.027	−0.090	−0.023	−0.040	−0.001	−0.006
America affected	0.068	0.121	0.104	0.146*	0.071	0.124	0.108

Notes: Table based entirely on author's own data. The table displays Pearson's correlation coefficients. Period of investigation: Jan. 1990–Mar. 2006 (195 months). Because of missing data, three countries include fewer months: AU 163, IR 166, GER 182. The calculation of 'all UN events' excludes the numbers of 'use of force with UN mandate' and 'without UN mandate' because the latter are a property of events, not events themselves.

The efforts of other international organisations to play a role in conflict mediation, prevention or intervention (e.g. the African Union in Somalia and Darfur, Sudan), and the diplomatic initiatives of international institutions, regional organisations and/or major powers to solve an escalating conflict, reach a ceasefire or negotiate a peace treaty, found a moderately positive echo in reporting. However, the numbers of interventions operated by individual states or institutions other than the UN, NATO or the EU do not correlate with the level of reporting on our issue of concern.

If one further collapses the event categories, the picture becomes even sharper: the mere number of all crisis events (outbreaks of war, massacres and mass killings, Islamist terrorist attacks) together correlate slightly negatively, but not significantly, with the intensity of reporting on wars and interventions. There are many conflicts in the world, but only some receive large-scale attention in the news, while the majority of these events are either briefly mentioned or covered at a very low level (Galtung and Holmboe Ruge 1965). All beginning interventions are less clearly associated to the level of reporting than NATO and EU interventions alone.

One could expect that varying issue salience, the degree to which a country is concerned by a conflict, and has a greater or lesser involvement in it, impacts on the amount of reporting in the media of this country on that topic. A country was considered to be involved in a conflict if the country participated in the diplomatic decision-making processes in the UN, NATO, EU or other settings; if its citizens were subject to atrocities or terrorist attacks abroad; or if it participated in a war or intervention. Table 4.3 shows that the involvement of the countries under study positively correlates comparatively strongly with the amount of newspaper coverage (Pearson's coefficients in most cases around 0.30). However, it is surprising that there is no single case where the involvement of a country has the highest impact on the amount of coverage of that country. For Ireland, the UK and the US, the correlation between involvement and the quantity of reporting is in fact the lowest of all countries under study. In the case of the US, this might result from the fact that the last remaining superpower is involved in almost all diplomatic events, so that this factor for the US does not vary to the same degree it does for others.

For the UK and Ireland, the comparatively limited association between involvement and the intensity of reporting might, however, indicate a more extroverted way of perceiving the world. The values for the non-NATO member Austria, which became an EU Member State only in 1995, point in the same direction: as in the other countries under study, Austrian media coverage corresponds most strongly to the involvement of the NATO members and big EU Member States. Parliamentary and presidential elections in one of the countries under study correlated minimally negatively with the intensity of reporting on wars and interventions – although the correlation was not significant.

It is also widely suspected that media attention varies according to the continent on which an armed conflict occurs (Galtung and Holmboe Ruge 1965). Coding of crisis events included geographical location. For diplomatic events, we coded by continent. Table 4.3 confirms the views prevalent in the literature: crises happening on the European continent are positively associated with the amount of news on wars and interventions on a moderate level in most countries under study, with the notable exception of the UK and the US. The correlation is most pronounced in the case of the Austrian media, most likely due to Austria's historical ties with Eastern and South-Eastern Europe. Similarly, the Dutch press reacted with more sensitivity to conflicts on the European continent, perhaps because of the country's traumatic experience in Srebrenica 1995 (for a detailed overview of the events leading up to the massacre in Srebrenica, see Annan 1999).

Conflict events in the Middle East correlate comparatively strongly with reporting in most countries under study. However, Austrian, French, and especially German quality newspapers' quantity of reporting on wars and interventions correlates at a much lower level with events in this region. Asian and African conflicts seem to be under-represented as well. Conflict events in Asia, Africa and the Americas are not even significantly correlated to the amount of reporting on wars and interventions.

One can therefore suspect that there is no automatic correlation between the frequency of certain types of crisis events and the issue-cycles. It seems that correlations increase with the co-occurrence of a series of inter-related factors: intensified media attention is attracted by selected events in selected parts of the world, in which the US and the European countries participate, and which attract a high level of diplomatic and institutional attention from important international organisations such as the UN, NATO and the EU.

In order to test this new hypothesis and to compare the obviously volatile curves in more detail, I conducted an ARIMA time-series analysis. Time-series analysis is an econometric statistical instrument for detecting long-time or seasonal trends hidden below the volatile image of the time series' sequence charts, to identify significant peaks (as well as sudden declines) in proportion to the overall variation.[9] The aim of the analyses is not to describe every single curve as neatly as possible, but to discover whether the same independent variables impact in a similar way on the quantity of reporting in the different countries, and to identify factors that influence several curves. It is doubtless possible to take the analysis of individual curves further. I do not therefore claim to have found the best model for each curve. Rather, my analysis aims at a transnational comparison of the broader structures of debate.

What we usually look for in time-series data, such as stock rates or unemployment rates, are general linear or non-linear *trends* – which we, for obvious reasons, hope slope upwards in the case of stock rates and downwards for unemployment rates. Moreover, we search for *seasonal patterns*, climatic patterns that cause unemployment to be lower in summer or wars to be started in March, for example.

Since this study is not limited to selected intervention episodes, but includes the continuous time period from January 1990 to March 2006, the data shed a differentiated light on the quantitative trajectory in media attention. What moves the overall issue-cycle and the specific issue-cycle on humanitarian military intervention?

The issue-cycles are not moved by inherent trends (linear or non-linear, upwards or downwards) over the whole time span of investigation. The observed issue-cycles rather resemble fever curves or financial data. They do not contain seasonal components. They seem to be driven by external events and also contain a considerable amount of 'noise' (random disturbances). They contain some extreme and several minor peaks. Moreover, at some points in time, structural breaks and even shocks occur, leading to a shock wave that vibrates before coverage returns to a 'normal' level. We may suspect from some of the curves that a few of these shocks (such as September 2001) even altered the 'normal' issue-cycle baseline.

As a consequence, simple classical time-series models cannot help us. We must turn instead to stochastic time-series models in order to separate the event-driven logic in the curves – if there is any – from noise (Eckstein 2006: Ch. 7; Thome 2005). I chose stochastic time series with autoregressive integrated moving-average (ARIMA) models.[10]

ARIMA models

ARIMA models are usually displayed in the form ARIMA (p,d,q). They include three components that model different effects of random disturbances or shocks.

- AR (p): the autoregressive component (p) indicates that each current value is a function of the specified number of previous values.[11] The stochastic process, it is assumed, has a long time memory for earlier events. Shocks have a – slowly diminishing – effect on the following values (Thome 2005: 80 ff.). For example, $p = 2$ specifies that the time-series values of the past two months have been used to predict the value for the current month.

- I (d): the value of the differencing (or integration) component (d) tells us how often one has to calculate the differences between the observed values and their preceding values in order to arrive at a 'stationary' series, one that varies around a constant and does not contain any trends (Eckstein 2006: 274; Thome 2005: 54). In order to calculate the AR and the MA component, the series has to be stationary. The differencing procedure filters trends and displays them as $d > 0$. For linear trends, the differencing procedure has to be done once ($d = 1$) and for nonlinear-quadratic trends twice ($d = 2$) (Eckstein 2006: 274).
- MA (q): in some stochastic processes, external events do not have a lasting effect (as modelled by the AR component above), but help to model short-term fluctuations (Thome 2005: 110ff). In such series, values are considered a function of deviations from the series mean in earlier observations. In such cases, it makes sense to include a moving-average component into the analysis. The number of moving-average orders (q) tells us how many deviations from the series mean for previous values (earlier observations) have been used to predict current values. For example, $q = 2$ specifies that the deviations from the series mean observed in the previous two months have been used to predict the value for the current month.

ARIMA models also allow for the inclusion of predictor variables and help to identify significant outliers. Some of the aggregated event-data already presented in the bivariate correlations were used as independent variables: The event-data time series serves as a predictor for the media content time series to be explained. This allows us to test which types of events impact on the curves to be explained. Events that do not follow the overarching dynamics will also be detected. Such outliers can be significant *pulse events* and *level shifts*, both either positive or negative, which is indicated by algebraic signs. *Pulse events (additive outliers)* are single extreme observations without lasting influence. *Level shifts* are single observations of a month with extreme reporting that cause a shift in the level of all subsequent observations for a constant. Both are of high relevance for the research questions.

Reading the statistical output

How should the statistical output be read? Of the various statistical outputs for the models estimated, the following measures are presented:

- The ARIMA (p,d,q) model.
- The goodness-of-fit of each model. Two measures are presented in the tables that summarise the models.
    - Stationary R-squared is a goodness-of-fit measure that compares the stationary part of the model to a simple mean model. This

measure is preferable to ordinary R-squared when there is a trend or seasonal pattern. However, this is not the case for most of the models estimated in this and the following sections (in most cases d = 0).
- Is a goodness-of-fit measure that estimates the proportion of the total variation in the series that is explained by the model. This measure is most useful when the series is stationary (d ≠ 0). Stationary R-squared and R-squared can be negative with a range of negative infinity to 1. Negative values mean that the model under consideration is worse than the baseline model. Positive values mean that the model under consideration is better than the baseline model.

- In order to check for structural links between the media content data on one hand, and dramatic conflict events as opposed to mundane institutional events on the other hand, the following event-data time series were chosen as predictors: the *number of all crisis events; number of all UN events; number of all NATO events*; and *number of all EU events*. It is reported whether some of them turned out significant and in which direction they impacted on media reporting.
- Outliers, or months that did not follow the general dynamics, are also reported.

The issue-cycles of wars and interventions are so volatile that the estimated ARIMA time-series models with the best fit were those that used the logarithms of the values to even the curves, which results in a better goodness-of-fit. ARIMA models with explanatory power between 69 per cent of the variation (IR, NL) and 86 per cent (GER) were estimated. In three countries we see a linear trend over time (GER, AU, FR). For Austria and France this limits the explanatory power of the models to 39 and 49 per cent, respectively. These values are satisfactory to highly satisfactory.

Among the aggregated event-data including the *number of all crisis events* (GER, IR)[12] and the *number of all NATO events* [13] were significant predictors in the ARIMA models estimated. Factors that turn out to be significant when the models have been estimated with evened (naturally logarithmised) values indicate extremely robust findings. The figures in the footnotes indicate the direction in which these predictors influenced the curves. In some cases, we see a shock pattern with an increase at the month of the concerned events or one month later (lag 1) and a decrease at the second month (lag 2). Table 4.4 shows the results of the ARIMA time-series models.

To give a reading example of this output, the ARIMA model for France, which used the aggregate event-type data as independent variables, had a comparatively low explanatory power of 49 per cent (R^2 for the stationary part = 0.485).[14] The model indicates that the stochastic process has a memory of three months ($p = 3$): the amount of coverage in any month is a function of

96 Comparing debates across nations

Table 4.4 ARIMA models for 'wars and interventions'

Time series (coverage)	ARIMA model description (all natural log)	R^2 for stationary part	R^2	Significant variables number of all:
GER	(0,1,1)	0.862	0.868	Crisis events
NL	(1,0,0)	0.767	0.690	NATO events
AU	(0,1,2)	0.390	0.716	NATO events
FR	(3,1,1)	0.485	0.781	NATO events
IR	(1,0,0)	0.688	0.689	Crisis events NATO events
UK	(0,0,6)	0.742	0.733	NATO events
US	(1,0,0)	0.793	0.742	NATO events

Notes: Table based entirely on author's own data. ARIMA models with aggregated event-type data as independent variables. Period of investigation: Jan. 1990–Mar. 2006 (195 months). Because of missing data, three countries include fewer months: AU 163, IR 166, GER 182.

the amount of coverage measured in the three previous months. The dynamics of the French issue-cycle dynamic is also characterised by short time fluctuations. The deviation of the amount of coverage in any month is influenced by the deviation of the previous month from the average level of coverage. Moreover, there is linear trend in the curve ($d = 1$) – over time reporting increases. The French issue-cycle also has a moving average component ($q = 1$), which is a memory of events that led to deviations from the series mean in the past – the last month's deviation contributes to predicting the value for the current month. The aggregated *number of all NATO events* also is a statistically significant predictor of the intensity of reporting on wars and interventions in the two French papers. The effect this factor adds to the already strong explanation of the ARIMA model consists of a slight increase in news coverage during months in which said events occur, as well as in the following month (lag 1). News coverage decreases thereafter (lag 2). This means there is a small shock wave going through the media in the face of NATO actions, and a large amount of reporting in the following month, but the second month after the shock witnesses reduced attention to the issue. Afterwards the level of reporting returns to normal – no further effects can be detected. Significant pulse events in the French issue-cycle occurred in August and September of 1990, as well as January and February of 1991. Most of these constitute peaks – short-term increases followed by normalisation. Only for September 1990 was a level shift detected: From this month on, the level of coverage increased permanently.

Which other months are characterised by significant peaks? Which events led to lasting level shifts in the overall coverage of wars and interventions? One first peak discharging into a level shift occurred in August 1990, when Iraq occupied Kuwait, drawing harsh condemnation from, amongst others, the UN and the Arab League and prompting the US to move troops to Saudi

Arabia (Operation Desert Shield). This peak is visible and significant for France, the UK and the US.[15] In January 1991, when the conflict escalated and a US-led coalition started bombing Iraq – partly with precision-guided munitions which shaped the televised media image of the conflict – another significant peak occurred. The UK and France participated in this coalition, while Germany supported it financially (Jacobs 1991) – one of the last examples of German 'cheque-book diplomacy'. In contrast to this official support, major peace demonstrations were organised in France and Germany. The Dutch newspapers belatedly experienced the level shift in reporting that had not yet been statistically significant at the beginning of the crisis. The aftershocks of these events are significant peaks in February (FR, UK). However, Iraq was not the only international crisis in January 1991. Civil wars in Angola (Arnold 2008a; James 2004: xxxiii) and a military coup in Haiti (Martin 1999: 713) also occurred, and may have contributed to the observed effect.

9/11 led everywhere to a rising interest in issues of war and interventions – the implications of the massive terrorist attacks on the World Trade Center in New York and the Pentagon in Washington for international relations and issues of war and peace were immediately discussed in the media. Almost all ARIMA models indicate a significant level shift in this month.[16] In the national and international arena, intense institutional and declaratory activities unfolded. By October, the war against the Taliban in Afghanistan had begun (Adamec 2003: 529) – causing a significant peak in some of the ARIMA models (FR, UK, US). Due to the extreme fluctuations in the issue-cycles on wars and interventions since September 2001, the most extreme and easily visible peak at the beginning of the Iraq War in March/April 2003 is only a significant outlier in the ARIMA model for the logarithmically transformed issue-cycle of the US press.

In a final step in the statistical analysis, I searched for a dynamic measure of difference and convergence across countries that can be calculated over time. At first sight, one could attempt to use the *standard deviation* as a measure for higher and lower degrees of similarity of the curves. However, in crisis periods – as compared with 'tranquil periods' – the mean as well as the standard deviation increase significantly.[17] Such phenomena have typically been observed in financial data and are considered to be due to a large increase in noise (random disturbances) in crisis periods (Corsetti et al. 2005). Therefore a convergence measure is needed, one that accounts for this interrelation. There are two alternative options: either one assumes a margin against which the curves compared are expected to converge; or one chooses a relative measure that tests whether the curves converge towards their common mean. I decided on the latter: because there is no reason to name any fixed value towards which convergence should be expected, I chose to calculate *sigma convergence*, the variation of all issue-cycles from their common mean (v = standard deviation/mean).[18] If the values of this coefficient move towards zero, dispersion decreases. Values larger than one

98 *Comparing debates across nations*

indicate that the standard deviation in the respective months was bigger than the mean. The coefficients multiplied by 100 can be read as deviation from the mean in per cent.

Figure 4.2 shows the results of this analysis, first for all countries under study and then for the EU countries only. We can see that the initial level of deviation is quite high. In January 1991 deviation decreased suddenly, coinciding with the beginning of international intervention in Iraq. For all countries the minimum variation is reached at the Iraq War-related peak in February 2003 (48 per cent deviation from the mean). In this month, the UN weapons inspector Hans Blix reported that Iraq had not fully cooperated with the inspections, and US, UK and Spanish pressure for a new resolution authorising the use of force against Iraq rose (Ghareeb and Dougherty 2004: xxxvii).

The maximum of deviation is reached with 128 per cent deviation from the mean in September 1992. This maximum of variance is probably due to developments in the Bosnian conflict, in combination with important domestic events in France and the UK that may have overshadowed other reporting in these countries.[19] In September 1992 the International Conference on the

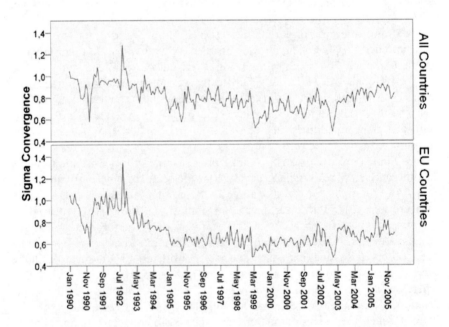

Figure 4.2 σ-convergence of the issue-cycles coverage on 'wars and interventions'
Notes: These figures are based entirely on the author's own data. The graph displays sequence charts of the deviation measure. Low values indicate less deviation, high values more deviation from the common mean. $N = 489,508$. Data aggregated on a monthly basis. Period of investigation: Jan. 1990–Mar. 2006 (195 months). Because of missing data, three countries include fewer months: AU 163, IR 166, GER 182.

Comparing debates across nations 99

Former Yugoslavia (ICFY) continued negotiations. In Bosnia, Serb forces made advances around Srebrenica, while UN observation of Serb artillery proved unable to end the shelling of Sarajevo (Annan 1999: 12–15; Burg and Shoup 1999: 213–215). The average deviation is 80 per cent.

If we exclude the US from the analysis, the results change slightly. The average level of deviation from the common mean of the issue-cycles decreases by 9 per cent, to 71 per cent. The minimum deviation is reached in February 2003 and February 1999 with 47 per cent and the maximum in September 1992 with 135 per cent. This means that the extremes are more pronounced than in the common convergence measure. However, on average the European issue-cycles deviate less from their common mean than with the US included. The convergence measure curves also show a clear downward trend from September 1992 to around February 1999 and an upward trend from then on. The first trend is much more pronounced for the EU countries only. The divergence trend is more pronounced if the US is included. The EU convergence curve also includes two additional significant outliers: in August 1990, coinciding with the Iraqi invasion of Kuwait and German reunification, we observe a negative level shift that is a decrease in variance for the EU curve only; in January 1991, when Operation Desert Storm began, there is a sudden decrease of variation. In September 1992, as in the analysis including the US, variance peaks significantly. In May 2003 there is a level shift upwards – from this month on, variance among the EU countries oscillates around a higher average level again.

Interim conclusions

The analysis substantiates the assumption that a common transnational debate on wars and interventions emerged after the end of the Cold War. The same issues of 'wars and interventions' were discussed at the same time across countries. Starting from a quite heterogeneous picture, similarity increased over time and was more pronounced among the EU countries. The observed issue-cycles resemble fever curves or currency exchange rates, in that they are driven by external events and contain a considerable amount of random 'noise'. However, analysis reveals some structure to the seemingly random pattern. As might be expected, news-breaking international crisis events, such as the Iraqi occupation of Kuwait in August 1990, the subsequent First Gulf War in 1991, the Kosovo crisis of mid-1999, and the beginning of the Iraq War 2003, were all intensively covered by the press in all countries under study, and led to simultaneous quantitative peaking of newspaper coverage. This indicates shared cross-national interest in events in which the respective countries are interdependently involved.

What one would not expect, however, is the countries' issue-cycles to be correlated strongly with each other at extremely high levels. Nonetheless, this intense correlation does not reflect the presence or absence of news values in any straightforward manner. The 'usual suspects' (i.e. outbreaks of war, massacres, instances of genocide or expulsion, Islamist terror attacks) of events pushing news coverage on wars and interventions do not correlate significantly with the monthly number of articles. The same is true for institutional reactions. UN, NATO and EU institutional events do not correlate more than moderately with the level of reporting on wars and interventions in the respective countries. The correlation is strongest for NATO and EU interventions – very rare events. Moreover, it is surprising that even national involvement has only a moderate impact on the issue-cycle in the country concerned.

We can conclude, therefore, that there is no automatic association between the frequency of certain types of crisis events and issue-cycles. Of the many conflicts in the world and of the many institutional events, only some selected events receive massive attention in the news, while the majority are only mentioned or are covered at a very low level. This is not to say that coverage is not event-driven; rather, that correlations seem to increase with the co-occurrence of a series of inter-related factors. Selected events in certain regions that engage in numerous diplomatic and institutional activities within important international organisations, and in which the US and the European countries participate, attract intense media attention.

This compound hypothesis could be indirectly supported with a set of ARIMA time-series analyses. The time series even of all dramatic international crisis events taken together is not a significant predictor of the issue-cycles. Of the aggregated event-data included, only the *number of all NATO events* – including the presumably 'mundane' meetings and summits – were significant independent variables.

Issue-cycles converge across countries in the 1990s. This trend is especially pronounced among the EU countries. However, deviation increases again after February 1999 – albeit on a much lower base level than at the start of our investigation. This divergence is somewhat more pronounced if the US is included than for the EU countries only, which indicates a certain transatlantic gap.

All these findings suggest a high sensitivity of the quality press in the countries under study to the same important international problems. This, in turn, creates awareness of an interdependent context and results in transnationally intertwined political communication. The intensity of newspaper coverage on war and intervention is driven by the same extraordinary crisis events, together with the institutional responses they generate in all countries under study. These initial findings must be kept in mind throughout the further analysis, and form the backdrop to my analysis of specific aspects of this coverage in the following sections.

The issue cycle of humanitarian military interventions

Cross-country and transatlantic similarities are even more likely to be found if one looks at the framing of international crisis events as normatively positively connoted 'humanitarian military interventions' as opposed to 'ordinary wars'. Here a degree of transatlantic drift and a polarised national debate can be expected. Figure 4.3 displays the sequence chart of the sub-sample issue-cycle of newspaper articles referring to humanitarian interventions. It includes all articles that discussed intervention in terms of an uninvolved third party intervening in an ongoing conflict in order to protect civilians from severe human rights abuses. This curve was generated using corpus-linguistic methods. Following the procedure described in Chapter 3, we created country-specific lists of typical phrases and collocations unambiguously belonging to the semantic field of humanitarian military interventions. These were particular specifications of 'troops' (e.g. 'UN troops', 'blue helmet'), 'force' (e.g. 'monitoring force'), 'forces' (e.g. 'contribute forces', KFOR, ISAF), 'missions' (e.g. 'military mission', 'peace-keeping'), 'strikes' (e.g. 'NATO air strikes'), 'operation', 'action' etc.

Altogether this sub-sample on humanitarian military interventions encompasses 108,677 articles. Newspaper articles using this more specific wording constitute approximately 20 per cent of all articles in France, the UK and the US, 25 per cent in Germany, and almost 30 per cent in the Netherlands, Ireland and Austria.[20]

At first sight, the intervention issue-cycles are even harder to interpret than the overall issue-cycle on 'wars and interventions' (compare Figure 4.3 with Figure 4.1). However, one can identify four waves of higher quantitative levels and several peaks: 1990–91 (Iraq/Kuwait); autumn 1992 to autumn 1996 (Balkan crises, African conflicts); 1999/2000 (Kosovo); 9/11 to 2004 (Afghanistan, Iraq War).

US and British newspapers have the highest quantity of articles on intervention, which is again due to their specific journalistic styles. On average the two US papers together ran 185 articles on interventions each month (see Table 4.5). The maximum was reached in October 2001, when the invasion of

Table 4.5 Descriptives of the issue-cycles on 'humanitarian military interventions'

Intervention	Minimum	Maximum	Sum	Mean	Standard deviation
GER	0	441	15,946	87.62	65.35
NL	2	231	9871	50.62	32.65
AU	0	135	3695	22.67	21.14
FR	4	344	12,097	62.04	48.62
IR	12	182	8018	48.30	31.68
UK	20	467	22,899	117.43	74.24
US	41	550	36,151	185.39	94.76

Notes: Table based entirely on author's own data. The table displays absolute numbers of articles (min, max, sum) per country over the period of investigation (Jan. 1990–Mar. 2006, 195 months). Because of missing data, three countries include fewer months: AU 163, IR 166, GER 182.

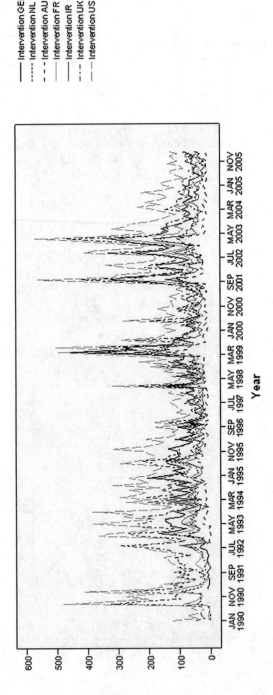

Figure 4.3 Issue cycles on 'humanitarian military interventions' (absolute numbers)
Notes: These figures are based entirely on the author's own data. $N = 108{,}677$, intervention sub-sample. Method used: corpus-linguistic frequency analysis, data aggregated on a monthly basis. Period of investigation: Jan. 1990–Mar. 2006 (195 months). Because of missing data, three countries include fewer months: AU 163, IR 166, GER 182.

Afghanistan began (Adamec 2003: 529). In the two British papers, about 117 articles on interventions were printed each month.

German, French and Irish papers also covered humanitarian military interventions extensively, although with somewhat lower absolute numbers of articles. On average, 88 (GER), 62 (FR), 50 (NL) and 48 (IR)[21] articles on interventions were printed per month. The Austrian press referred to interventions least often. The two Austrian newspapers published only 24 articles per month on interventions. Unlike the coverage on war *and* interventions, March 2003 was no longer the month with the maximum coverage. Instead, April 1999 took centre stage for most countries.[22] In the German and Austrian newspapers, there were no articles on humanitarian military interventions in some months.[23]

Besides the news-breaking crisis events already visible in the overall issue-cycle (Figure 4.1), another group of conflicts – mainly in Africa – now become visible as simultaneous peaks (Figure 4.3): the international reactions to crises in Somalia 1992/93 and 1995 (Arnold 2008g: 331–338); the genocide in Rwanda 1994 (Twagilimana 2007: xxxii–xxxv); and the civil war in Sierra Leone in the late 1990s (Arnold 2008f: 320–325; Fyle 2006) seem to have been consistently labelled as interventions rather than wars.

Even if the curves at first sight seem less harmonious than the overall issue-cycles, the correlations between them are almost as distinct as the overall issue-cycles on 'wars and interventions'. All curves correlate highly significantly with each other, ranging from slightly more than 0.70 (AU/US, AU/UK, NL/UK, NL/US), to values around 0.80 among the continental European countries, to 0.90 between the Irish and the British papers, as well as those from the US (see Table 4.6). On one hand, this is an indicator for synchronous debates about the normative justification (or lacking normative justification) of some military conflicts as interventions for a humanitarian purpose. On the other hand, the correlation coefficients indicate less

Table 4.6 Bivariate correlations of the issue-cycles on 'humanitarian military interventions' (Pearson's coefficients)

Intervention				Intervention			
	GER	NL	AU	FR	IR	UK	US
GER	1	0.813**	0.873**	0.849**	0.840**	0.787**	0.842**
NL	0.813**	1	0.791**	0.807**	0.830**	0.736**	0.736**
AU	0.873**	0.791**	1	0.804**	0.781**	0.728**	0.715**
FR	0.849**	0.807**	0.804**	1	0.813**	0.820**	0.809**
IR	0.840**	0.830**	0.781**	0.813**	1	0.896**	0.859**
UK	0.787**	0.736**	0.728**	0.820**	0.896**	1	0.914**
US	0.842**	0.736**	0.715**	0.809**	0.859**	0.914**	1

Notes: Table based entirely on author's own data. The table displays Pearson's correlation coefficients. Period of investigation: Jan. 1990–Mar. 2006 (195 months). Because of missing data, three countries include fewer months: AU 163, IR 166, GER 182.

inter-correlation than among the overall issue-cycles. This constitutes an indicator for slightly more cross-national differences – or, more precisely, more transatlantic differences – when we focus not just on the conflicts as such, but on their normative dimension.

Did the issue-cycle of humanitarian military interventions respond to the same type of events in the countries under study? Table 4.7 shows the correlations of the coverage and aggregated event-data. As in the case of the overall issue-cycle, the figures indicate that the mere monthly numbers of certain types of crisis events do not correlate significantly with the monthly number of articles on interventions.

UN institutional (re-)actions do not correlate straightforwardly with the reporting on interventions. It is not the normal institutional acts of the UN (passing resolutions, summits, beginning UN interventions), but rather extraordinary UN events and the use of force without a UN mandate that correlate at a low to moderate level with the intensity of news coverage on interventions and debates questioning the legitimacy of foreign interventions – especially in the post-neutral countries of Austria and Ireland. Even the aggregated numbers of all UN events do not correlate with the level of coverage of humanitarian military interventions as 'just wars'.

Stronger correlations, though still only at a medium level, can be observed with regard to NATO interventions in most of the countries under study. The Pearson's coefficients indicate that knowing whether NATO intervenes in a conflict predicts the direction of change in the intervention issue-cycles in between 42 (US) and 47 per cent (FR) of the cases. With regard to 'ordinary wars' and 'interventions' together, the difference between the US and the EU is stronger, which suggests that NATO is for the US media what the ESDP has become for the European media: the first port of call for multilateral security policy for normative purposes. The numbers of NATO summits do not correlate significantly with the curves. Extraordinary NATO events, however, are of moderate importance in the European countries under study, except the UK. All NATO events together are moderately and positively correlated with the quantity of articles invoking humanitarian intervention with its attendant positive connotations. This effect is again much weaker for the US and strongest for Austria and Germany. However, this may be a statistical artefact caused by the enormous peaks associated with the Kosovo intervention and the Iraq War.

The number of EU activities seems to correlate positively, albeit at a very low level, with the issue-cycles on 'humanitarian military interventions'. The correlation is strongest for France (0.23 for beginning EU interventions and 0.22 for all EU events). For all countries, EU institutional activities seem to be associated with the issue-cycle less than in the overall issue-cycle. This may be partly due to the fact that the EU often acted not alone, but in broader multilateral settings (such as the so-called 'Contact Groups' during the Bosnian and Kosovo conflicts). Summits outside of the regular purview of the UN, NATO and EU, in which regional organisations and/or major (regional)

Table 4.7 Bivariate correlations between the issue-cycles of 'humanitarian military interventions' and aggregated event-data (Pearson's coefficients)

	Intervention						
	GER	NL	AU	FR	IR	UK	US
Number of UN Resolutions	0.013	0.135	0.064	0.066	0.123	0.140	0.164*
Number of other UN events	0.193**	0.246**	0.223**	0.197**	0.194*	0.216**	0.216**
Number of all UN events	−0.003	0.141*	0.043	0.047	0.062	0.129	0.178*
Number of use of force without UN mandate	0.117	0.086	0.369**	0.189**	0.311**	0.221**	0.199**
Number of beginning NATO interventions	0.464**	0.445**	0.457**	0.468**	0.440**	0.434**	0.424**
Number of other NATO events	0.272**	0.275**	0.335**	0.264**	0.218**	0.164*	0.158*
Number of all NATO events	0.413**	0.396**	0.457**	0.395**	0.351**	0.309**	0.301**
Number of EU summits	0.169*	0.162*	0.176*	0.187**	0.125	0.107	0.148*
Number of beginning EU interventions	0.184*	0.160*	0.149	0.225**	0.172*	0.183*	0.146*
Number of other EU events	0.070	0.184**	0.172*	0.154*	0.175*	0.110	0.156*
Number of all EU events	0.136	0.188**	0.156*	0.221**	0.095	0.063	0.085
Number of other summits	0.299**	0.205**	0.329**	0.330**	0.296**	0.164*	0.157*
Number of all interventions	0.203**	0.233**	0.236**	0.224**	0.232**	0.265**	0.310**
Number of all crisis events and all EU, NATO and UN events	0.238**	0.311**	0.351**	0.299**	0.283**	0.232**	0.250**
Involvement Austria	0.261**	0.358**	0.266**	0.335**	0.172*	0.176*	0.259**
Involvement Germany	0.355**	0.405**	0.411**	0.409**	0.328**	0.283**	0.330**

106 Comparing debates across nations

	Intervention						
	GER	NL	AU	FR	IR	UK	US
Involvement France	0.303**	0.385**	0.364**	0.364**	0.277**	0.256**	0.296**
Involvement Ireland	0.185*	0.264**	0.209**	0.275**	0.152	0.141*	0.217**
Involvement Netherlands	0.357**	0.418**	0.385**	0.405**	0.323**	0.278**	0.337**
Involvement UK	0.313**	0.373**	0.363**	0.397**	0.305**	0.270**	0.310**
Involvement US	0.319**	0.379**	0.380**	0.339**	0.344**	0.335**	0.372**
Number of parliamentary and presidential elections	–0.085	–0.082	–0.051	–0.108	–0.164*	–0.075	–0.018
Europe affected	0.219**	0.308**	0.315**	0.241**	0.173*	0.132	0.209**
Middle East affected	0.045	0.112	0.108	0.167*	0.144	0.201**	0.196**
America affected	0.111	0.132	0.129	0.139	0.091	0.158*	0.168*

Notes: Table based entirely on author's own data. The table displays Pearson's correlation coefficients. Period of investigation: Jan. 1990–Mar. 2006 (195 months). Because of missing data, three countries include fewer months: AU 163, IR 166, GER 182. Rows with no significant results have been eliminated for better readability. The full list of events included in the test can be seen in Table 4.3.

powers try to solve an escalating conflict diplomatically, reach a ceasefire or arrive at a peace treaty, are moderately and highly significantly associated with the issue-cycles on humanitarian military interventions.

If one further collapses the event categories, it becomes clear that the numbers of crisis events alone, and the numbers of institutional events of any type, do not matter. However, the *number of all interventions* [24] as well as the *number of all crisis events and all EU, NATO and UN events* [25] correlate moderately and highly significantly with the issue-cycles in the different countries under study. The mere numbers of all crisis events (outbreaks of war, massacres, Islamist terrorist attacks) do not even correlate significantly with the intensity of the debate on humanitarian military interventions.

Does the involvement of the nation state in which a newspaper is published in crisis events and institutional reactions correlate with the issue-cycle? In Table 4.7 we can also see that the involvement of our countries under study correlates positively at a comparatively high level with the amount of newspaper coverage (Pearson's coefficients in most cases around 0.30). However, it is surprising that there is only one case – the Netherlands – in which a country's involvement has the highest impact on the amount of articles that refer to the normative concept of humanitarian military interventions in the press of this country. One can suspect that this too may be an artefact of the Dutch experience at Srebrenica. For Ireland and the UK, the correlation between national involvement and the quantity of reporting is the lowest of all countries under study – for Ireland it is not even significant. This low correlation between national involvement and the intensity of debate about and reporting on interventions may indicate a very extroverted way of perceiving the world. The coefficients for the Netherlands point in the same direction. The Dutch media seem sensitive not only to Dutch involvement, but to Western involvement more broadly. Parliamentary and presidential elections in one of the countries under study correlated minimally negatively with the intensity of the debate on humanitarian military interventions – the correlation was significant only for Ireland.

Does media debate on humanitarian military interventions vary according to the continent on which an armed conflict takes place (or in relation to which international institutions and organisations react)? Table 4.7 reveals that crises happening on the European continent are positively associated with the number of articles dealing with interventions. This association is moderate for Austria and the Netherlands (Pearson's coefficient 0.30), rather weak for France, Germany and the US (0.20), and very weak for Ireland (less than 0.20). It is not significant for the UK. However, geographical correlation in the data is comparatively strong. Conflicts (or institutional events related to conflicts) in the Middle East are moderate and significant only for the issue-cycles of the former colonial powers in this region (FR, UK) and the US. Conflict events in the Americas are significantly correlated to the amount of debate on interventions in the UK and US – and then only at a weak level (less than 0.20).

Again, there seems to be no automatic link between the frequency of certain types of crisis events, institutional events or conflict characteristics, and the issue-cycles of articles referring to the normative concept of humanitarian military interventions. NATO interventions, the participation of the countries under study in the conflicts, and that the armed conflicts in question take place on the European continent correlate most strongly with the level of reporting on interventions.

In order to test the robustness of this finding and to compare the obviously highly volatile curves in more detail, I again conducted a set of time-series analyses. As previously, some aggregated event-data, the *number of all crisis events*, the *number of all UN events*, the *number of all NATO events*, and the *number of all EU events*, were included as independent variables into the analysis and outliers were calculated. Table 4.8 displays the condensed results of the ARIMA models concerning news on interventions in the normative sense.

The issue-cycles of humanitarian military interventions were also so volatile that the values were logarithmically smoothed for the curves of all countries except Germany and Austria. ARIMA models with explanatory power

108 *Comparing debates across nations*

Table 4.8 ARIMA models for 'humanitarian military interventions'

Time series (intervention)	ARIMA model description	R^2 for stationary part	R^2	Significant variables number of all:
GER	(1,0,5)	0.732	0.732	NATO events
NL	(0,1,1) (natural log)	0.498	0.548	NATO events
AU	(0,0,2)	0.671	0.671	NATO events
FR	(1,0,0) (natural log)	0.619	0.652	NATO events
IR	(1,0,0) (natural log)	0.377	0.455	NATO events
UK	(1,0,0) (natural log)	0.449	0.442	NATO events
US	(1,0,0) (natural log)	0.539	0.480	NATO events

Notes: Table based entirely on author's own data. ARIMA models with aggregated event-type data as independent variables. Period of investigation: Jan. 1990–Mar. 2006 (195 months). Because of missing data, three countries include fewer months: AU 163, IR 166, GER 182.

between 44 per cent of the variation (UK) and 73 per cent (GER) were estimated. These values are satisfying. Of the aggregated event-data included in the analysis, only the *number of all NATO events* was significant.[26]

Which months are characterised by significant peaks? Which events led to lasting level shifts in the debate on humanitarian military interventions? The first upwards peak occurred in August 1990 in two of the countries under study for which electronic newspaper articles were available at this early time (FR, US), while August marks an upwards level shift for the Netherlands. This increase in debate refers clearly to the Iraqi occupation of Kuwait and the resulting diplomatic activities. The next outliers can be detected in the Dutch media in September 1992 and December 1993, and constitute short-term peaks. In September 1992, the ICFY continued negotiations. In Bosnia, Serb forces made advances around Srebrenica, while UN observation of Serb artillery proved unable to end the shelling of Sarajevo (Annan 1999: 12–15; Burg and Shoup 1999: 213–215). In February 1998, the Kosovo conflict rapidly unfolded on the diplomatic level as the first news about violent incidents made international headlines. Such pulses are also visible in the German and Dutch media in February 1998, as well as the German and Austrian coverage in April 1999. In March and April 1999, Special European Council summits on Kosovo were held, and several EU Member States participated in sanctions against Belgrade and contributed to the enforcement of the weapons embargo (Central European & Eastern Adriatic Research Group 1999: 45–65). The fledgling ESDP developed rapidly in parallel. EU foreign ministers supported the stationing of a peacekeeping force in Kosovo on 8 April 1999. The last significant outlier during the period under investigation is seen in January 2003 in the Austrian issue-cycle. In that month, transatlantic and inner-European tensions rose over the question of Iraq (Pond 2005: esp. 42–49). In January the first European Union Police Mission in Bosnia and Herzegovina also began.

Do the curves highlight either convergence or divergence processes? The two graphs in Figure 4.4 show the results of the convergence analysis first for all countries under study and then for the EU countries only.

We can clearly see a process of convergence from autumn 1991 to March 1999 and – at a slower pace – increasing divergence from March 1999 onwards. Both trends are clearer for the EU countries only than for the upper graph, which includes the US. The minimum variation (42 per cent deviation from the mean) was reached in April 1999 at the height of the Kosovo War. The maximum variation (123 per cent deviation from the mean) was reached in September 1992, when developments in Bosnia coincided with momentous domestic events in France and the UK and variation was also greatest in the overall sample. Variation displays a marked peak in January 1990, when UN Resolution 771 was passed with the aim of ensuring humanitarian aid delivery in Bosnia.[27] Overall, the average variation was 74 per cent deviation from the mean.

Excluding the US from the convergence measure, the average level of variation is more than 10 per cent less (62 per cent deviation from the mean). Excluding the US, the minimum variation (34 per cent deviation from the

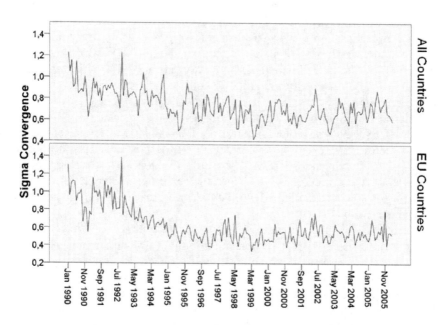

Figure 4.4 σ-convergence of the issue-cycles on 'humanitarian military interventions'
Notes: These figures are based entirely on the author's own data. The graph displays sequence charts of the deviation measure. Low values indicate less deviation, high values more deviation from the common mean. $N = 489{,}508$, $n = 108{,}677$. Data aggregated on a monthly basis. Period of investigation: Jan. 1990–Mar. 2006 (195 months). Because of missing data, three countries include fewer months: AU 163, IR 166, GER 182.

mean) was reached in March 1999, in the midst of NATO's intervention in Kosovo, and the maximum variation (139 per cent deviation from the mean) was reached in September 1992 – similarly to the overall issue-cycle on wars and interventions together. The EU convergence curve also includes three significant outliers: a negative peak indicating high similarity in October 1990 (Rwanda),[28] and two positive peaks indicating more divergence in April 1991 (Iraq)[29] and September 1992 (Bosnia). Only the last peak is also significant for the σ-convergence curve that includes the US.

Interim conclusions

Was the intensity of transnational political communication, and the degree of awareness of being cross-nationally involved in an interdependent problem-solving attempt, more distinguished for the normative part of the debate, that is, articles that frame ongoing armed conflicts in the positively connoted terms of a 'humanitarian + military intervention' in the sense of our definition? Was there more European coherence and a large transatlantic gap? The convergence measure is the strongest indicator for this expectation. We observed a process of increased synchronisation in the intensity of reporting from the first Iraq war to the Kosovo intervention and – at a low level and a much slower pace – somewhat increasing divergence again after the Kosovo crisis. On average, the deviation between the intervention issue-cycles was clearly lower than in the overall debate, and it was even lower for the EU countries only. Thus we observe a transatlantic discourse and within it an even tighter European one.

This finding is also mirrored by the very high correlations among the countries' issue-cycles on humanitarian military interventions. On one hand, this indicates very synchronous debates about the normative justification of some military conflicts as interventions for a humanitarian purpose. On the other hand, there are somewhat larger transatlantic differences – when the reporting on conflicts and the debate about their normative dimension are taken into consideration.

The transnational discussion on 'humanitarian military interventions' was certainly not restricted to a European community of communication. It is surely part of Western, if not global, news coverage, attention cycles and discourse. A substantial part of this debate on the use of military force focuses on four major conflicts: the Gulf War, the Kosovo conflict, the toppling of the Taliban regime in Afghanistan, and the 2003 Iraq War. These crises appear to be particularly contested, and consequently reporting on them is characterised by a 'mixed' wording. Some articles frame them as wars; others frame them as (possible) cases of intervention, or dispute their legitimacy with reference to the normative concept of humanitarian military intervention; and some use both terms.

Besides the news breaking crises visible already in the overall issue-cycle on 'wars and interventions', another group of conflicts – mainly in Africa – became visible as simultaneous peaks because these crises, when they were discussed, were consistently labelled as interventions. We thus observe four waves of heightened attention: 1990/01 (Iraq/Kuwait), autumn 1992 to autumn 1996 (Balkan crises, African conflicts), 1999/2000 (Kosovo), and 9/11 to 2004 (Afghanistan, Iraq War). March 2003, however, was no longer the month with the maximum coverage – indicating that the 2003 Iraq War was – especially in the continental European countries – decisively not framed in terms of a humanitarian military intervention, but as an 'ordinary war' for self-interested reasons.

As with the overall issue-cycles, the issue-cycles on the normative concept of 'humanitarian military interventions' do not automatically correlate with the mere frequency of certain types of crisis events, institutional reactions or conflict characteristics. The highest correlations were found with respect to NATO interventions, the participation of the countries under study in the conflicts and the location of the conflict on the European continent. These correlations, however, remained at a moderate level. However, the time-series analysis confirmed that monthly numbers of NATO events is a significant predictor for the issue-cycles of 'humanitarian military interventions' in all countries under study, but that the number of dramatic, presumably highly newsworthy crisis events are not.

The visibility of Europe and the EU

The same issues of 'wars and interventions' respectively 'humanitarian military interventions' have been discussed at the same time in all countries. The synchronous peaking of the curves and the sensitivity of the curves to the same event-types and individual events identified with the correlation analysis and with time-series analyses indicate – despite some national differences – that the debates have been transnationally intertwined. We took further steps and described the dynamics of the issue-cycles, what triggered them, and whether they became more similar over time. The third indicator for transnational political communication is 'similar aspects of relevance'. In this section I sketch the role Europe, and more specifically the EU, played in the reporting on armed conflicts and the normative debate about the use of military force after the end of the Cold War.

What role did Europe play in the debates on wars and humanitarian military interventions after the end of the Cold War? Was it visible at all? In political communication research, the term 'visibility' refers to the quantity of occurrence of a specific actor, frame or topic in the media and therefore the expected public awareness of it. An actor is 'visible' to the audience when it regularly and to sufficient degrees appears in the news (Kantner et al. 2008: 7). The degree and quality of visibility is often taken as an indicator of the attention and the importance attributed to a specific actor during the process of news selection:

> The amount, placement, and length of EU stories can provide insights into how much importance journalists ascribe to the coverage of European affairs.
>
> (Peter et al. 2003: 307)

Yet how much 'visibility' is necessary for an actor to be noted, or even acknowledged, by the audience is contested. Some authors use a rule of thumb: if in 10 per cent of the contributions to a topic a certain content element (an issue, frame or actor) is present, it is visible (Gamson 1992: 197). other authors search for a measure of appropriate presentation as comparing the 'real-world' share in influence that the EU assumes in economic and political terms with its share in societal and media activities (Beisheim et al. 1999; Gerhards 2000).

It is uncontested, however, that the media visibility of an actor is an important precondition for the media's and the audience's awareness of it. Only when an issue or actor is on the agenda can people develop reasoned arguments and expectations about it. Accordingly, 'visibility' can be taken as a first and preliminary indicator for the study of the publicly perceived importance of Europe and the EU. In political communication research, the degree and quality of the visibility of an actor or topic are usually measured with the help of the following indicators: the frequency of news stories or parts of news stories dedicated to the actor/topic under study (Downs 1972); the length and elaborateness of those reports or commentaries; and their placement in more or less prestigious newspaper or programme sections (*priming*) (Iyengar and Kinder 1987). A limitation of these indicators is that most of them are bound to qualitative content analysis (scanning of topics, sections and so on by human coders). Human coding secures high internal validity of the research results produced, but at the same time it limits researchers to a manageable effort in relation to reading and interpretation.

To determine efficiently the visibility of Europe, and more specifically the EU, in a newspaper corpus as large as the one used for this study, quantitative methods should be used. However, those quantitative methods should be much more sensitive to the contextual meaning of the counted word clusters than classic keyword-based approaches, and they should be generated semi-automatically in order to save time and lower costs. This calls for a well balanced combination of quantitative and qualitative methods (King et al. 1994). In order to detect how visible Europe was in the media discourse on 'wars and interventions', and on 'humanitarian military interventions' in particular, our corpus-based approach was used, which includes several qualitative steps. We began by counting how many newspaper articles mentioned 'Europe' in the different countries, using classical keyword searches of words such as 'Europe', 'European', 'Europeans', 'EU', 'Brussels' in all possible grammatical forms in the respective languages. In a second step, all respective word-clusters were checked for unambiguous references to the European context, to ensure, for instance, that 'Brussels' was used as shorthand for an

EU institution and not to designate the Belgian capital. Identifications of Europe as geographical space, as a place of origin of (national) politicians, and as part of the names of different European regional organisations (the EU being just one of them), were not excluded at this level. The selected search-words were applied in a text-mining procedure to retrieve all those articles from the text-corpus in which at least one of the keywords was mentioned at least once. This procedure was applied to the whole sample and to the sub-sample of articles that referred to 'humanitarian military interventions'.

How often 'Europe' is mentioned varies with the issue-cycles, but if we look at the percentages, we see interesting shifts. In both samples 'Europe' is mentioned more frequently in the EU countries (most often in AU and FR, least often in the UK) than in the US. In the intervention sub-sample, all newspapers mention 'Europe' in at least one-third of all articles, which is a very high share. However, this overall figure again masks significant variation. The British papers mentioned 'Europe' almost as rarely as the US papers. The frequency with which Europe is mentioned is 5–12 per cent lower in the US than in the EU countries in the overall sample, and between 5 and 7 per cent lower in the intervention sub-sample. Here, however, it makes sense to distinguish the continental European countries from the UK, where the newspapers refer to Europe only 1 per cent more often than in the US (Table 4.9). While at the beginning of the analyses in this study the US and the UK always had the highest numbers of articles, in later measures the US and UK figures drop so dramatically that the absolute numbers – despite stemming from a larger base – are below those of the continental European countries. The relative

Table 4.9 Share of articles mentioning 'Europe' in the two samples

Country	'Europe' in the overall sample		'Europe' in the intervention sub-sample	
	Absolute numbers	%	Absolute numbers	%
GER	21,183	33.43	6158	38.62
NL	12,070	34.79	3832	38.82
AU	4745	37.39	1515	41.00
FR	22,688	35.61	5272	43.58
IR	8731	30.84	3056	38.11
UK	32,606	28.59	8046	35.14
US	42,922	24.86	12,180	33.69
Σ	**144,945**		**40,059**	

Notes: Table based entirely on author's own data. The table displays the absolute numbers of articles as well as their percentage within the two samples. Period of investigation: Jan. 1990–Mar. 2006 (195 months). Because of missing data, three countries include fewer months: AU 163, IR 166, GER 182.

shares of references to the concepts of Europe, the EU, and EU identity (as we will see in later sections) are considerably lower in the US and the UK than in the other countries.

This indicates that 'Europe' was highly visible in the debate on 'wars and interventions' and on 'humanitarian military interventions' since the end of the Cold War, appearing in more than 10 per cent of articles on these topics. In the overall sample, 'Europe' was mentioned in every third article; in the intervention sub-sample, it was referred to in at least every fourth article in every country – except the UK and the US, where the share was some percentage points lower.

This difference is even more pronounced if one excludes from the analysis all simply geographical references as well as all other uses of 'Europe' that do not unambiguously refer to the European Union and its institutions, political actors and policies. To arrive at the frequencies of references to *the EU and its institutions in the sense of EU politics* for each country, another, much more specific set of word-cluster lists had to be generated according to the procedures described in Chapter 3. These word-clusters were again inductively identified with a qualitative research procedure based on a concordance analysis. All collocations of 'Europe', 'European', 'Europeans', 'Brussels' and so on that occurred at least 15 times in a language were checked manually in order to decide whether they were used unambiguously with respect to the EU and its institutions, instead of the 'broader Europe' or simple geographical references to the continent. Such geographical references also include references to 'Eastern Europe', South-Eastern Europe', and 'European capitals'. All expressions that *always* or *sometimes* refer to Europe in a larger political or geographical context were excluded at this stage, since they are in our terminology, only *numerical identifications* in space and time, which are not telling for my research questions. By this method, all word clusters that unambiguously signified the EU context could be isolated. In this way, we were able to generate large lists of word clusters that mirrored the entire universe of EU multi-level politics. These terms included expressions for the different levels, representatives and mechanisms of EU internal politics, among them:

- terms for *EU institutions*: including the official names of the EU and its predecessors, names and abbreviations of EU bodies, their representatives and sub-entities (e.g. 'European trade ministers', 'eurozone', 'marché unique', 'ECOFIN'); EU rules (e.g. 'European standards', 'European norms'), symbols (e.g. 'European flag') and documents (e.g. 'Maastricht Treaty', 'Treaty of Maastricht'); paraphrases (e.g. 'l'Europe communautaire', 'club européen'); the processes of supra-national *policy-making in Brussels* ('on the European level', 'accord de Bruxelles', 'calendrier européen') and *intergovernmental Europe* (e.g. 'European leaders', 'European embassies', 'responsables européens');

Comparing debates across nations 115

- terms for EU-internal *mutual observation, intra-EU and EU-transatlantic relations* (e.g. 'European partners', 'our European friends', 'other European states', 'le reste de l'Europe');
- terms referring to the newspapers' home country's relation to Brussels and its EU policy (e.g. 'confiance dans l'Europe', 'bataille européenne', 'imposed by Brussels');
- terms for the *EU policy of candidate states* (e.g. 'European future of', 'European aspirations');
- terms for the *EU's appearance and actions at the international level* (e.g. 'European position', 'European criticism', 'European failure', 'the Europeans', 'par l'Europe'), the *EU's international relations* (e.g. 'between Europe and America', 'relations russo-européennes', 'towards Europe'), and the institutionalised *common foreign, development and security policies* (CFSP/ESDP) (e.g. 'European aid', 'force de reaction rapide européenne'); and finally
- terms for the (rather technical process) of *European integration* (e.g. 'European process', 'Europeanisation', 'construction européenne'), the *intellectual struggles, visions, and myths of European integration* (e.g. European debate, European project, European founding fathers), and fragments of clauses in which 'Europe' appeared as a grammatical subject that, in our data, unambiguously referred to the EU ('Europe must', 'Europe should', 'Europe will').

Altogether, 74,488 articles referred to 'EU institutions' as operationalised in the corpus-linguistic retrieval procedure. The share of those articles from the whole sample was by far the lowest in the US-American papers, where it constituted less than 9 per cent. Among the EU countries under study, the share varied from 14 per cent (UK) to around 26 per cent (AU). Within the intervention sub-sample, the share of articles that also referred to the EU and its institutions was much higher than in the overall sample in all countries. In the European newspapers, the EU occurs in between 20 and 30 per cent of all newspaper articles on humanitarian military interventions, and even in the US (where the EU was not very visible in the overall sample) it was mentioned in 16 per cent of the articles on this normatively distinguished type of armed conflict. This suggests the EU is much more visible with respect to humanitarian military interventions than with regard to the use of military force in general. This is a first empirical indicator for a normative role perception of the EU in international affairs, and will be good news for those interested in the perceived character of the EU as a 'normative power' (Bicchi 2006; Diez 2005; Larsen 2014; Lucarelli and Fioramonti 2011; Manners 2002; Sjursen 2006; Whitman 2011). This link between the normative concept of 'humanitarian military intervention' and the EU is most pronounced in France and the neutral member states (AU, IR) at about 30 per cent (Table 4.10).

Table 4.10 Share of articles mentioning 'EU institutions' in the two samples

Country	'EU institutions' in overall sample		'EU institutions' as % of 'Europe' in overall sample	'EU institutions' in intervention sub-sample		'EU institutions' as % of 'Europe' in intervention sub-sample
	Absolute numbers	%		Absolute numbers	%	
GER	12,787	20.18	60.36	4,241	26.60	68.87
NL	7,056	20.34	58.46	2,532	25.65	66.08
AU	3,264	25.72	68.79	1,137	30.77	75.05
FR	14,444	22.67	63.66	3,919	32.40	74.34
IR	5,656	19.98	64.78	2,263	28.22	74.05
UK	16,080	14.10	49.32	4,869	21.26	60.52
US	15,201	8.80	35.42	5,917	16.37	48.58
Σ	74,488			24,878		

Notes: Table based entirely on author's own data. The table displays absolute article numbers as well as their percentage value within the two samples. Moreover, their share among articles that refer to 'Europe' has been calculated. Period of investigation: Jan. 1990–Mar. 2006 (195 months). Because of missing data, three countries include fewer months: AU 163, IR 166, GER 182.

In the continental European countries, references to the EU and its institutions are present in two-thirds of the articles that contain any references to 'Europe' in the overall sample (Table 4.10). In Austria it is even almost 70 per cent. In the UK, about every second article that mentions 'Europe' refers to it just in a geographical sense, and in the US press non-EU related meanings of 'Europe' prevail in almost two-thirds of the articles mentioning 'Europe'. If we look only at the articles of the intervention sub-sample, the share of references to the EU among all articles referring in any sense to 'Europe' increases by approximately 10 per cent in every country. Hence the role of the EU becomes more important and visible when newspapers discuss humanitarian military interventions.

Interim conclusions

Europe and the EU in its institutional sense were remarkably visible 'aspects of relevance' in newspaper articles on 'wars and interventions', and even more so in press reporting on 'humanitarian military interventions' in the EU countries. Of all articles problematising 'wars and interventions', more than a third referred to Europe in some way – except the UK and the US, where Europe clearly mattered less. In the normative part of the debate on 'humanitarian military interventions', Europe played some role in almost 40 per cent of the articles – again, except in the UK and the US, where the share was closer to a third. Using a detailed analysis to distinguish the share of explicit references to the EU from a broader use of the term 'Europe' revealed that, in the continental European countries, references to the 'EU and its institutions' are present in about two-thirds (and more: FR, AU, IR) of the articles that contain any references to Europe in the overall sample, and about 70 per cent (more in the case of FR, AU, IR) in the intervention sub-sample. In the British, and even more so in the US media, the EU has a clearly lower share within those articles that refer to 'Europe'. This means that in the US and the UK, 'Europe' has a much more general and geographical meaning than in continental Europe. Thus the publics of the (continental) European countries seem to share an awareness that they, as Europeans, have a common problem in coming to terms with the new international situation after the end of the Cold War.

4.2 EU identity references: *commercium* and *communio*

European identity over time

Having shown that there is a common transnational and European debate, and that the European Union's place in international crisis politics is an important issue of concern, especially in the continental European countries, this section addresses a more specific aspect of relevance. I investigate how intensely European identity mattered in public debates. '*European identity*' in the following refers to the EU only, not to a broader Europe identity, and I also distinguish between collective identity in the sense of a particularistic $we_{2/commercium}$- or $we_{2/communio}$-identity of the EU and its citizens.

In order to determine the number of newspaper articles referring to European identity (hereafter '*EU identity*') for each country, another set of very detailed word-cluster lists had to be generated using the procedures described in Chapter 3. This procedure ensured that those collocations signifying a particularistic European identity could be isolated. Ambiguous expressions most other studies would include, that is, those that refer to the EU but also to a larger Europe (e.g. 'European values', 'European civilisation'), and expressions that refer to a broader entity (e.g. 'European home', 'Christian Europe'), were excluded. The article numbers identified in this section therefore represent a very conservative measure of how many references to EU identity were made in the context of issues of wars and humanitarian military interventions. The final lists included a broad variety of word-clusters:

- expressions signifying visions, myths and concepts of European integration, terms used for the discussion and intellectual debate about European values and identity (e.g. 'European debate', 'European project', 'European founding fathers' etc.);
- subject clauses expressing modality and probability as well as fragments of clauses in which the EU appeared as a grammatical subject ('l'Europe devrait', 'Europe must', 'Europe should', 'Europe will', 'Europe could', 'Europe would have', 'que l'Europe puisse' etc.) and their negations; and
- explicit talk about 'us Europeans' or self-references as 'we Europeans'.

118   *Comparing debates across nations*

Altogether, almost 12,000 articles referred to European identity as operationalised in the corpus-linguistic retrieval procedure. The share of those articles from the whole sample was by far the lowest in the US-American papers (not even 1 per cent). Among the EU countries under study, the share varied from 6 per cent (FR) to about 2 per cent (UK, IR) (see Table 4.11). Within the sub-sample of articles that speak of 'humanitarian military interventions' as a normative concept, the share of articles that also refer to European identity is higher than in the overall sample in all countries except the Netherlands (see Table 4.11). This hints towards a European identity in which the EU is – at least in part – seen in the press as a 'normative' or 'civilian power' (Bull 1982; Duchêne 1972, 1973; Manners 2002; Maull 2002; Mitzen 2006; Whitman 1998) and not as a self-interested global power using force for its own economic or geopolitical interests. This coupling between the normative concept of 'humanitarian military intervention' and the concept of 'EU identity' (EU ID) seems to be strongest in the French newspapers, where 9 per cent of all articles that refer to humanitarian military interventions also mention European identity.

Table 4.11 also shows the extent to which 'identity' is present in the articles that mention 'Europe' in a broad sense. The proportions point in the same direction and are even more pronounced. In the French papers, 17 per cent of the articles in which 'Europe' is mentioned also contain expressions of 'EU identity'. Within the intervention sub-sample, every fifth article on Europe contains EU identity expressions. For the other EU countries, the figure is

Table 4.11 Share of articles mentioning 'EU identity' in the two samples

Country	'EU identity' in overall sample (Absolute numbers)	%	'EU identity' as % of 'Europe' in overall sample	'EU identity' in intervention sub-sample (Absolute numbers)	%	'EU identity' as % of 'Europe' in intervention sub-sample
GER	2,088	3.29	9.86	620	3.89	10.07
NL	1,142	3.29	9.46	316	3.20	8.25
AU	578	4.55	12.18	185	5.01	12.21
FR	3,876	6.08	17.08	1097	9.07	20.81
IR	637	2.25	7.30	262	3.27	8.57
UK	2,033	1.78	6.24	567	2.48	7.05
US	1,490	0.86	3.47	586	1.62	4.81
Σ	**11,844**			**3,633**		

Notes: Table based entirely on author's own data. The table displays absolute article numbers, their respective shares in the two samples as well as the percentage share of the respective articles among those articles that refer to 'Europe' in a broad sense. Period of investigation: Jan. 1990–Mar. 2006 (195 months). Because of missing data, three countries include fewer months: AU 163, IR 166, GER 182.

between 6 and 12 per cent in the overall sample, and between 7 and 12 per cent in the intervention sub-sample. These are very high numbers given that we are talking here about everyday newspaper reporting and not only special features, editorials or intellectual discourses. The US again lags far behind these numbers. The share of EU identity among those articles referring to Europe tells us to what degree speakers and journalists explicitly used expressions that address the EU as a particularistic community in the sense of a we$_{2/commercium}$ or a we$_{2/communio}$ and did not just numerically identify something happening on the European continent or the EU institutions. In most countries this share is substantial, and even a little higher within the intervention sub-sample than in the overall sample.[30]

Is there a change in the intensity of references to 'EU identity' over time *within* those articles that refer to Europe in one or the other way? Table 4.12 shows that, for the overall sample in all countries except the UK and the US, the percentage of EU-identity articles among those that refer in one way or the other to Europe is continuously increasing. The UK and the US are the only two countries where the share of explicit references to European identity was lowest in the second period (1996–2000). This phase was characterised by a more proactive European stance towards international missions – something the US had called for in the early 1990s – and by increasing participation of EU Member States in international missions. In the case of the Kosovo intervention, this took the form of a NATO mission without a UN mandate. The CFSP was taking shape in this period, and after the Kosovo intervention the institutionalisation of the ESDP became possible and progressed rapidly.

Table 4.12 Share of 'Europe' articles that mention 'EU identity' in the two samples (in %)

Country	\multicolumn{6}{c}{Articles mentioning 'EU identity'}
	Overall sample			Intervention sub-sample		
	1990–95	1996–2000	2001–06	1990–95	1996–2000	2001–06
GER	14.0	16.0	17.5	12.9	15.8	14.9
AU	10.9	17.8	19.0	8.9	17.3	18.3
NL	13.0	15.1	18.8	9.5	12.1	15.8
FR	25.9	27.1	27.2	23.9	30.5	29.2
IR	8.5	9.7	13.3	7.2	10.4	15.7
UK	12.4	11.8	13.3	10.2	11.1	14.0
US	10.3	8.3	10.2	9.8	9.3	10.5

Notes: Table based entirely on author's own data. The table displays the percentage values of articles that address 'EU identity' in the two samples for three distinct phases within the period of investigation. The figures are based on the word-cluster-based analysis and are given as percentage of total newspaper articles (overall sample: $N = 489{,}508$ and intervention sub-sample, $N = 108{,}677$). Period of investigation: Jan. 1990–Mar. 2006 (195 months). Because of missing data, three countries include fewer months: AU 163, IR 166, GER 182.

'Hard-line Atlanticists' (Howorth 2007: 42) at that time feared that ESDP could weaken NATO (see e.g. Cimbalo 2004; Menon 2003), and this may be the reason for the relative absence of references to 'EU identity' in the two most Atlanticist countries in the sample.

In the third period, which was dominated by the events following 9/11 and the Iraq War, the old levels of EU-identity references were reached again in the UK and the US. In general we see again a transatlantic cleavage: French, Austrian, Dutch and German media use EU-identity phrases to a much higher degree than the Irish, British or US-American papers. France here is at all times the country with the largest share of EU-identity rhetoric. Almost every third article on wars and interventions that refers to Europe in whatever sense contains references to the EU as a particularistic community.

Comparing the share of EU-identity articles among articles referring in some way to Europe between the overall and within the intervention sub-sample Table 4.12 points out that only in France (second and third period) and Ireland (third period) is the share of EU-identity articles higher in the intervention sub-sample than in the overall sample. The French press remains the one with the largest share of EU-identity rhetoric, and this exceptional position becomes even more pronounced in the intervention sub-sample. In the German (third period) and Dutch papers (first and second period), the share is even lower than that of the same measure within the overall sample. In all other cases the percentages are basically stable.

Most countries now show a pattern of continuously increasing percentage EU-identity references over the three periods. France, the country with the by far highest degree of EU-identity references, and Germany are the EU member states where an increase from period one to period two, and a minimal decrease from period two to period three, can be observed. This may hint towards a certain disappointment about the EU's future role in the emerging international order in the post 9/11 and Iraq War context. In the US papers there is basically no difference over time: when articles refer to Europe, one in ten of them also uses expressions referring to the EU as a particularistic community.

All these tendencies, however, are not continuous trends in terms of absolute numbers, but are due to the characteristics of the framing of individual conflicts that dominated the different periods in the media debate. Figures 4.5 and 4.6 display the absolute numbers of articles that addressed the EU as a particularistic community over time on a monthly basis and reveal that there are no simple linear trends in the curves.

The uneven share of articles referring to 'EU identity' in the different countries changes the proportions of the time-series data between the countries. In the earlier results presented in this chapter, the US papers published by far the most articles and the US chart was always depicted as the upper curve in the issue-cycles. With regard to EU identity and the later results here, the US curve is no longer the dominant curve. In France, the UK and Germany, references to EU identity are more frequent. There are only two exceptions to this pattern: within the intervention sub-sample in May 1993

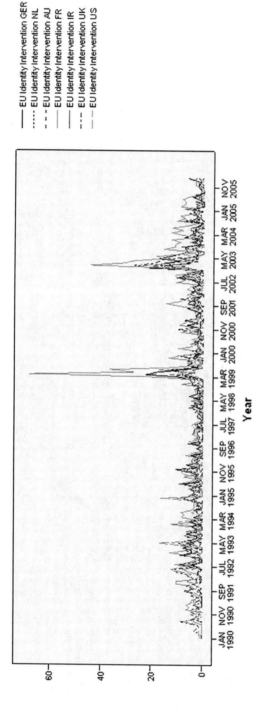

Figure 4.5 Sequence chart of 'EU identity' in the overall sample (absolute numbers)
Notes: These figures are based entirely on the author's own data. N = 489,508, overall sample; n = 11,844. Method used: corpus-linguistic frequency analysis, data aggregated on a monthly basis. Period of investigation: Jan. 1990–Mar. 2006 (195 months). Because of missing data, three countries include fewer months: AU 163, IR 166, GER 182.

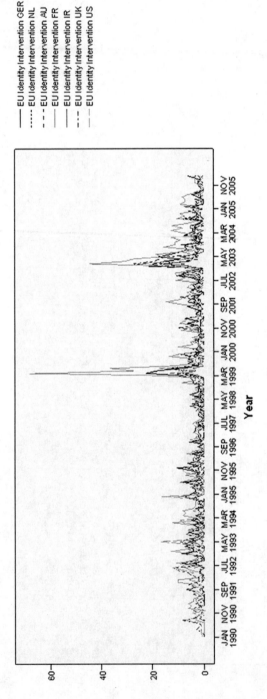

Figure 4.6 Sequence chart of 'EU identity' in the intervention sub-sample (absolute numbers)
Notes: These figures are based entirely on the author's own data. $N = 108,677$, intervention sub-sample; $n = 3633$. Method used: corpus-linguistic frequency analysis, data aggregated on a monthly basis. Period of investigation: Jan. 1990–Mar. 2006 (195 months). Because of missing data, three countries include fewer months: AU 163, IR 166, GER 182.

(when escalating violence in Bosnia led to intense political reactions), and in December 1994 (when Hutu refugees began returning after the Rwandan Patriotic Front victory in Rwanda)[31], where the US newspapers appealed to EU identity more frequently than any of the other countries.

On average, the two French newspapers referred to EU identity in 20 articles on 'wars and interventions' each month. In Germany and the UK, the figure is more than ten articles per month. In the two US newspapers it is about eight articles monthly. Ireland reaches a similar level, while the Dutch and Austrian papers display smaller absolute numbers. There are several months when no article addresses EU identity as operationalised in the word-cluster lists. The months with the highest absolute numbers of articles referring to EU identity coincide with the lead-up to war in Iraq in February 2003 (GER, NL, AU, IR, UK, US) and with the intervention in the Kosovo in April 1999 (FR) (Table 4.13). In the intervention sub-sample, the months with the highest number of articles thematising EU identity are April 1999 (GER, FR), June 1999 (AU) and February 2003 (AU, NL, IR, UK, US) (Table 4.14).

These peaks of identity discourse in the problem-oriented general debate come as no surprise. April to June 1999 marked the Kosovo crisis, the months of the NATO bombing of the Former Republic of Yugoslavia (Central European & Eastern Adriatic Research Group 1999). A common European interest in stability in the Balkans, its experience of finding itself as an – incapable – foreign policy actor, as well as ethical questions related to participation in an intervention without UN mandate, each gave much reason for contestation.

February 2003 also demarcates an extreme peak. This month saw escalating tensions between the governments of the EU Member States regarding US plans for a 'pre-emptive' war against Iraq, and led – in the face of the obviously conflicting normative positions of the EU Member States and their

Table 4.13 Descriptives of 'EU identity' in the overall sample

Country	'EU identity' in overall sample				
	Minimum	Maximum	Sum	Mean	Standard deviation
GER	0	72	2,088	11.47	12.26
NL	0	48	1,142	5.86	5.86
AU	0	34	578	3.55	4.93
FR	1	129	3,876	19.88	19.31
IR	0	35	637	3.84	4.55
UK	0	76	2,033	10.43	8.94
US	0	67	1,490	7.64	7.07

Notes: Table based entirely on author's own data. The table displays absolute articles numbers (min, max, sum) per country over the period of investigation: Jan. 1990–Mar. 2006 (195 months). Because of missing data, three countries include fewer months: AU 163, IR 166, GER 182.

124 *Comparing debates across nations*

Table 4.14 Descriptives of 'EU identity' in the intervention sub-sample

Country	'EU identity' in intervention sub-sample				
	Minimum	Maximum	Sum	Mean	Standard deviation
GER	0	22	620	3.43	3.75
NL	0	17	316	1.62	2.19
AU	0	13	185	1.16	1.99
FR	0	67	1,097	5.63	7.43
IR	0	15	262	1.58	2.04
UK	0	27	567	2.91	3.43
US	0	25	586	3.01	3.52

Notes: Table based entirely on author's own data. The table displays absolute article numbers (min, max, sum) per country over the period of investigation: Jan. 1990–Mar. 2006 (195 months). Because of missing data, three countries include fewer months: AU 163, IR 166, GER 182.

lack of ability to act coherently – to an intensified debate on the legal foundations of the use of force and on European identity (Renfordt 2007a, 2007b). The most important events in this sequence were the following. At the celebrations for the fiftieth anniversary of the Élysée Treaty between France and Germany, President Jacques Chirac and Chancellor Gerhard Schröder proposed further initiatives to strengthen the ESDP. By invoking visions of the European Union as a counterweight to the US (22 January), they ensured a frosty reception in the US, where their proposals were dismissed as the views of 'Old Europe' by US Secretary of Defence Donald Rumsfeld, while the 'new Europe' would support the US. On 30 January, the heads of government of eight EU Member States (the Czech Republic, Denmark, Spain, Hungary, Italy, Poland, Portugal and Britain) called for Europe and the US to 'stand united'. In the 'Letter of the Eight' they expressed support for the American view of the situation, demanded that '[w]e must remain united in insisting that his regime is disarmed',[32] and called for the UN Security Council to credibly enforce its resolutions against Iraq. On 6 February, the Vilnius group joined the 'Eight' in expressing their solidarity with the Bush government and the planned US-led invasion of Iraq.

However, citizens all over Europe were less divided on the issue than their governments. On 15 February, massive peace demonstrations took place all over Europe. The philosophers Jacques Derrida and Jürgen Habermas welcomed them as the birth of a European public sphere (Habermas and Derrida 2003) and as expression of shared European values regarding foreign policy on the level of the EU and its citizens.

The diplomatic quarrels on all levels of the international system, however, went on in February 2003, yet the EU did not find a common position at the Extraordinary European Council Meeting on the Iraq issue (17 February). In the press conference after the meeting, Jacques Chirac admonished the Central and Eastern European accession states for 'miss[ing] a good opportunity to remain silent' (17 February) (Pond 2005: esp. 42–49):

> I shall nevertheless make one comment [...]. As regards the candidate countries – I'm not talking about countries which aren't candidates – honestly, I think they have behaved somewhat irresponsibly. Because being a member of the European Union nevertheless requires a minimum of consideration for the others, a minimum of consultation. If on the first difficult issue you start giving your point of view irrespective of any consultation with the entity you want to join, then that isn't very responsible behaviour. At any event, it's not very good manners. So I believe they have missed a good opportunity to remain silent.
>
> (Chirac 2003)

This was publicly perceived as a manifestation of deep divisions between the old and the new Member States, and as further proof that the EU was deeply divided and unable 'to speak with one voice'. Once again, this became visible on the international stage when Britain on one hand, and France, Germany and Russia on the other, circulated contradictory proposals in the UN Security Council in the same month. The foundations for common European foreign and security policies seemed to be entirely lacking. It was widely assumed that internal disruption weakened the EU as a foreign policy actor.

One month later, on 19 March, the US-led coalition – actively supported by the UK, Poland, Spain and Italy – attacked Iraq. On 9 April Baghdad fell.[33] Some European governments began to repair what could be repaired and to regain the initiative. France, Germany, Belgium and Luxembourg met at the Quadripartite summit on 29 April 2003 and discussed the operational bases of the ESDP. On this occasion, the EU-4 'appeared to make very ambitious noises. Many analysts at the time feared that the four intended to forge ahead with the project for a vastly ambitious European defence capacity – in the absence of any British restraining influence.' (Howorth 2007: 47).

Of course, this provoked at first another wave of anger (and mockery on the 'praline summit') from US and UK foreign policy makers (Howorth 2007: 111f.). Yet, on the EU policy level, these events were followed by intense diplomatic efforts to clarify the situation (Jopp and Sandawi 2003; Menon 2004) and to arrive at a common set of basic understandings about foreign policy problem definitions, common European interests and aims, as well as shared normative principles regarding the ESDP. This finally resulted in the adoption of the European Security Strategy, entitled 'A Secure Europe in a Better World' (European Union 2003) on 20 June – an event far less visible in the press than the conflicts that preceded it. The peak in the number of articles referring to the EU as a particularistic community, found in the different countries in spring 2003, mirrors perfectly the intensity of passionate public debate on European identity surrounding this sequence of institutional events concerning the beginning of the Iraq War.

126 *Comparing debates across nations*

Do the curves peak simultaneously? Correlations between the national curves are very high (Pearson's coefficients between 0.84 FR–NL and 0.65 FR–US), albeit somewhat lower than the correlations for the overall issue-cycle and the intervention sub-sample. This effect may be due to the fact that the graphs represent much lower overall numbers.

Within the intervention sub-sample correlations decreased further (between 0.45 IR–AU and 0.70 GER–FR) so that some of them even remained at a medium level (Table 4.16). Bivariate correlations in the earlier parts of this study were higher. This indicates that notions of EU identity are not as synchronously invoked as the issue-cycles of 'wars and interventions' and 'humanitarian military interventions'.

Table 4.15 Bivariate correlations of 'EU identity' in the overall sample (Pearson's coefficients)

'EU identity' in overall sample	'EU identity' in overall sample						
	GER	NL	AU	FR	IR	UK	US
GER	1	0.797**	0.824**	0.832**	0.747**	0.752**	0.648**
NL	0.797**	1	0.753**	0.839**	0.746**	0.754**	0.652**
AU	0.824**	0.753**	1	0.775**	0.746**	0.683**	0.681**
FR	0.832**	0.839**	0.775**	1	0.742**	0.752**	0.641**
IR	0.747**	0.746**	0.746**	0.742**	1	0.826**	0.757**
UK	0.752**	0.754**	0.683**	0.752**	0.826**	1	0.786**
US	0.648**	0.652**	0.681**	0.641**	0.757**	0.786**	1

Notes: Table based entirely on author's own data. The table displays Pearson's correlation coefficients. Period of investigation: Jan. 1990–Mar. 2006 (195 months). Because of missing data, three countries include fewer months: AU 163, IR 166, GER 182.

Table 4.16 Bivariate correlations of 'EU identity' in the intervention sub-sample (Pearson's coefficients)

'EU identity' in intervention sub-sample	'EU identity' in intervention sub-sample						
	GER	NL	AU	FR	IR	UK	US
GER	1	0.569**	0.695**	0.702**	0.505**	0.577**	0.561**
NL	0.569**	1	0.571**	0.696**	0.457**	0.520**	0.531**
AU	0.695**	0.571**	1	0.689**	0.454**	0.517**	0.561**
FR	0.702**	0.696**	0.689**	1	0.526**	0.579**	0.572**
IR	0.505**	0.457**	0.454**	0.526**	1	0.630**	0.593**
UK	0.577**	0.520**	0.517**	0.579**	0.630**	1	0.655**
US	0.561**	0.531**	0.561**	0.572**	0.593**	0.655**	1

Notes: Table based entirely on author's own data. The table displays Pearson's correlation coefficients. Period of investigation: Jan. 1990–Mar. 2006 (195 months). Because of missing data, three countries include fewer months: AU 163, IR 166, GER 182.

Did the frequency of references to EU identity respond to the same types of events in the countries under study? Tables 4.17 and 4.18 show the correlations of the numbers of articles that referred to EU identity and the aggregated event-data in the overall sample and the intervention sub-sample.

The crude monthly numbers of crisis events are not significantly or even negatively correlated with the monthly numbers of articles mentioning EU identity. UN, NATO and EU events are rather moderately correlated to the curves with the exception of the *number of beginning NATO interventions* (Pearson's coefficients ranging from 0.34 AU to 0.15 UK); the *number of beginning EU interventions* (0.35 FR to 0.21 US); and the *number of all EU events* together (0.40 FR to 0.22 UK). Again, the involvement of one of the EU countries under study in diplomatic or military actions is highly significantly correlated to the curves of 'EU identity' at a stable moderate-to-high level. The correlation is always strongest for the French and weakest for the British media. We see comparatively strong correlations between the German, Dutch, Austrian and French frequencies of EU identity and the involvement of other EU countries (including IR and UK). This pattern is, conversely, much less developed for the Irish and British papers. This means that even in the US newspapers, crisis management events in which EU Member States are involved correlate more clearly with the number of references to the EU as a particularistic community than in the UK and Ireland.

This substantiates the idea that the press in the continental EU member states places EU identity in a context of common foreign policy actions – including the use of military force – of the EU member states. In the British and Irish papers this connection is not developed in the same way, while the US papers take a middle-ground position. The US media talk much less about EU identity than the press in the EU member states, but when they do talk about it, there is a quite strong correlation to the involvement of the UK,

Table 4.17 Bivariate correlations of 'EU identity' in the intervention sub-sample (Pearson's coefficients)

'EU identity' in intervention sub-sample	'EU identity' in intervention sub-sample						
	GER	NL	AU	FR	IR	UK	US
GER	1	0.569**	0.695**	0.702**	0.505**	0.577**	0.561**
NL	0.569**	1	0.571**	0.696**	0.457**	0.520**	0.531**
AU	0.695**	0.571**	1	0.689**	0.454**	0.517**	0.561**
FR	0.702**	0.696**	0.689**	1	0.526**	0.579**	0.572**
IR	0.505**	0.457**	0.454**	0.526**	1	0.630**	0.593**
UK	0.577**	0.520**	0.517**	0.579**	0.630**	1	0.655**
US	0.561**	0.531**	0.561**	0.572**	0.593**	0.655**	1

Notes: Table based entirely on author's own data. The table displays Pearson's correlation coefficients. Period of investigation: Jan. 1990–Mar. 2006 (195 months). Because of missing data, three countries include fewer months: AU 163, IR 166, GER 182.

Table 4.18 Bivariate correlations between 'EU identity' in the intervention sub-sample and aggregated event-data (Pearson's coefficients)

	'EU identity' in intervention sub-sample						
	GER	NL	AU	FR	IR	UK	US
Number of other UN events	0.191**	0.162*	0.170*	0.139	0.185*	0.228**	0.156*
Number of all UN events	0.106	0.012	0.003	0.038	0.011	0.092	0.145*
Number of use of force without UN mandate	0.031	0.115	0.173*	0.121	0.029	0.161*	0.150*
Number of beginning NATO interventions	0.262**	0.383**	0.370**	0.366**	0.132	0.216**	0.280**
Number of other NATO events	0.203**	0.108	0.149	0.307**	0.099	−0.008	0.152*
Number of all NATO events	0.280**	0.246**	0.296**	0.394**	0.163*	0.102	0.254**
Number of EU summits	0.167*	0.075	0.216**	0.223**	0.089	0.092	0.131
Number of WEU/CFSP/ESDP events	0.110	0.167*	0.131	0.184*	0.125	0.038	0.081
Number of beginning EU interventions	0.240**	0.193**	0.128	0.203**	0.117	0.186**	0.130
Number of other EU events	0.151*	0.156*	0.224**	0.181*	0.217**	0.165*	0.224**
Number of all EU events	0.226**	0.217**	0.299**	0.304**	0.208**	0.129	0.194**
Number of other summits	0.206**	0.104	0.229**	0.272**	0.161*	0.163*	0.105
Number of all interventions	0.226**	0.134	0.172*	0.176*	0.046	0.188**	0.207**
Number of all crisis events and all EU, NATO and UN events	0.244**	0.232**	0.270**	0.321**	0.165*	0.136	0.273**
Involvement Austria	0.321**	0.358**	0.310**	0.336**	0.199*	0.176*	0.234**
Involvement Germany	0.372**	0.352**	0.373**	0.431**	0.263**	0.227**	0.339**
Involvement France	0.338**	0.322**	0.332**	0.413**	0.250**	0.206**	0.302**
Involvement Ireland	0.278**	0.286**	0.285**	0.311**	0.213**	0.180*	0.263**
Involvement Netherlands	0.354**	0.351**	0.370**	0.428**	0.251**	0.208**	0.314**
Involvement UK	0.345**	0.326**	0.342**	0.420**	0.244**	0.237**	0.316**

	'EU identity' in intervention sub-sample						
	GER	NL	AU	FR	IR	UK	US
Involvement US	0.266**	0.204**	0.211**	0.305**	0.164*	0.163*	0.268**
Europe affected	0.255**	0.271**	0.340**	0.266**	0.111	0.120	0.267**
Middle East affected	0.025	0.069	0.076	0.054	0.066	0.143*	0.093

Notes: Table based entirely on author's own data. The table displays Pearson's correlation coefficients. Period of investigation: Jan. 1990–Mar. 2006 (195 months). Because of missing data, three countries include fewer months: AU 163, IR 166, GER 182. Rows with no significant results have been eliminated for better readability. The full list of events included in the test can be seen in Table 6.

the Netherlands, Germany and France, which are more or less perceived as the EU – a collective actor with common interests and ethical obligations.

The involvement of the US correlates only weakly with the number of articles mentioning European identity, indicating that public reflection on European identity in the EU member states is rather self-sufficient and not dependent on the systematic demarcation of differences from the US or distinction from the US as the 'other'. This finding flies in the face of a long line of theorising about collective identities, beginning with Carl Schmitt, which assumes that groups need an 'other' in the sense of an enemy in order to develop a political identity (Schmitt 1996). Many authors in the debate on European identity share this view, even if they would not go as far as Schmitt in that they do not share the view that the 'other' must be seen as an existential enemy.[34] Their 'other' can also be a partner in controversies. However, if EU identity-formation during the period under investigation had occurred in demarcation against an American 'other', we would observe much stronger correlations.

Other parts of the world also do not serve as 'others'. Among all regions, it is conflicts on the European continent (the Balkan wars) that correlate at all significantly and on a weak level with the frequencies of references to EU identity.[35] In the context of conflicts in the Middle East, EU identity peaks significantly, albeit at a low level in the Netherlands, Austria, Ireland and the US – an effect of the Iraq War 2003.

Do these findings change if we reduce the search to the sub-sample of articles referring to the normative concept of humanitarian military interventions (Table 4.18)? The initial international crisis events have disappeared from the list of significant correlations. Extraordinary UN events matter now – especially in the British, German and Irish press. A variety of NATO and EU events also correlate significantly, but mostly at a weak level, with the frequencies of expressions of 'EU identity'. The *number of beginning NATO interventions* (moderate correlation in NL, AU, FR); the *number of all NATO events* (moderate correlation for FR, AU); the aggregated *numbers of all EU events* (moderate correlation in FR, AU); and the *number of all crisis events and all EU, NATO and UN events* (moderate correlation for FR, US, AU) are linked more strongly to EU identity than other event-types.

The involvement of other EU countries correlates on a moderate level (on a 0.30 level) with the numbers of articles that refer to both humanitarian military interventions and European identity in the continental European countries. These correlations are again usually highest for the French media.[36] Expressions referring to 'EU identity' in the Irish and British media correlate much less strongly with both national and European involvement in diplomatic events or interventions. However, one cannot say the British and Irish press decidedly avoid EU identity rhetoric. As we have seen above, the US media use this vocabulary much less; nevertheless, the correlation of its use resembles the continental European media much more than Ireland and the UK.

Regarding the strength of correlations, the US is again a median case: the more the European countries take international action in the domain of humanitarian military interventions, the more the US press addresses the EU as an acting unit and uses expressions that refer to 'EU identity' (moderate correlations around 0.30). The involvement of the US in return correlates to a much lower, albeit significant and positive degree with the curves. Notions of 'EU identity' are much more likely to be invoked in the context of humanitarian military interventions on the European continent (weak correlation in all countries except France, where the correlation is moderate) than comparable conflicts in any other region of the world. This is likely to be due to the Balkan wars that in the 1990s dominated the debate on humanitarian military interventions for much of the period under investigation.

Are certain types of crisis or institutional event significant predictors in the ARIMA time-series models? By including the aggregated event-data as independent variables in the analysis, quite satisfying models could be estimated for the frequencies of 'EU identity' in the overall issue-cycle. Only the French curve had to be logarithmically smoothed. For the German, French and US curves, linear trends were detected ($d = 1$). The explanatory power of the estimated ARIMA models ranged from only 36 per cent of the variation (FR) to 91 per cent (GER). The condensed results of the time-series analysis are shown in Table 4.19.

Of the aggregated event-data, the *number of all NATO events* was a significant predictor for all but one model (the Irish),[37] while here also the *number of all EU events* was significant in all models except for the Austrian and British.[38] This indicates that, especially if large strategic or moral questions are debated at the EU level, this is very well reflected in the media of the different countries. The *number of all crisis events*[39] and the *number of all UN events*[40] were significant in the British and US models, respectively.

For the monthly numbers of articles mentioning EU identity in the intervention sub-sample, the estimated ARIMA models have a somewhat lower explanatory power, ranging from 55 per cent (UK) to 85 per cent (AU) (see Table 4.20). None of the models rests on smoothed values.

The *number of all EU events* (GER, FR, IR)[41] and the *number of all NATO events* (all models except GER)[42] are significant predictor variables for several countries, while the *number of all UN events* is significant only in the

Table 4.19 ARIMA models for 'EU identity' in the overall sample

Time series	'EU identity' in overall sample			
	ARIMA model description	R^2 for stationary part	R^2	Significant variables number of all:
GER	(0,1,1)	0.757	0.905	EU events NATO events
NL	(1,0,0)	0.754	0.754	EU events NATO events
AU	(0,0,1)	0.873	0.873	NATO events
FR	(0,1,3) (natural log)	0.365	0.647	EU events NATO events
IR	(1,0,0)	0.793	0.793	EU events
UK	(0,0,2)	0.656	0.656	crisis events NATO events
US	(0, 1, 1)	0.738	0.720	UN events EU events NATO events

Notes: Table based entirely on author's own data. ARIMA models with aggregated event-type data as independent variables. Period of investigation: Jan. 1990–Mar. 2006 (195 months). Because of missing data, three countries include fewer months: AU 163, IR 166, GER 182.

Table 4.20 ARIMA models for 'EU identity' in the intervention sub-sample

Time series	'EU identity' in intervention sub-sample			
	ARIMA model description	R^2 for stationary part	R^2	Significant variables number of all:
GER	(4,0,0)	0.657	0.657	EU events
NL	(1,0,0)	0.609	0.609	NATO events
AU	(0,0,2)	0.845	0.845	NATO events
FR	(1,0,0)	0.782	0.782	EU events NATO events
IR	(1,0,0)	0.573	0.573	EU events NATO events
UK	(1,0,0)	0.554	0.554	NATO events
US	(1,0,0)	0.632	0.632	UN events NATO events

Notes: Table based entirely on author's own data. ARIMA models with aggregated event-type data as independent variables. Period of investigation: Jan. 1990–Mar. 2006 (195 months). Because of missing data, three countries include fewer months: AU 163, IR 166, GER 182.

US model.[43] Individual months that are characterised by significant peaks in several countries are April to June 1999 – the months of the NATO bombing of the Former Republic of Yugoslavia (Central European & Eastern Adriatic Research Group 1999). January and February 2003 also demarcate extreme peaks with upward level shifts in Germany, the Netherlands, Great Britain and the US.

Since there are several months in which no article addresses EU identity as operationalised in the word-cluster lists, it makes no sense to conduct the σ-convergence analysis. It would bring about confusing results: extreme months with very high or with no references to EU identity would seem to indicate high degrees or similarity, whereas everything in between would seem to indicate deviance – compared with the outliers. Therefore the results could not be interpreted.

Interim conclusions

European identity mattered in transnational discourse. Despite the very conservative measure applied, almost 12,000 articles referring to EU identity were identified. The figures were very high in the continental European countries and highest in the French media, where 6 per cent of all articles on wars and interventions used expressions of EU identity. In the US papers, by contrast, European identity was virtually invisible. The UK and Ireland lay in the middle. Within the intervention sub-sample, the share of articles referring to EU identity was usually higher than in the overall sample. One can interpret this as an indicator for a shared perception of 'EU identity' in the field of foreign and security policy as a 'normative' or 'civilian power'.

However, even if this shows that identity aspects overall have mattered, those aspects feature only as a side-aspect in an event- and problem-oriented discourse. On one hand, this is certainly normal for news reporting, since readers want to be informed first of all about the important issues at stake and – usually – do not want to be bombarded with identity politics. On the other hand, it seems that in the course of news reporting, identity aspects were addressed (in the sense of references to the EU as a particularistic community), especially in the context of the Kosovo crisis and the Iraq War.

The share of articles mentioning EU identity among those articles that referred to 'Europe' in a very broad sense show these relations even more clearly. Distinguishing three time periods characterised by important conflict events and by important steps in the process of institutionalisation of ESDP within the period of investigation, one can see an increase of identity references. The exceptions were for the overall sample the UK and the US, which referred more to EU identity in the early 1990s than in the late 1990s, and reached the old levels again in the new century. Within the intervention sub-sample, the British media show the same upwards trend as the other EU countries, while in the US media there is quasi-no change in the EU-identity share among the articles that refer to Europe in general.

Turning back to the data aggregated on a monthly base, the curves of the frequencies of references to EU identity are characterised by two common large peaks: the Kosovo conflict in spring 1999 and the Iraq War in early 2003. Besides these there are some smaller peaks, some of which are shared and some not clearly visible in all the countries. Yet on the whole, the curves develop quite simultaneously even if the correlations are somewhat lower than those for the issue-cycles. This suggests that aspects of EU identity do not occur as synchronously as the overall debate on 'wars and interventions' and 'humanitarian military interventions'. The measures of EU identity have high volatility since the media appeal to strongly varying degrees of EU identity, and they do so mainly in the context of important institutional decisions and diplomatic conflicts.

Which predictors of the intensity of EU identity rhetoric could be identified? The frequencies of references to 'EU identity' did not respond to certain types of crisis event, but correlated with institutional events (e.g. beginning NATO interventions, beginning EU interventions and the overall intensity of institutional activities of the EU). National involvement in diplomatic or military activities did not correlate strongly with the quantity of references to EU identity, but there was a clear pattern of receptiveness towards mutual involvement. We observed quite strong correlations between the German, Dutch, Austrian and French frequencies of EU identity and the involvement of the EU countries (including IR and UK) in crisis-management activities.

The invocation of 'EU identity' in the Irish and British papers, however, did not correlate strongly with the involvement of other EU Member States. As already seen with regard to the findings on references to Europe in general, the EU as an institutional actor in particular, and here regarding European identity discourse, we observe a clear and consistent pattern of British distance and scepticism towards the European Union. The Irish press meanwhile either shares this distance or orientates itself – for media-economic reasons and linguistic similarity – quite strongly toward the British discourse.

The press in the continental EU member states obviously puts EU identity into a context of common or at least coordinated foreign policy actions of the EU Member States. Interestingly, for the US we found a quite strong correlation between the quantity mentioning 'EU identity' and the involvement of the UK, the Netherlands, Germany and France in diplomatic or military actions. The US media seem to perceive those NATO Member States together as 'the EU', which in those instances is addressed in terms of a collective actor with a particularistic identity. Moreover, because of the way in which we operationalised EU identity, this acts as evidence supporting the idea that the US press also conceptualises this collective actor as possessing common interests and ethical obligations upon which it should act.

Within the intervention sub-sample, the correlations between the numbers of articles that referred to EU identity and the aggregated event-data were slightly weaker. Again, references to EU identity were linked not to certain types of crisis event, but rather to international institutional events (UN,

NATO, EU and the sum of all crisis and institutional events together). EU identity correlated with the involvement of other EU countries for the continental EU Member States and – surprisingly – the US, but much less in the Irish and British media. Talk about EU identity correlated for most countries with the conflicts and conflict-related events on the European continent. This means that the part of the debate on humanitarian military interventions that involved identity aspects has been shaped significantly by the Balkan conflicts in the 1990s.

Conducting ARIMA time-series analyses including the event-data as independent variables confirmed that notably the *number of all NATO events* as well as the *number of all EU events* were significant predictors for the intensity of pragmatic problem-solving debates and ethical discourses about a shared European self-understanding. The analysis of outliers again shows that the Kosovo crisis and the Iraq war in spring triggered exceptionally intense identity reflections in the media. European identity became important, especially in the context of the Balkan wars and the Iraq War 2003, when a painful lack of identity and collective agency was perceived. From a hermeneutic-pragmatist identity-based theoretical point of view, this is not surprising. Humans don't talk about themselves out of the blue, but only in those moments when they feel insecure, ashamed or confused about the roles they want to assume.

Commercium *and* communio *aspects of European identity*

In the previous section we saw that references to the EU as a particularistic community consistently occurred in the European press in the debate on wars and humanitarian military interventions, albeit – with the exception of France – at a rather low level. EU identity mattered over time. The aggregation of the results into three periods within the overall time period already provided initial indications that the different crisis events matter for whether and how European identity was addressed. In this section, the interrelations between *commercium* and *communio* aspects of European identity are explored in more detail. For this purpose, the phrases included in the word-cluster lists for the corpus-linguistic text-retrieval procedures of 'EU identity' were further refined, differentiated and completed. Mutually exclusive lists of word-clusters referring to the EU either as a *commercium* or as a *communio* were created. Ambiguous expressions were left out. The list for the EU as a *commercium* now included:

- expressions of *role-expectations* addressed to the EU as an actor, among them fragments of subject-clauses (e.g. 'Europe must', 'the European Union should/needs/might/has to/wants', 'from a European perspective', 'Europe's role', 'the EU's role', 'European voice', 'presence/absence de l'Europe', 'Handlungsfähigkeit Europas', 'rol/falen/uur/zwakte van de Europese Unie');

Comparing debates across nations 135

- expressions delineating an *EU-specific action space* (e.g. 'European problem', 'a real European solution', 'European responsibility', 'europaeische Herausforderung', 'europaeisches Thema');
- phrases that relate to *European interests* (e.g. 'ambitions of the EU', 'Europe's influence', 'Europe's weakness', 'Europe's failure', 'capacite europeenne', 'puissance de l'Europe', 'impuissance de l'Europe', 'credibilite de l'Europe', 'interets de la communaute europeenne', 'Ohnmacht Europas', 'europaeische Emanzipation').

The articles referring to the EU as a *communio* were identified by using those search terms of the 'EU identity' lists that referred to:

visions, models and rhetoric related to the *project of European integration* as well as *self-identifications* of the Europeans as Europeans (e.g. 'we the Europeans', 'European dream/project/identity/unity', 'as Europeans we', 'themselves as Europeans', 'United States of Europe', 'Europe of nation states', 'closer union', 'federal/integrated Europe', 'opt for Europe', 'European consciousness', 'enthusiasm for Europe', 'Europeanism', 'vision of Europe', 'the European ideal', 'for the future of Europe', 'malaise europeenne', 'paysage europeen', 'victoire de l'Europe', 'l'idee europeenne', 'normes europeennes', 'l'Europe des hommes', 'l'Europe de la defense', 'europaeische Prinzipien', 'europaeische Sache/Rhetorik/Diskurs/Selbstverstaendnis', 'europese weg', 'identiteit van europa', 'europese bewustzijn', 'gemeenschappelijk europa').

all terms included were identified inductively, drawing on terms that were frequently used in the newspapers. Table 4.21 presents the share of articles in

Table 4.21 Share of articles that mention the EU as a *communio* or *commercium* (%)

Country	Overall sample		Intervention sub-sample	
	communio	commercium	communio	commercium
Germany	2.1	1.5	2.0	2.2
Austria	2.1	2.7	2.0	3.0
Netherlands	2.7	0.6	2.5	0.7
France	5.0	2.0	7.1	3.7
Ireland	1.3	1.0	1.7	1.7
UK	1.1	0.7	1.2	1.4
US	0.5	0.3	0.9	0.7

Notes: Table based entirely on author's own data. The table displays the shares of references to the EU as *communio* and *commercium* within the two samples. The figures resulted from the word-cluster-based analysis and are given in percentage of total newspaper articles (overall sample, $N = 489,508$; intervention sub-sample, $N = 108,677$). Period of investigation: Jan. 1990–Mar. 2006 (195 months). Because of missing data, three countries include fewer months: AU 163, IR 166, GER 182.

each country that mention the EU as a *communio* or as a *commercium*, respectively. In many articles the EU is mentioned as both a *communio* and a *commercium*. Because of such overlaps, the figures for *communio* and *commercium* added together are sometimes slightly higher than the 'EU identity' figures in the previous section.

Within the overall-sample, the expressions referring to the EU as a *communio* occurred in more articles than phrases referring to the EU as a pragmatic *commercium* – except in Austria. This dominance of a conception of particular identity that refers to a shared ethical self-understanding and a common project is most pronounced in the French and Dutch press, but is also present in the US media. However, in the US-American newspapers, references to the EU as a particularistic community in general are virtually absent. The prevalence of the EU as a *communio* in the data is surprising, since one would expect the pragmatic recourse to the EU to be more frequent than the normatively more demanding ethical one. Within the EU member states, European identity in both aspects is mentioned least in the UK and Ireland.

Within the intervention sub-sample, the shares remain virtually constant for the EU as a *communio* (GER, AU, NL, UK) (see Table 4.21). They are higher than in the overall sample only for the US, Ireland and – especially – France. The shares of articles in which the EU is referred to as a *commercium*, however, increase clearly (GER, FR, IR, UK, US). Only in the Austrian and Dutch media do they remain the same in the intervention sub-sample. In the English-speaking countries (IR, UK, US) and Germany, the EU is mentioned almost exactly as often in terms of a *communio* as in terms of a *commercium*. Overall, the difference between Germany, Austria and the Netherlands on one hand, and Ireland and the UK on the other, decreased. France remains the country with by far the highest percentage of references to the EU as a community in both the *communio* and the *commercium* sense.

In order to explore these interrelationships, it is worth looking further at the *communio* and *commercium* portion according to different time periods. To avoid distortions, the two identity types were related to the baseline of articles containing 'EU identity' references at all. If EU identity is addressed, in which phases do which aspects of it dominate? Table 4.22 displays these relations for the overall sample. Regarding cross-country differences, Austria is the only country where *commercium*-expressions occur more frequently than *communio*-expressions in all three time periods. Austria is also the country with the least references to the EU as a *communio* and the most references to the EU as a *commercium* (as a percentage of all references to EU identity over all three time periods). In all other countries, *communio*-expressions score as high as, or higher than, *commercium* expressions. The Dutch media present the opposite picture: here we find the highest percentage of references to the EU as a *communio* and the lowest percentage of references to the EU as a *commercium*. The US media do not exhibit any special features. The range of different percentage values is highest in the second and

Table 4.22 Share of 'EU identity' articles that mention the EU as a *communio* and/or as a *commercium* in the overall sample (%)

Country	communio	commercium
1990–95		
GER	63.3	46.9
AU	48.8	55.8
NL	86.8	13.5
FR	84.5	29.7
IR	58.7	50.4
UK	61.3	47.3
US	68.4	37.5
1996–2000		
GER	58.9	54.8
AU	45.6	62.6
NL	85.1	17.6
FR	81.4	33.5
IR	52.9	52.9
UK	63.9	43.7
US	63.3	42.8
2001–06		
GER	67.5	43.3
AU	49.6	58.6
NL	83.4	22.3
FR	81.8	34.0
IR	65.5	43.7
UK	71.7	37.8
US	73.7	31.0

Notes: Table based entirely on author's own data. The table displays the changing proportions of articles referring to the EU as a *communio* or a *commercium* as a share of those articles referring to 'EU identity' for three distinct time periods within the period of investigation. Since articles can refer to the EU as both a *communio* and a *commercium*, the values do not add up to 100 per cent. Period of investigation: Jan. 1990–Mar. 2006 (195 months). Because of missing data, three countries include fewer months: AU 163, IR 166, GER 182.

lowest in the third period distinguished. The 9/11 and Iraq War context is generally characterised by a proportional increase of EU-*communio* rhetoric in all countries.

Table 4.22 illustrates the changing percentage distributions of references to the EU as a *communio* and as a *commercium*. The countries are characterised by somewhat different patterns. In German and Austrian reporting, the *communio* aspect of EU identity decreases while references to the EU as a *commercium* increase during the second period, which was dominated by the Kosovo conflict and the start of the institutionalisation of the ESDP. By contrast, in the Dutch and French media the percentage of *commercium* expressions for the EU increases over time. This distinguishes them from the English-speaking countries, which see a trend towards slightly more *communio* rhetoric at the expense of *commercium* expressions.

Do the proportions change within the more specific discourse on humanitarian military interventions? Table 4.23 lists the proportions of the two identity aspects for the intervention sub-sample. Interestingly, and against my expectations, the predominance of *communio* rhetoric within articles that refer to the EU as a particularistic community is absent in most countries under study in the first and second periods. This may be a reflection of the fact that, when the debate was more directly focused on interventions, it implied the possibility that countries would have to send troops. In this context, the pragmatic aspects of a *commercium*, a problem-solving community that cooperates on the basis of some common interests (which co-exist with other idiosyncratic motives of the members), move to the fore. In the first and second periods, visions of the EU as a community with a shared ethical self-understanding dominate among references to EU identity in only three countries (NL, FR, US).

Regarding cross-country differences, the Dutch media – closely followed by the French – tend most strongly towards EU-as-*communio* expressions. The Irish media meanwhile – closely followed by the British, Austrian and German – prefer EU-*commercium* expressions in the first period after the end of the Cold War. In the second period, the French overtake the Dutch media in terms of the share of EU-as-*communio* expressions. Only in the third period does the appeal to the EU as a *communio* become overwhelming. For Ireland and the UK, it is only in the context of the Iraq War that the EU is addressed in terms of a *communio* more frequently than as a *commercium*. Only two countries are left in which *commercium*-terms score higher than EU-as-*communio* expressions (GER, AU). The range of percentage differences in each category between the countries is broad, but it decreases continuously from period to period.

The data reported in Table 4.23 allow for the distinction of three patterns of change regarding the distribution of the two identity aspects over time. German and Austrian papers prefer *commercium* over *communio* terms in all phases. Dutch and French papers consistently prefer *communio* terms, but their use of *commercium* terms increases. Ireland, the UK and the US instead are characterised by an increase in the use of *communio* at the expense of *commercium* expressions, a change that is particularly marked in the post-9/11 and post-Iraq War context. These shifts and changes are related to the public interpretation of the international crisis situations prevalent during the respective time periods.

Another way to substantiate this interpretation is to establish which conflict areas were mentioned in the newspaper articles with the EU as a

Table 4.23 Share of 'EU identity' articles that mention the EU as a *communio* and/or a *commercium* in the intervention sub-sample (%)

Country	communio	commercium
1990–95		
GER	51.7	59.9
AU	44.4	55.6
NL	82.5	18.8
FR	80.7	37.2
IR	38.3	66.0
UK	41.7	63.8
US	55.2	51.6
1996–2000		
GER	51.0	60.2
AU	35.7	65.7
NL	78.8	25.3
FR	80.7	38.0
IR	44.9	60.3
UK	43.1	65.1
US	54.5	51.7
2001–06		
GER	54.9	57.0
AU	44.3	59.8
NL	78.8	21.9
FR	75.7	45.2
IR	65.7	43.8
UK	60.5	49.8
US	71.5	33.2

Notes: Table based entirely on author's own data. The table displays the changing proportions of articles referring to the EU as a *communio* or a *commercium* as a share of those articles referring to 'EU identity' for three distinct time periods within the period of investigation. Since articles can refer to the EU as both a *communio* and a *commercium*, the values do not add up to 100 per cent. Period of investigation: Jan. 1990–Mar. 2006 (195 months). Because of missing data, three countries include fewer months: AU 163, IR 166, GER 182.

particularistic community in the *commercium* and/or the *communio* sense. In order to construct a simple but efficient measure for the crisis countries concerned, this time we retrieved the grammatically neutralised country names and important conflict provinces with a simple keyword search.[44] Within only those articles that referred to 'EU identity', the strengths of the co-occurrences of all possible pairs of conflict countries and European identity in the *commercium*- and the *communio*-dimension in the newspaper articles (e.g. 'Bosnia and Rwanda', 'EU-as-*communio* and Bosnia') was calculated as pairwise overlap of the set union. We considered it if the overlap was at least 10 per cent.

Table 4.24 represents selected conflicts and how they co-occurred with references to the EU as a *commercium* or a *communio* for the individual countries under study. Which conflicts were most frequently connected to either EU-as-*commercium* or EU-as-*communio* type identity? The picture is strikingly uniform. Very strong connections emerged between countries involved in a conflict scenario with each other, or were a result of multiple conflicts occurring at the same time (e.g. Croatia/Slovenia or Palestine/Israel). Yet for some countries the co-occurrence of Iraq and the EU as a *communio* was the strongest of all. This was the case in the overall sample for France (35 per cent), Germany (38 per cent), the Netherlands (42 per cent) and the US (40 per cent). Similarly, the connection between Bosnia and the EU as a *commercium* was strongest in one case, the US, in the intervention sub-sample (40 per cent). The conflict locations that co-occurred with EU-as-*commercium* phrases in at least 10 per cent of the articles of the set union were Bosnia, Iraq, Kosovo and other conflicts in the former Yugoslavia. Also, Israel was mentioned in many cases in connection with calls for the EU to act or appeals to its interests in the region (*commercium* sense) (GER, FR, IR, UK, US).

Afghanistan, Bosnia, Iraq, Kosovo and Yugoslavia – including its former parts – were the conflict locations which were frequently discussed in the same articles that contain expressions of European identity in its *communio* sense. Within the intervention sub-sample, articles that mentioned Afghanistan co-occurred with the 'EU as *communio*' in at least 10 per cent of the articles of the set union. This was the case in all countries under study. However, in the overall sample this link occurred in no country. Hence this conflict was clearly and unanimously seen as an intervention challenging European identity in the ethical sense. Israel was mentioned much less frequently in connection with the EU as a *communio* than in connection with the EU as a *commercium*. Only in the Netherlands and the US – in both samples – and in Germany and the Netherlands – in the intervention sub-sample – was Israel more clearly and emphatically related to European identity.

Interim conclusions

The concepts of pragmatic problem-solving community (*commercium*) and ethical community of values (*communio*) developed in Chapter 2 were fruitfully employed in the corpus-linguistic analysis. The share of expressions of the EU as a *commercium* or as a *communio* were low – which is good news insofar as it shows that, contrary to some allegations, 'Europeans' not only practised narcissistic navel-gazing but very much tried to talk about the problems at stake. Interestingly, the EU was presented somewhat more in terms of a *communio* than in terms of a *commercium* in the overall debate, while

Table 4.24 The EU as *commercium* and/or *communio* in relation to different crises

Country	commercium conflicts	communio conflicts
Overall sample		
GER	Bosnia, Iraq, Israel, Kosovo, Yugoslavia	Bosnia, Iraq, Kosovo, Yugoslavia
NL	Bosnia, Iraq, Kosovo	Bosnia, Iraq, Israel, Kosovo, Yugoslavia
AU	Bosnia, Iraq, Kosovo, Yugoslavia	Bosnia, Iraq, Kosovo, Serbia, Yugoslavia
FR	Bosnia, Iraq, Israel, Kosovo, Serbia, Yugoslavia	Bosnia, Iraq, Kosovo, Serbia, Yugoslavia
IR	Bosnia, Iraq, Israel, Kosovo, Palestine, Serbia, Yugoslavia	Bosnia, Iraq, Kosovo, Yugoslavia
UK	Bosnia, Croatia, Iraq, Israel, Kosovo, Serbia, Yugoslavia	Bosnia, Iraq, Yugoslavia
US	Bosnia, Croatia, Iraq, Israel, Kosovo, Serbia, Yugoslavia	Bosnia, Iraq, Israel, Kosovo, Yugoslavia
Intervention sub-sample		
GER	Bosnia, Iraq, Kosovo, Macedonia, Serbia, Yugoslavia	Afghanistan, Bosnia, Iraq, Israel, Kosovo, Macedonia, Serbia, Yugoslavia
NL	Bosnia, Iraq, Kosovo, Macedonia, Yugoslavia	Afghanistan, Bosnia, Croatia, Iraq, Israel, Kosovo, Serbia, Yugoslavia
AU	Bosnia, Iraq, Kosovo, Macedonia, Yugoslavia	Afghanistan, Bosnia, Iraq, Kosovo, Yugoslavia
FR	Afghanistan, Bosnia, Croatia, Iraq, Kosovo, Macedonia, Serbia, Yugoslavia	Afghanistan, Bosnia, Croatia, Iraq, Kosovo, Macedonia, Serbia, Yugoslavia
IR	Bosnia, Iraq, Kosovo, Serbia, Yugoslavia	Afghanistan, Bosnia, Iraq, Kosovo, Yugoslavia
UK	Bosnia, Croatia, Iraq, Israel, Kosovo, Macedonia, Serbia, Yugoslavia	Afghanistan, Bosnia, Iraq, Kosovo, Serbia, Yugoslavia
US	Bosnia, Croatia, Iraq, Kosovo, Macedonia, Serbia, Yugoslavia	Afghanistan, Bosnia, Croatia, Iraq, Kosovo, Serbia, Yugoslavia

Notes: Table based entirely on author's own data. It displays a listing of those conflicts that strongly co-occurred with references to the EU as a *communio* or a *commercium*. It includes only conflicts that displayed at least a 10 per cent overlap of the set union of the articles referring to the conflict and those referring to the respective identity dimension. Period of investigation: Jan. 1990–Mar. 2006 (195 months). Because of missing data, three countries include fewer months: AU 163, IR 166, GER 182.

within the normatively framed part of the debate the picture was mixed. In some countries *communio* while in others *commercium* expressions of European identity predominated. This contradicts the idea that political communities resemble a *commercium* most of the time and that this is sufficient for political integration (Habermas 1998: Ch. 9). Only further qualitative-hermeneutic in-depth analysis will help in explaining which considerations of the speakers in the public cause this finding; whether it is a particular feature of the debate on wars and interventions at the time studied, or whether this is a more stable finding; and what exactly explains country-specific differences.

Also, over time no trends concerning the relative shares of *communio* and *commercium* aspects of EU identity could be identified. The logic seems to be rather case-dependent, because if one matches the important conflicts with the two types of expression of European identity, one sees that often EU identity is invoked in both senses. The conflicts in the former Yugoslavia as well as the Iraq War 2003, for example, challenged the EU as a problem-solving community (*commercium*) as well as an ethical community (*communio*). During the period of investigation, the Afghanistan intervention was the only case in which the press of the different countries referred to the EU overwhelmingly as a community of values (*communio*). At least at the beginning, the NATO mission in Afghanistan seems to have been seen by many as the ideal-typical humanitarian military intervention. Since then, of course, this picture has changed.

The Israel–Palestine conflict, in contrast, was one in which the EU was most systematically referred to as a pragmatic problem-solving community (*commercium*). This long-lasting conflict, with its many waves of hope and disillusionment, has been discussed in a more 'technical', problem-solving manner. Perhaps this is because the Europeans do not see the EU as a norm-shaper in relation to the conflict parties which seem to orient themselves towards very different ethics, while the geographical proximity of the conflict still nourishes the perception of 'sitting in one boat' and having therefore to support common peace initiatives if proposed and accepted.

Notes

1 All statistics have been calculated with SPSS.
2 For estimates on political news reporting in several European quality newspapers, see Trenz (2004: 298). For this study it was not possible to arrive at similar estimates, because newspaper formats and styles of each paper may have changed over the length of the period of investigation. It was thus not possible to estimate the average number of articles on political issues in general and relate this to the intensity of reporting on wars and interventions.
3 The minimum values were: May 1990 (UK), June 1990 (FR), November 1991 (GER), September 1992 (NL, IR), January 1993 (AU), February 1997 (US) and December 1997 (UK).
4 In August 1998, Russia issued a statement that any request for Security Council authorisation to use force in Kosovo would be met by a Russian veto. In September 1998, the Security Council passed Resolution 1199, which did not, however,

Comparing debates across nations 143

authorise the use of force through any of the usual formulas. No further Security Council authorisation was sought (O'Connell 2000: 76).
5   For a listing of events related to the development of CFSP/ESDP, see http://europa.eu/about-eu/eu-history/1990-1999/1999/index_en.htm (28/01/2015).
6   The UN administration was established by Resolution 1244.
7   The significance of correlations may be slightly overestimated when applied to time series that share a common trend. However, as the ARIMA time-series analysis shows, most of the time-series data gathered for this study are not characterised by trends.
8   In the calculation of 'all UN events' the numbers of 'use of force with UN mandate' and 'without UN mandate' are excluded.
9   The time series analysis was conducted with the SPSS expert modeller. In a preparatory heuristic ARIMA analysis I tested all corpus-linguistically generated time series for overall trends and seasonal components. It was confirmed that there were almost no overall trends. Very few of the curves in this study are characterised by a linear trend. In the ARIMA models used, the differencing procedure displays linear trends as $d = 1$. The initial checks confirmed that there were also no seasonal components in the various curves to be explained. For all further analyses seasonal components were therefore excluded.
10 For the mathematical notation of ARIMA models, see https://ciser.cornell.edu/sasdoc/saspdf/ets/chap30.pdf (28/01/2015).
11 However, the driving force of the process is random events that prevent the autoregressive series from stagnating at an equilibrium level (Thome 2005: 110).
12 In Germany, a month with a higher *number of all crisis events*, however, led to a downward move in reporting in the same month (GER (− at lag 0)). In Ireland the effect went in the same direction as the predicting event time series (IR (+ at lag 0)).
13 NL (+ at lag 0 and lag 1), AU (+ at lag 0 and lag 2), FR (+ at lag 0 and lag 1, − at lag 2), IR (+ at lag 0 and lag 1, − at lag 2), UK (+ at lag 0), US (+ at lag 0 and lag 1, − at lag 2).
14 If $d \neq 0$ we look for the stationary R^2, otherwise the simple R^2.
15 Austrian, German and Irish newspapers are missing at that early moment of the period under study.
16 September and October 2001 are not statistically significant in the ARIMA model for the Netherlands.
17 I displayed the sequence charts of the means and the standard deviations of all media content time series used in this study (for all countries as well for the EU countries only). The pattern was found in all curves: at the peaks of the sequence charts, the common mean of the national curves, as well as the standard deviation of the national curves for this indicator, peak simultaneously.
18 The advantage of the sigma-convergence measure is that it does not assume convergence towards a postulated value, but instead calculates whether the variation from the common mean decreases over time (Higgins et al. 2003). It is a common measure in econometrics because it allows for the assessment of dynamic processes of convergence and divergence, without assuming a fixed standard value to which different time series should converge (see e.g. Barro, et al. 1991; Dreger and Kholodilin 2007).
19 In France, the Maastricht referendum on 20 September is likely to have monopolised press attention. In Britain, currency speculations prompted the devaluation of sterling and the British exit from the European Exchange Rate Mechanism.
20 This section draws on ideas published elsewhere (Kantner 2014; 2015). I am grateful to the publishers for their kind permission for me to reproduce it here.
21 Only one newspaper was available for Ireland.
22 The maximum months are April 1999 (GER, NL, AU, FR, IR), October 2001 (US) and March 2003 (IR, UK).

144 *Comparing debates across nations*

23 No articles on humanitarian military interventions could be identified in November 1991 (GER) and December 1992, January 1993 and April 1993 (AU). The minimum values for NL (January–March 1990) and FR (May 1990) are also close to zero. In the English-speaking countries the numbers do not fall as dramatically. The minimum months were February 1990 (UK), May 1990 (US) and February 1997 (IR).
24 The correlation coefficients range from 0.20 (GER) to 0.31 (US). The association is by far the weakest in the case of the German issue-cycle, which may indicate a higher selectivity to individual events instead of classes of events.
25 The correlation coefficients range from 0.25 (US) to 0.35 (AU).
26 GER (+ at lag 0 and lag 1), NL (+ at lag 0 and lag 1), AU (+ at lag 0 and lag 1), FR (+ at lag 0 and lag 1), IR (+ at lag 0 and lag 1, – at lag 2), UK (+ at lag 0 and lag 1), US (+ at lag 0 and lag 1).
27 The immediate time after the fall of the Iron Curtain also saw the gradual breakdown of the USSR. Early in 1990, Soviet troops occupied Baku (Azerbaijan) under a state-of-emergency decree issued by Mikhail Gorbachev. Violent confrontations occurred. Hence the West could not be sure how peacefully the transformation in the East – especially the multi-ethnic states – would proceed.
28 In October 1990, the Rwandan Patriotic Front began its offensive and the Habyarimana regime called for international support (Adelman and Suhrke 1996; Twagilimana 2007: xxxii).
29 In April 1991, Iraqi forces succeeded in crushing a series of uprisings following military defeat in the Gulf War and international action was taken to address the developing refugee crisis (Ghareeb and Dougherty 2004: xviii). However, in spring 1991 the situation in Yugoslavia also began to escalate.
30 The exceptions are the Dutch and Austrian newspapers, where the share of 'EU identity' within the articles that refer to 'Europe' in a broad sense decreases slightly but remains constant in the intervention sub-sample.
31 Opération Retour was launched in December 1994. The situation of the Hutu refugees received significant international attention since the refugee camps became a new power-base for the perpetrators of the genocide. Attempts to encourage displaced Hutu civilians to return ran aground when a Hutu government in exile was created in Zaire (Adelman and Suhrke 1996: Ch. 6.3; Twagilimana 2007: xxv).
32 For the text of the 'Letter of the Eight' see www.globalpolicy.org/component/content/article/168/36565.html (28/01/2015).
33 By 1 May the war seemed over when President George W. Bush declared the war ended (Ghareeb and Dougherty 2004: xxxvii).
34 Especially in qualitative study, the 'other' is often seen as a necessary ingredient for any collective identity (Bishop and Jaworski 2003; Castano,et al. 2003; Stråth 2000).
35 This correlation is weaker for Ireland, and for the UK it is not significant.
36 There is one exception: the involvement of the neutral Member State Austria correlates slightly more strongly with the frequencies of 'EU identity' phrases in the Dutch media.
37 GER (+ at lag 0), NL (+ at lag 0, lag 1 and lag 2), AU (+ at lag 0 and lag 1), FR (+ at lag 0, – at lag 1, + at lag 2), UK (+ at lag 0), US (+ at lag 0).
38 GER (+ at lag 0), NL (– at lag 0, + at lag 1), FR (+ at lag 0), IR (+ at lag 0), US (+ at lag 0 and lag 1).
39 UK (+ at lag 0).
40 US (– at lag 0).
41 GER (+ at lag 0), FR (+ at lag 0), IR (+ at lag 0).
42 NL (+ at lag 0 and lag 1), AU (+ at lag 0 and lag 2), FR (+ at lag 0, – at lag 1, + at lag 2), IR (+ at lag 0, – at lag 4), UK (+ at lag 0), US (+ at lag 0, – at lag 2).

43 US (+ at lag 0, – at lag 4).
44 The selection of the conflict areas included in this measure did not just draw on our initial sampling-strategy but was guided by the results of the analysis of the human coding also conducted for other parts of the research project later published elsewhere (Grabowsky 2010; Renfordt 2011).

5 Reality and identities 'under construction'

In recent decades, new international threats and challenges of the post-Cold War era have emerged, which have had to be comprehended and institutionally digested by all international actors. Key international problems, such as the return of civil wars – even on the European continent – catastrophic terrorism, the Iraq War 2003, and experiences of failing international crisis management taught Europeans the hard way that they had to find new security strategies, develop their capabilities, and build common institutions for dealing with the new security threats of the twenty-first century. In this context, foreign, security and defence policy also became the subject of institutionalisation efforts at the EU level.

This study has investigated the dynamics of transnational collective sense-making of international crisis events from a hermeneutic-pragmatist and language-analytical perspective in connection with constructivist International Relations theory. It focused on the discourse on war and humanitarian military interventions as it unfolded before the eyes of ordinary citizens after the end of the Cold War, so as to investigate whether transnational (transatlantic and/or European) debates took place in the face of international crisis events, and whether these events resulted in European identity-formation.

To do so, this study introduced a number of new concepts. *Transnational political communication* was conceptualised as collective-sense making process in the context of emergent interdependent problems – problems often not yet seen by a significant number of actors as their *common* problems, which necessitate political-institutional solutions. Transnational political communication takes place when people across national borders have the opportunity to make up their mind about the *same political issues* at the *same time* under *similar aspects of relevance* – no matter whether in face-to-face interactions or via which media. This means that people do not need to consume exactly the same media content in the same language(s) or presented from the same partisan 'perspectives'. What matters is the thematically intertwined communication about the same problematic issues. I further distinguished ideal-typically between two types of identity and two types of identity discourse: *pragmatic problem-solving debates*, in which *problem-solving communities* (*commercium*) may emerge on one hand; and *ethical discourses*, in which the ethical foundations of collective problem-solving practices are debated and in which a *shared ethical self-understanding* (*communio*) may be created on the other.

The members of particularistic we$_{2/commercium}$ groups draw on a collective identity in the sense of a shared interpretation of their situation or the awareness of being involved in a cooperative enterprise. They consider themselves to be 'sitting in the same boat' – whether they like it or not, the perceived problem is their *common* problem. With regard to international crisis events, this type of conviction could include shared threat perceptions, the experience of being affected by the external consequences of crisis events such as refugee streams, or the perceived risk of the destabilisation of whole regions. This type of shared conviction does *not*, however, include common ethical convictions: the members follow diverse desires and purposes and do not see themselves as pursuing a common, ethically motivated project. They may organise and institutionalise their cooperation and regulate it normatively with prescriptive norms, yet when the perception of collectively facing a difficult situation fades away, they may decide not to continue cooperation.

Members of particularistic we$_2$-groups in the sense of a we$_{2/communio}$ share more than some practical interests: they try to find answers to key ethical questions concerning the 'good life' and 'what is good or better for *us* to do'. The answers to these ethical questions are organised around certain collective goods, which characterise this shared conception of a 'good life' (Tietz 2001: 113–124). We generally call these collective goods 'values'. Members of a we$_{2/communio}$ can become involved in a common ethical project such as, for instance, to secure human rights for people in distant places (because we lose some of our self-respect if we do not help when we could) or to foster a law-based world order. Only collective identities in this normative sense consist of a widely shared ethical self-understanding of the individual members.

This study started with six hypotheses. Against the mainstream of research on transnational political communication in the European Union (which still holds that political discourses in different countries follow their own idiosyncratic logic, which results in strong national differences in media attention to the relevant issues), I *hypothesised firstly* that there is a transnational debate on wars and humanitarian military interventions in which the *same issues* are discussed at the *same time*. I assumed that this would be observable in very similar issue-cycles across countries. Moreover, I expected convergence between the countries' degrees of awareness paid to the issue over time. Since wars and interventions in tendency are global problems, I did not expect much transatlantic difference.

The study shows clearly that issues of wars and humanitarian military interventions were discussed synchronously by Europeans and Americans. Public political communication was intensely intertwined thematically across all countries studied. These are important findings. While other pragmatist-constructivist contributions in International Relations theory stress the piecemeal, incremental and 'experimental' character of problem-solving, institution-building and collective learning processes beyond the nation state on a meta-theoretical level (Albert and Kopp-Malek 2002; Bohman 2002; Cochran 2002), this study made the collective communication- and action-oriented contribution of John Dewey productive for the study of change in international relations. It has shown that transnational debates in fact take place as my reading of John Dewey (1927) would predict: We$_1$ communicate across borders about transnationally interdependent issues. In light of these findings, the widespread scepticism towards the possibility of transnational political mass communication (Gerhards 2001; Graf von Kielmansegg 1996; Grimm 1995) is not justified.

The debate was characterised by highly *simultaneous issue-cycles* in all countries under study. The *same issue* was discussed not only at the *same time* but also with the same shifts in intensity across nations. In all countries, the Iraq War (March 2003) received the most coverage. Additional simultaneous peaks of media attention could be observed in relation to the Iraq/Kuwait crisis (August 1990 and the first three months of 1991), the Kosovo crisis (April–June 1999), as well as 9/11 and the following intervention in Afghanistan (September/October 2001). This indicates an event-driven transnational and transatlantic (possibly even global) debate on the changing international constellations and the question of what kind of international crisis management activities are needed. There was, moreover, a remarkable process of convergence in the intensity of debate between September 1992 and the beginning of the Kosovo conflict, which was even more pronounced among the EU countries. However, those who have documented processes of intra-European divergence (Pütter and Wiener 2007) are partially right too: when radical decisions about the direction of further policies were at stake during the two most controversial crises, we can observe increasing differences in the level of attention paid to the issue. After a continuous period of convergence until February 1999 (Kosovo), a slight process of divergence set in among the European countries, exacerbated by the clash over the Iraq War in March 2003. The war resulted in a slight upwards level shift in the average degree of deviance between the countries. Within the group of the European countries, the similarity of the issue-cycles was higher and the convergence period was more pronounced.

Putting in doubt the view that political discourses in different countries are more or less incommensurable with each other with regard to their frames of interpretation (most explicitly, Greven 2000), with my *second hypothesis* I suspected that *similar aspects of relevance* – which does not imply that opinions are necessarily shared – would be observable, and that the higher the density of interdependence and interaction in the policy field, the more pronounced similarity would be. I therefore expected the part of the discourse that addresses the normative framing of the (possible) use of military force as 'humanitarian military intervention' to be more similar and more convergent among the EU countries. Consequently, I expected clear transatlantic differences in this area of debate.

The *interpretative framing* of a part of the overall debate as a normatively positively connoted type of armed conflict, namely a humanitarian military intervention by uninvolved third parties for the sake of the protection of the lives and human rights of the civilian population of the crisis countries, was present in all countries under study. Again, the issue-cycles of all countries correlated very strongly – albeit slightly less than the overall issue-cycles. The intensity of the debate followed a very erratic pattern driven by external events instead of inherent trends. We could identify four waves of heightened media attention with several peaks: 1990/01 (Iraq/Kuwait); autumn 1992 to autumn 1996 (Balkan crises, African conflicts); 1999/2000 (Kosovo); and 9/11 to 2004 (Afghanistan, Iraq War). March 2003 was no longer the month with the maximum coverage – indicating that the Iraq War was – especially in the continental European countries – not framed in terms of a humanitarian military intervention, but was discussed as an 'ordinary war' for self-interested reasons. In fact, after the Iraq War 2003 the debate on humanitarian military interventions decreased dramatically, either as an abrupt level shift or in the form of a steep downwards trend. This supports the contention that the Iraq War severely and lastingly damaged the normative credibility of the political-philosophical distinction between 'ordinary wars' and 'humanitarian military interventions'.

The *'big' crises* were presented in the media with a 'mixed wording': some articles addressed them in terms of ordinary wars, some in terms of humanitarian military interventions, and some in both terms. Besides these breaking-news crisis events that constituted the peaks in the overall issue-cycle on 'wars and interventions', another group of *'minor' conflicts* – mainly in Africa – became visible as simultaneous peaks in the normatively framed part of the debate: these events were, when they were discussed, consistently labelled as interventions. This observation was only possible based on the continuous rather than case-by-case approach of this study.

The convergence analysis provided strong support for the assumption of decreasing inner-European and increasing transatlantic differences. On average, the deviation for the normatively framed part of the debate was clearly lower than in the overall debate for all countries under study. This was very pronounced among the EU countries: the difference between the curves for the sub-sample on humanitarian military intervention was about 10 per cent lower than for the overall sample. Moreover, a process of convergence could be observed from autumn 1991 to March 1999. This trend was again more pronounced among the EU countries.

This contributes another important insight to the debate on transnational political communication. We can conceptualise transnational political communication across borders, but it makes sense to specify different degrees of intensity of this communicative intertwinement according to different degrees of interdependence and political interaction in the policy areas under investigation. This approach provides a bridge between the literature on global public spheres, which in general is very optimistic about the prospects of transnational political communication and the possibilities of transnational democracy, and the overwhelmingly sceptical literature on European public spheres, which tends to hold that transnational European communication lags behind national public spheres.

With a *third hypothesis* I suspected that debate is focused on concrete problems. The problem-focus was operationalised according to the theory of news values as parallel time-series of the number of certain event-types per month. The theory of news values holds that specific *event-types* with high news values receive disproportionate media attention (Buckalew 1969/70; Eilders 2006; Galtung and Holmboe Ruge 1965; Östgaard 1965; Schulz 1976; Staab 1990) and 'drive' the issue-cycle. However, I assumed there is no automatic relation between the existence of crisis events and their becoming perceived as a public problem (Dewey 1927; Hilgartner and Bosk 1988) and that problem-focus can be alternatively operationalised as *individual crisis events* and episodes that 'drive' the debate. Both options were tested based on a statistical time-series analysis including event data external to the media discourses analysed (as proposed by Rosengren 1970, 1974).

In what ways did events drive the debate? The issue-cycles of 'wars and interventions' and of 'humanitarian military intervention' in particular responded to the same *individual crisis events* and not to certain *types* of dramatic crisis events as the literature maintained. If certain *types of events* matter at all in a systematic fashion,[1] it was the accumulated number of all NATO events and, to a lesser degree, the number of all EU events. The '*additivity hypothesis*' (Galtung and Holmboe Ruge 1965: 71; Rosengren 1974: 145), which holds that events scoring highly on several news factors take centre stage in terms of public attention, proved right in a surprising fashion: dramatic events alone – even those in 'elite nations' – do not *per se* result in heightened media attention, but crisis events followed by immediate and massive international reactions by different international actors (mainly NATO and the EU) are discussed in detail by the media. The more various international actors do in response to a crisis, the more media attention the crisis receives. Conversely, this means that conflicts on which the institutionalised international community remains silent are also forgotten by the media. Studying the journalistic news production process, other researchers have arrived at the same conclusion (see e.g. Holm 2002). International activity contributes to a process by which some conflicts become more 'important' than others.

One could object that the reverse 'causal logic' could also be at work: as the 'CNN effect' hypothesises, media coverage may set the political agenda, forcing politicians to react to events for which the media has created an audience (for a critical overview of this literature see Gilboa 2005; Livingston 1997). However, since institutions are less flexible in their reactions than the media – because it takes time to organise summits, prepare a humanitarian military intervention or reorganise security organisations – and since this study worked with monthly aggregated data and found simultaneous peaking of media coverage and institutional reactions, it is very unlikely that the media systematically 'drove' the crisis-management activities. It is much more likely that the media follow the political dynamics, even if some degree of mutual interaction and reinforcement is possible. Supporting this interpretation, other case-by-case analyses find that, although under some conditions the media may exert a strong influence on intervention decisions, this logic is not dominant (Robinson 2000a, 2000b).

Regarding the intensity of references to a European identity in the media, institutional events took centre stage as structural 'drivers' of the debate as well: NATO and EU events (including interventions, but also 'boring' or mundane summits, CFSP/ESDP activities, etc.) proved to be relevant predictors across all time-series models, both in the overall issue-cycles and in the normatively framed part of the debate on humanitarian military intervention. In contrast, dramatic crisis events (outbreaks of wars, massacres and terrorist attacks) and UN events each were only significant in a single country's time series. Of course, institutional events are usually interrelated with certain crisis events. Those dramatic crisis events on which our common institutions act become focus points of political communication and perhaps even identity discourses. This was the case with the first Iraq war 1990/91, the Kosovo conflict, 9/11 and the beginning of the NATO missions in Afghanistan, and the Iraq war of 2003.

The theory of news values hence predicts the right events for the wrong reasons. It is not so much the conflict event in itself (or the features journalists ascribe to it) that catches attention, provokes reflections on our identity, and renders some events more important than others, but rather the accumulated media attention paid to the conflict *and* the respective actions of diverse international actors, their controversies and institution-building attempts in reaction to the conflict. In other words, the 'news-value effect' is not due to *one* event that journalists cover but to an *interrelated chain of events* including many mundane institutional ones that together make up for a story which becomes more and more likely to leave lasting traces in our institutional orders at the national, European, transatlantic or global level. Other crisis events, such as the genocide in Rwanda and the civil war in Somalia, or even geographically close conflicts such as the secessionist provinces of the former Soviet Union, received some UN attention but did not, by far, capture the same degree of complex institutional attention as the crises that were significant in this study.

Since interdependence and interaction is assumed to be higher among the EU countries than across the Atlantic, drawing on Dewey (1927) I *hypothesised fourthly* that Europe in general, and the EU in particular, would be much more present in the European media than in the US. Indeed, Europe in a broad sense was surprisingly visible in the debate. In the overall sample more than every third article referred to Europe in all countries except the English-speaking countries of Ireland, the UK and the US. In the normatively framed part of the debate, approximately every fourth article mentioned Europe – except in the UK and the US, where Europe was less visible.

152   Reality and identities 'under construction'

With respect to the visibility of the EU in particular, the gap between the US and the UK on one hand, and the other European countries on the other, increased. In the EU countries, the EU and its institutions were addressed in about every fifth article in the overall sample and in every third article in the normatively framed part of the discourse referring to humanitarian military interventions. In the US, by contrast, the EU was mentioned in only 9 per cent of the articles and 16 per cent of the humanitarian military intervention articles. The UK scored higher than the US, but clearly lower than the other EU countries. In the EU countries – again with the exception of the UK – most of the articles that referred to Europe in a broad sense were concerned with the EU more narrowly. This means that 'Europe' widely became a synonym for the EU in the European media. In the UK this finding is less pronounced. In the US media, Europe is mainly a geographical category.

These findings support the pragmatist-constructivist contention that problem-solving communities and their piecemeal, incremental and 'experimental' problem-solving attempts transcend the national level (Albert and Kopp-Malek 2002; Bohman 2002; Cochran 2002; Dewey 1927). In principle, a global public is possible (see e.g. Bohman 1998; Dryzek 1999: 44; Rabinder 1999; Stichweh 2003; Volkmer 2003). However, there is a gradient in interaction density which influences the intensity of thematical intertwinement of political communication and determines which problem-solving communities and international institutions are highlighted. Therefore, in a pragmatist-constructivist framework, the possible extension of problem-solving communities was expected and empirically confirmed to correspond to the range of political, legal and economic interdependence (Brunkhorst 2002; Kantner 2004b: Ch. 5; Zürn et al. 2007). This view adds a medium position to the existing literature on transnational political communication and builds a bridge between the two extremes: public political communication is neither contained within the nation state nor does it spread evenly beyond it. It develops with different intensity according to different degrees of mutual interdependence and interaction.

Thus we can clearly observe that transnational political communication on important problems takes place, and that the European Union – formerly not considered an international actor – has assumed some importance in international crisis politics. Did this also contribute to European identity-formation? We can say that the broad stream of transnational political communication is made up of two smaller flows: *pragmatic problem-solving debates* on one hand, and European *ethical discourses*, in which a particular community of the Europeans as Europeans develops shared ethical convictions, on the other.

Hypothesis five, moreover, stated that if a European identity emerged over the time period investigated, this should result in an increase of expressions of European identity in the EU countries. One should also be able to observe a convergence among the EU media in this respect over time. Using a very conservative measure that excluded any ambiguous expressions of European interests or European values that might also refer to broader Europe, this study found evidence for a European identity discourses – in both senses – within the discussions on wars and humanitarian military intervention. Almost 12,000 articles referring to 'EU identity' were identified for the period of investigation from January 1990 to March 2006. Their share of the debate was always low. The Europeans did not mainly talk about themselves *instead* of the international problems at stake, as some critics alleged (Kagan 2003). Identity was far from being of central concern in the debate – with interesting country differences pointing in the direction of the hypothesis. It was highest in France, followed by the other continental European countries, then Ireland and the UK, and finally the US papers, where such references were almost invisible. The higher salience of expressions of EU identity in the normatively framed part of the discourse on humanitarian military interventions nicely confirms a (self-)perception of EU identity in the field of foreign and security policy as a 'normative' or 'civilian power' (Bull 1982; Duchêne 1972, 1973; Manners 2002; Maull 2002; Mitzen 2006; Whitman 1998).

Contrary to my expectations, there was no pronounced upwards trend in the absolute volume of references to European identity. The time-series models detected linear trends only for the German, French and US cases, and only within the overall sample. However, the share of identity expressions was substantial within those articles that referred in some way to Europe and increased over the three phases of the debate for most countries, rising from the early 1990s over the late 1990s to higher levels in the first half-decade of the new millennium. The UK (in the overall sample) and the US were the only exceptions to this trend. The British media displayed significant distance from Europe, the EU and questions of European identity; for the American media these features were – as expected – of less relevance with regard to content.

Expressions of European identity peaked during the most controversial and most intensively debated conflicts, Kosovo 1999 and Iraq 2003. NATO and EU events, moreover, proved to have a systematic influence on the intensity of EU identity discourse. As for the issue-cycles, one can conclude that event-chains of crisis and institutional events together triggered the debate. In attempting to confront and come to terms with serious international issues, Europeans invariably also faced the challenge of what these crises meant for them and their collective self-understanding.

In a final *sixth hypothesis* drawing on Dewey (1927), I expected that new collective identities emerge in two ways, as a pragmatic problem-solving community (*commercium*) and ethical community of values (*communio*). I assumed to find a stronger presence of the EU as a *commercium* than as a *communio* in the debate, since with Habermas (1998b: Ch. 9) I hold that political communities resemble a *commercium* most of the time, and that this is sufficient for political integration. This expectation could not be confirmed in this study. All in all, the EU was presented somewhat more in terms of a *communio* than in terms of a *commercium* in the overall debate, while within the normatively framed part of the debate, counter-intuitively, the picture was mixed. Sometimes *communio*, sometimes *commercium* expressions of European identity predominated. The EU as *communio* clearly prevailed over the EU as a *commercium* only in France, the Netherlands and (on a much lower level) the US. Over time, no clear trends with regard to the relative shares of *communio* and *commercium* aspects of EU identity could be discovered. While the US referred to the EU and to European identity on a very low level, if they mentioned it, they, like the EU countries, did so largely in *communio* terms – especially in the context of the Iraq War 2003 – and, surprisingly, to a greater extent than EU countries such as Ireland, the UK, Austria and even Germany.

The analysis showed that the differentiated conceptual tools developed in the theoretical sections on collective identities could be fruitfully employed for the empirical study, although they led to somewhat surprising findings. Further research – also with qualitative-hermeneutic methods – should be directed to finding out why this is the case. Today I can only speculate that, perhaps in the context of the more general debate on (ordinary) wars and interventions, speakers in the public appeal to the values of a *communio* in order to give orientation to the larger audience, while in specifically *ethical debates* they feel a strong need to hint also at manifest interests in order to show that their views are not only morally coherent but also workable and in the well understood self-interest of the community they address.

A meaningful pattern, however, emerges if one relates the references to European identity to the important conflicts: the conflicts in the former Yugoslavia as well as the Iraq War 2003 challenged the EU as both a problem-solving community (*commercium*) and an ethical community (*communio*). During the period of investigation, only in the context of the Afghanistan intervention did the press of the various countries refer to the EU overwhelmingly as a community of values (*communio*). It seems that 'European identity' in the *communio*-aspect was taken for granted and appealed to. This may be a reflection of the fact that this intervention did not directly involve (perceived) European interests, constitute a direct threat, or threaten immediate negative externalities. Without these factors, which would likely have been discussed in pragmatic debate, *commercium* concerns for the problematic situation took a back seat to universalistic and ethical considerations. Quickly, however, the mission in Afghanistan came to be discussed far less favourably (Aday 2010; Daxner and Neumann 2012; Ringsmose and Børgesen 2011; Schüßler and Heng 2013) and in the course of later conflicts such as Libya, Syria and the Ukraine, the final illusions concerning humanitarian military interventions seem to have passed away.

By contrast, in discussions of the Israel–Palestine conflict, the EU is most clearly addressed as a pragmatic problem-solving community (*commercium*). Often discussed in connection with other conflicts in the Middle East as part of a problem-diagnosis, the limited influence of the EU on the conflict parties, the long history of attempts to find a negotiated solution, and the highly politicised international profile of the conflict may result in a strong focus on 'technical' problem-solving. In line with the theoretical arguments developed in this study, *commercium*-expressions of collective identity are to be expected.

More qualitative-hermeneutic in-depth analysis of particular conflicts, concepts or event-chains and their lasting effects in the debate on wars and humanitarian military interventions are certainly needed to further substantiate the findings of this study. At this point, I can only advertise the qualitative research conducted by our research team using the same corpus (Biegoń 2010; Grabowsky 2010; Kantner 2014, 2015; Kantner et al. 2008; Renfordt 2009: 207–212). These and other qualitative (and quantitative) analyses will contribute further to a better understanding of the communicative processes in which a European answer to identity questions such as 'who are we?' and 'who do we want to be?' in world politics is emerging.

The inner-European and transatlantic comparisons conducted support the pragmatist-constructivist assumption that there is a gradient with regard to varying density of transnational public political communication, which follows the density of political interaction and interdependence. The large degree of transatlantic similarity in the intensity of debate that addressed the normatively connoted concept of humanitarian military intervention points towards the existence of a Western '*corridor of normative convictions*' oriented around universalistic principles. Within this 'corridor', we argue about the correct interpretation of the empirical facts concerning a concrete international crisis, the appropriateness of certain courses of action, and sometimes the authenticity of our motives and intentions (Habermas 1984, 1987). However, the differences between the European countries tended to be smaller than transatlantic differences. In these countries, Europe, the EU and its institutions, as well as European identity, clearly played a more important role within the normatively framed part of the debate. This points towards the differentiation of a narrower European '*corridor of normative convictions*' within the Western one, marked by a dedication to a more specific interpretation of universalistic principles, support for multilateralism, a preference for civilian and diplomatic means of conflict solutions over military ones. In tendency, Europe was portrayed in the European media as a 'civilian power' (Bull 1982; Duchêne 1972, 1973; Manners 2002; Maull 2002; Mitzen 2006; Whitman 1998), but a 'civilian power' which also has military means at its disposal if all other options fail (Börzel and Risse 2007; Sjursen 2006; Stavridis 2001).

Within this narrower European '*corridor of normative convictions*', Europeans hold different opinions about many empirical and ethical questions, and what role Europe should play in international crisis events and world politics in general (Kantner 2006; Meyer and Zdrada 2006; Overbeck 2014) – the important lines of conflict, however, divide each national public too. A collective identity in both the pragmatic and the ethical sense does not mean that conflicts disappear. The hope that 'identity' would make things easier – as articulated by many analysts (Etzioni 2007: 31; Herrmann and Brewer 2004: 3; Risse 2004: 250; Taylor 1995: 204; Vobruba 1999) – will certainly be disappointed. Ethical discourses occur because 'we$_2$' have different views on problematic practical and ethically controversial issues. Our common ethical understandings about security and defence should not be imagined as a single set of maxims or narrowly defined policy position. Differences will remain. We need common procedures and institutions precisely in order to deal with those differences (for the proceduralist model of the public sphere, see Habermas 1998b: Ch. 9). Intra-European conflicts can be expected to be an ongoing feature of European political life, but they are not insurmountable obstacles to collective action – such as further European political integration in the field of the Common Foreign and Security Policy (CFSP). In a liberal democratic community, it is possible to agree upon common policies without 'speaking with one voice'.

The transnational public debates studied are very likely to have provided important background conditions for the rapid development of the European Security and Defence Policy (ESDP) after the end of the Cold War (for similar intuitions see e.g. Baumgartner and Mahoney 2008; Duffield 2007; Finnemore 2004; Finnemore and Sikkink 1998, 2001; Mansbridge et al. 2012; Schmidt 2010). They show the emergence of similar horizons of awareness and perception of issues of war and intervention: shared European perceptions of what are the most important international problems and actors; a sense of common responsibility of the Europeans as Europeans 'sitting in the same boat' and having in some way to contribute to problem-solutions; and last, but not least, common ethical self-understandings as to which values should guide – or limit – their international policy. In particular, the Yugoslav wars and the Iraq War 2003 gave rise to widely shared expectations towards the EU – a discursive background that allowed policy makers to push for the quite rapid institutionalisation of ESDP since 1998.

The problem-related nature of pragmatic problem-solving debates and ethical discourses found in this study has far-reaching implications for the question of a European identity. It implies that identity-politics campaigns are very likely to miss their aims. Why should modern, self-conscious and possibly sceptical citizens be impressed by someone attempting to impose an artificial 'identity' on them? Instead, citizens discover ethically relevant aspects of selected controversial issues. A *shared ethical self-understanding* emerges in the group members' discourses about important policy issues. The only thing that can be done in order to strengthen the EU as we$_{2/communio}$ is to openly debate and tackle the controversial issues that the broader public deems highly important, and to openly discuss policy alternatives and choices. Collective identities in the *commercium-* and the *communio*-aspect cannot 'be created' out of the blue by more or less creative intellectuals, PR specialists or politicians. There is a 'reality' out there that – even if we have to interpret it and to argue about what can be done about the problems and to which ethics we bind our actions – delimits which 'narratives' are perceived as plausible and which are not. Needless to say, human convictions can always be wrong. Occasionally, the wrong decisions will be reached. Our choices today will be our common past tomorrow – burdened with guilt or giving us reason for pride in our achievements. The future European identity will arise both from the crises that we face and overcome, and from the challenges we fail to. A new reflexive political tradition can develop only in the course of the emerging history of our cooperative problem-solving efforts.

Note

1 An event type was considered to 'matter' if its aggregated event-type variable was a significant predictor in the ARIMA models, i.e. if it added explanatory power to the model beyond the long-time (autoregressive component) and the short-term (moving average component) memory inherent in the issue cycles.

Technical Appendix

Sample characteristics

Table A1 Sample characteristics

Country	Newspaper	Digital availability	Missing time periods	Cleaned full sample	'Intervention' sub-sample
US	The Washington Post	1990-01-01 to 2006-03-31	No missing years/months	80,532	17,703
	The New York Times	1990-01-01 to 2006-03-31	No missing years/months	92,140	18,448
United Kingdom	The Times and The Sunday Times	1990-01-01 to 2006-03-31	No missing years/months	61,946	12,023
	The Guardian	1990-01-01 to 2006-03-31	No missing years/months	52,111	10,876
Germany	Frankfurter Allgemeine Zeitung (FAZ)	1993-01-02 to 2006-03-31	1990–92	24,142	6,520
	Süddeutsche Zeitung	1991-02-11 to 2006-03-31	1990 1991: Jan.	39,232	9,426
The Netherlands	De Volkskrant	1995-01-03 to 2006-03-31	1990–94 1995: Oct.	12,434	3,342
	NRC Handelsblad	1990-01-08 to 2006-03-31	2002: Aug.	22,255	6,529
Ireland	The Irish Times	1992-06-01 to 2006-03-31	1990–91 1992: Jan.–May	28,313	8,018

Country	Newspaper	Digital availability	Missing time periods	Cleaned full sample	'Intervention' sub-sample
France	Le Monde	1990-01-01 to 2006-03-31	No missing years/months	42,641	8,158
	Les Echos	1993-01-05 to 1996-12-30	French conservative papers: 1990–92	942	215
	Le Figaro	1997-01-09 to 2006-03-31	1994: Jul.–Dec. 1995: Jan.–May; Jul.–Dec. 1996: Jan. 1990–96	20,129	3724
Austria	Die Presse	1993-05-03 to 2006-03-31	1990–92 1993: Jan.–Apr.	7527	2259
	Der Standard	1992-09-17 to 2006-03-31	1990–91 1992: Jan.–Aug. 1993: May–Dec 1994: Jan.–Jun. 2000: Jan.–Feb. 2003: May	5164	1436
Σ				489,508	108,677

Source: author's own data.

Note: The 'intervention sample' is a sub-sample of the cleaned full sample generated by means of a sophisticated word-cluster search.

Summary of the results of the statistical analyses

Table A2 Overview for the results: 'wars and interventions', 'humanitarian military interventions', 'Europe'

	'Wars and interventions' overall sample	'Humanitarian military interventions' sub-sample	'Europe' Overall	'Europe' Intervention
Visibility	489,508	108,677	144,945	40,059
Major peak	Mar. 03	Oct. 01 (US) Apr. 99 (GER, NL, AU, FR, IR) Mar. 03 (UK, IR)	Mar. 03 (GER, NL, IR, UK, US) Feb. 03 (AU) Apr. 99 (FR)	Apr. 99 (all)
Lowest correlations among countries (Pearson's coefficients)	0.76 US/GER	0.72 US/AU	0.79 US/NL	0.68 UK/GER
Highest correlations among countries (Pearson's coefficients)	0.95 US/UK	0.91 US/UK	0.94 AU/GER	0.87 US/UK
Correlations with aggregated events*	NATO interventions EU interventions Involvement AU Involvement GER Involvement UK Involvement US	NATO interventions All NATO events Involvement Germany Involvement France Involvement Netherlands Involvement UK Involvement US	NATO interventions All NATO events EU interventions All crisis events and all EU, NATO and UN events Involvement Austria Involvement Germany Involvement France Involvement Netherlands Involvement UK Involvement US	NATO interventions All NATO events All crisis events and all EU, NATO and UN events Involvement Germany Involvement France Involvement Netherlands Involvement UK Involvement US Europe affected

	'Wars and interventions' overall sample	'Humanitarian military interventions' sub-sample	'Europe' Overall	'Europe' Intervention
ARIMA model**	Number of all NATO events	Number of all NATO events	Number of all crisis events Number of all EU events Number of all NATO events	Number of all NATO events
Significant outlier months***	Aug. 90 Jan. 91 Sep. 01	Aug. 90	None	Apr. 99 Feb. 03
σ-convergence all****, trend	80% Convergence Sep. 92–Feb. 99 Slight divergence since Feb. 99	74% Convergence autumn 91–Mar. 99 Constant since Mar. 99	69% Convergence Aug. 92–Aug. 95 Slight convergence since Aug. 95	65% Convergence Aug. 92–Aug. 95 Constant since Aug. 95 Major peak Oct. 97
σ-convergence EU****, trend	71% Convergence Sep. 92–Feb. 99 Slight divergence since Feb. 99	62% Convergence autumn 91–Mar. 99 Constant since Mar. 99	69% Convergence Aug. 92–Aug. 95 Constant since Aug. 95	61% Convergence Aug. 92–Feb. 96 Constant since Feb. 96 Major peak Oct. 97

Notes: *This table is based entirely on the author's own data. The table includes only event-types with high (Pearson's coefficient ≥0.30) correlations for four or more countries.
**Aggregated event categories were used as independent variables. The table records only variables that were significant for at least three countries.
***The table records only months that were significant for at least three countries' ARIMA models; months belonging to the same crisis are listed together.
****The percentage values indicate the mean deviation from the common mean. Lower percentages therefore indicate a lower level of deviation.

162 *Technical Appendix*

Table A.3 Overview of the results: 'EU and its institutions', 'EU identity'

	'EU and its institutions'		'EU identity'	
	Overall	Intervention	Overall	Intervention
Visibility	74,488	24,878	11,844	3633
Major peak	Apr. 99 (FR) Feb. 03 (AU, IR, US) Mar. 03 (GER, NL, UK)	Apr. 99 (GER, AU, FR, IR) Feb. 03 (NL) Aug. 92 (UK) May 93 (US)	Apr. 99 (FR) Feb. 03 (GER, NL, AU, IR, UK, US)	Apr. 99 (GER, FR) Jun. 99 (AU) Feb. 03 (AU, NL, IR, UK, US)
Lowest correlations among countries (Pearson's coefficients)	0.69 US/GER	0.51 UK/GER	0.64 US/FR	0.45 IR/AU
Highest correlations among countries (Pearson's coefficients)	0.92 AU/GER	0.84 FR/AU	0.84 FR/NL	0.70 GER/FR
Correlations with aggregated events*	NATO interventions EU interventions All crisis events and all EU, NATO and UN events Involvement Austria Involvement Germany Involvement France Involvement Ireland Involvement Netherlands Involvement UK	NATO interventions All NATO events All crisis events and all EU, NATO and UN events Involvement Germany Involvement France Involvement Netherlands Involvement UK Involvement US	All EU events Involvement Austria Involvement Germany Involvement France Involvement Netherlands Involvement UK	Involvement Austria Involvement Germany Involvement France Involvement Netherlands Involvement UK
ARIMA model**	Number of all EU events Number of all NATO events	Number of all EU events Number of all NATO events	Number of all EU events Number of all NATO events	Number of all EU events Number of all NATO events
Significant outlier months***	None	Apr. 99 Feb. 03	Apr. 99, Jun. 99 Jan. 03, Feb. 03	Apr. 99, Jun. 99 Jan. 03, Feb. 03

	'EU and its institutions'		'EU identity'	
	Overall	Intervention	Overall	Intervention
σ-convergence all****, trend	55% Convergence Sep. 92–Aug. 95 Constant since Aug. 95	59% Convergence Sep. 92–Jan. 97 Constant since Jan. 97	78% No trend	98% No trend
σ-convergence EU****, trend	60% Convergence Sep. 92–Aug. 95 Slight divergence since Aug. 95	61% Convergence Sep. 92–Jan. 97 Constant since Jan. 97	80% No trend	101% No trend

Notes: *This table is based entirely on the author's own data. The table includes only event-types with high (Pearson's coefficient ≥0.30) correlations for four or more countries.
**Aggregated event categories were used as independent variables. The table records only variables that were significant for at least three countries.
***The table records only months that were significant for at least three countries' ARIMA models; months belonging to the same crisis are listed together.

References

Adamec, L.W. (2003) *Historical Dictionary of Afghanistan*, 3rd edn, Lanham, MD: Scarecrow Press.
Aday, S. (2010) 'Chasing the bad news: an analysis of 2005 Iraq and Afghanistan war coverage on NBC and Fox News channel', *Journal of Communication*, 60(1): 144–164.
Adelman, H. and Suhrke, A. (1996) *Early Warning and Conflict Management, The International Response to Conflict and Genocide: Lessons from the Rwanda Experience 2*, Joint Evaluation of Emergency Assistance to Rwanda Steering Committee, Copenhagen, www.oecd.org/countries/rwanda/50189764.pdf (accessed 28/01/2015).
Adler, E. (2002) 'Constructivism and international relations', in W. Carlsnaes, T. Risse and B.A. Simmons (eds), *Handbook of International Relations*, London: Sage, pp. 95–118.
Adler, E. (2005) 'Imagined (security) communities. Cognitive regions in International Relations', in E. Adler (ed.), *Communitarian International Relations. The Epistemic Foundations of International Relations*, London: Routledge, pp. 185–206.
Adler, E. and Barnett, M.N. (eds) (1998) *Security Communities*, Cambridge: Cambridge University Press.
Albert, M. and Kopp-Malek, T. (2002) 'The pragmatism of global and European governance: emerging forms of the political "beyond Westphalia"', *Millennium – Journal of International Studies*, 31(3): 453–471.
Alexander, J.C. (2002) 'On the social construction of moral universals: the 'Holocaust' from war crime to trauma drama', *European Journal of Social Theory*, 5(1): 5–85.
Annan, K. (1999) *Report of the Secretary General pursuant to General Assembly resolution 53/35: The Fall of Srebrenica*, UN Document A/54/549, United Nations, New York, www.un.org/en/ga/search/view_doc.asp?symbol=A/54/549 (accessed 30/01/2015).
Antaki, C., Billig, M., Edwards, D. and Potter, J. (2002) 'Discourse analysis means doing analysis: a critique of six analytic shortcomings', submission to *Discourse Analysis Online*, www.shu.ac.uk/daol/articles/v1/n1/a1/antaki2002002-paper.html (accessed 28/01/2015).
Apel, K.-O. (1988) *Diskurs und Verantwortung*, Frankfurt: Suhrkamp.
Arendt, H. (1965) *On Revolution*, Harmondsworth: Penguin.
Arnold, G. (2008a) 'Angola', in *Historical Dictionary of Civil Wars in Africa*, 2nd edn, Lanham, MD: Scarecrow Press, pp. 31–46.
Arnold, G. (2008b) 'Chronology', in *Historical Dictionary of Civil Wars in Africa*, 2nd edn, Lanham, MD: Scarecrow Press, pp. xxiii–xxvii.
Arnold, G. (2008c) 'Congo, Democratic Republic of: Africa's Great War', in *Historical Dictionary of Civil Wars in Africa*, 2nd edn, Lanham, MD: Scarecrow Press, pp. 97–111.

References

Arnold, G. (2008d) 'Darfur', in *Historical Dictionary of Civil Wars in Africa*, 2nd edn, Lanham, MD: Scarecrow Press, pp. 138–143.

Arnold, G. (2008e) 'Liberia', in *Historical Dictionary of Civil Wars in Africa*, 2nd edn, Lanham, MD: Scarecrow Press, pp. 208–217.

Arnold, G. (2008f) 'Mozambique', in *Historical Dictionary of Civil Wars in Africa*, 2nd edn, Lanham, MD: Scarecrow Press, pp. 243–252.

Arnold, G. (2008g) 'Sierra Leone', in *Historical Dictionary of Civil Wars in Africa*, 2nd edn, Lanham, MD: Scarecrow Press, pp. 317–325.

Arnold, G. (2008h) 'Somalia', in *Historical Dictionary of Civil Wars in Africa*, 2nd edn, Lanham, MD: Scarecrow Press, pp. 328–343.

Arnold, G. (2008i) 'Sudan', in *Historical Dictionary of Civil Wars in Africa*, 2nd edn, Lanham, MD: Scarecrow Press, pp. 353–366.

Austin, J.L. (2009) *How to do Things with Words. The William James Lectures delivered at Harvard University in 1955*, Oxford and New York: Oxford University Press.

Baker, P. and McEnery, T. (2005) 'A corpus-based approach to discourses of refugees and asylum seekers in UN and newspaper texts', *Journal of Language and Politics*, 4(2): 197–226.

Barbato, M. (2000) 'Chronologie der Europäischen integration 1999', in W. Weidenfeld and W. Wessels (eds), *Jahrbuch der Europäischen Integration 1999/2000*, Bonn: Europa Union Verlag, pp. 471–488.

Bärenreuter, C., Oberhuber, F., Krzyzanowski, M., Schönbauer, H. and Wodak, R. (2005) 'Debating the European Constitution. What went wrong?', *Journal of Language and Politics*, 4(2): 227–271.

Barro, R.J., Sala-i-Martin, X., Blanchard, O.J. and Hall, R.E. (1991) 'Convergence across states and regions', *Brookings Papers on Economic Activity*, (1): 107–182.

Baumgartner, F.R. and Mahoney, C. (2008) 'Forum section: The two faces of framing: individual-level framing and collective issue definition in the European Union', *European Union Politics*, 9(3): 435–449.

Baur, N. and Lahusen, C. (2004) 'Sampling process-generated data: the case of newspapers', paper presented at the ISA RC 33Sixth International Conference on Social Science Methodology: 'Recent Developments and Applications in Social Research Methodology', 16–20 August, Amsterdam, www.mes.tu-berlin.de/fileadmin/fg224/Baur_Lahusen-SamplingProcessGeneratedData.pdf (accessed 28/01/2015).

Bayley, P. and Williams, G. (eds) (2012) *European Identity: What the Media Say*, Oxford: Oxford University Press.

Beck, U. (2007) *Weltrisikogesellschaft*, Bonn: Bundeszentrale für politische Bildung.

Beck, U. and Grande, E. (2007) *Das kosmopolitische Europa*, Frankfurt: Suhrkamp.

Beisheim, M., Dreher, S., Walter, G., Zangl, B. and Zürn, M. (1999) *Im Zeitalter der Globalisierung? Thesen und Daten zur gesellschaftlichen und politischen Denationalisierung*, Baden-Baden: Nomos.

Bellamy, A.J. (2009) *Responsibility to Protect: The Global Effort to End Mass Atrocities*, Cambridge: Polity Press.

Benoit, K., Laver, M. and Mikhaylov, S. (2009) 'Treating words as data with error: uncertainty in text statements of policy positions', *American Journal of Political Science*, 53(2): 495–513.

Benson, L. (2001) *Yugoslavia: A Concise History*, Basingstoke and New York: Palgrave.

Bicchi, F. (2006) '"Our size fits all": normative power Europe and the Mediterranean', *Journal of European Public Policy* 13(2): 286–303.

References

Biegoń, D. (2010) *European Identity Constructions in Public Debates on Wars and Military Interventions*, RECON Online Working Paper 2010/02, Oslo: ARENA, www.reconproject.eu/projectweb/portalproject/RECONWorkingPapers2010.html (accessed 28/01/2015).

Biehl, H. (2001) 'Wendepunkt Kosovo? Sicherheitspolitische Einstellungen in den alten und neuen Ländern', SOWI-Arbeitspapier, Strausberg, www.mgfa-potsdam.de/html/einsatzunterstuetzung/downloads/ap128.pdf (accessed 28/01/2015).

Billig, M. (1988) 'Methodology and scholarship in understanding ideological explanation', in C. Antaki (ed.), *Analysing Everyday Explanation: A Casebook of Methods*, London: Sage, pp. 199–215.

Bishop, H. and Jaworski, A. (2003) '"We beat 'em": nationalism and the hegemony of homogeneity in the British press reportage of Germany versus England during Euro 2000', *Discourse & Society*, 14(3): 243–271.

Bjola, C. (2005) 'Legitimating the use of force in international politics: a communicative action perspective', *European Journal of International Relations*, 11(2): 266–303.

Böckenförde, E.-W. (1991) *Recht, Staat, Freiheit*, Frankfurt: Suhrkamp.

Bohman, J. (1998) 'The globalization of the public sphere, cosmopolitan publicity and the problem of cultural pluralism', *Philosophy and Social Criticism*, 24(2/3): 199–216.

Bohman, J. (2002) 'How to make a social science practical: pragmatism, critical social science and multiperspectival theory', *Millennium – Journal of International Studies*, 31(3): 499–524.

Born, H. and Hänggi, H. (eds) (2004) *The 'Double Democratic Deficit': Parliamentary Accountability and the Use of Force under International Auspices*, London: Ashgate.

Börzel, T.A. and Risse, T. (2007) 'Venus approaching Mars? The EU as an emerging civilian world power', EUSA Conference, 17–19 May, Montreal.

Bretherton, C. and Vogler, J. (1999) *The European Union as a Global Actor*, London: Routledge.

Brubaker, W.R. and Cooper, F. (2000) 'Beyond "identity"', *Theory and Society*, 29(1): 1–47.

Brunkhorst, H. (2002) 'Globalising democracy without a state: Weak public, strong public, global constitutionalism', *Millennium – Journal of International Studies*, 31(3): 675–690.

Bruter, M. (2004) 'Civic and cultural components of a European identity: A pilot model measurement of citizens' levels of European identity', in R.K. Herrmann, T. Risse and M.B. Brewer (eds), *Transnational Identities. Becoming European in the EU*, Lanham, MD: Rowman & Littlefield, pp. 186–213.

Bruter, M. (2005) *Citizens of Europe? The Emergence of a Mass European Identity*, London: Palgrave Macmillan.

Buchanan, A. and Golove, D. (2002) 'Philosophy of international law', in J. Coleman and S. Shapiro (eds), *The Oxford Handbook of Jurisprudence & Philosophy of Law*, Oxford: Oxford University Press, pp. 868–934.

Buckalew, J.K. (1969/70) 'News elements and selection by television news editors', *Journal of Broadcasting*, 14(1): 47–54.

Bull, H. (1977) *The Anarchical Society*, New York: Columbia University Press.

Bull, H. (1982) 'Civilian power Europe: a contradiction in terms?', *Journal of Common Market Studies*, 21(1/2): 149–165.

Burg, S.L. and Shoup, P.S. (1999) *The War in Bosnia-Herzegovina: Ethnic Conflict and International Intervention*, Armonk, NY and London: M.E. Sharpe.

References

Carlsnaes, W. and Smith, S. (eds) (1994) *Foreign Policy in the New Europe*, London: Sage.

Carlsnaes, W., White, B. and Sjursen, H. (eds) (2004) *Contemporary European Foreign Policy*, London: Sage.

Castano, E., Sacchi, S. and Gries, P.H. (2003) 'The perception of the other in international relations: evidence for the polarizing effect of entitativity', *Political Psychology*, 24(3): 449–468.

Caygill, H. (2001) 'Perpetual police? Kosovo and the elision of police and military violence', *European Journal of Social Theory*, 4(1): 73–80.

Central European & Eastern Adriatic Research Group (1999) *Kosovo Chronology: 1997 to the End of the Conflict*, Research and Analytical Papers, London: Foreign & Commonwealth Office, www.fco.gov.uk/resources/en/pdf/pdf5/fco_pdf_kosovochronolgy (accessed 28/12/2008; no longer available online).

Checkel, J.T. (1998) 'The constructivist turn in International Relations theory', *World Politics*, 50(2): 324–348.

Chesterman, S. (2002) 'Legality versus legitimacy: humanitarian intervention, the Security Council, and the rule of law', *Security Dialogue*, 33(3): 293–307.

Chirac, M.J. (2003) 'Extraordinary European Council – press conference by M. Jacques Chirac, President of the Republic, Brussels 17.02.2003', Newsroom, London, www.ambafrance-uk.org/Extraordinary-European-Council.html (accessed 22/12/2008; no longer available online).

Cimbalo, J.L. (2004) 'Saving NATO from Europe', *Foreign Affairs*, 83 (6), www.foreignaffairs.com/articles/60275/jeffrey-l-cimbalo/saving-nato-from-europe (accessed 28/01/2015).

Citrin, J. and Sides, J. (2004) 'More than nationals: how identity choice matters in the new Europe', in R.K. Herrmann, T. Risse and M.B. Brewer (eds), *Transnational Identities. Becoming European in the EU*, Lanham, MD: Rowman & Littlefield, pp. 161–185.

Clausen, J.A. (ed.) (1968) *Socialization and Society*, Boston, MA: Little, Brown and Company.

von Clausewitz, C. (1984) *On War*, Princeton, NJ: Princeton University Press.

Cochran, M. (2002) 'Deweyan pragmatism and post-positivist social science in IR', *Millennium – Journal of International Studies*, 31(3): 525–548.

Cole, J. and Cole, F. (1997) *A Geography of the European Union*, London: Routledge.

Commission of the European Communities (2005) *Communication from the Commission to the Council, the European Parliament, the European Economic and Social Committee and the Committee of the Regions. The Commission's Contribution to the Period of Reflection and Beyond: Plan-D for Democracy, Dialogue and Debate*, Brussels: Commission of the European Communities, http://eur-lex.europa.eu/legal-content/EN/TXT/PDF/?uri=CELEX:52005DC0494&from=EN (accessed 28/01/2015).

Corsetti, G., Pericoli, M. and Sbracia, M. (2005) '"Some contagion, some interdependence": more pitfalls in tests of financial contagion', *Journal of International Money and Finance*, 24(8): 1177–1199.

Culpeper, J. (2009) 'Keyness: words, parts-of-speech and semantic categories in the character-talk of Shakespeare's Romeo and Juliet', *International Journal of Corpus Linguistics*, 14(1): 29–59.

Czempiel, E.-O. (1999) 'Europa und die Atlantische Gemeinschaft', *Aus Politik und Zeitgeschichte*, (B1/2): 12–21.

References

Czempiel, E.-O. (2002) *Neue Sicherheit in Europa. Eine Kritik an Neorealismus und Realpolitik*, Frankfurt: Campus.

Davidson, D. (1991) *Inquiries into Truth and Interpretation*, Oxford: Clarendon Press.

Daxner, M. and Neumann, H. (eds) (2012) *Heimatdiskurs. Wie die Auslandseinsätze der Bundeswehr Deutschland verändern*, Bielefeld: Transcript Verlag.

Delanty, G. (1995) *Inventing Europe: Idea, Identity, Reality*, London: Macmillan.

Delanty, G. and Rumford, C. (2005) *Rethinking Europe. Social Theory and the Implications of Europeanization*, London: Routledge.

Dembinski, M. and Wagner, W. (2003) 'Europäische Kollateralschäden. Zur Zukunft der europäischen Außen-, Sicherheits- und Verteidigungspolitik nach dem Irak-Krieg', *Aus Politik und Zeitgeschichte*, (B31/32): 31–38.

Deutsch, K.W. (1954) *Political Community at the International Level. Problems of Definition and Measurement*, Garden City, NY: Doubleday.

Deutsch, K.W., Burrell, S.A., Kann, R.A., Lee, M.J., Lichterman, M., Lindgren, R.E., Loewenheim, F.L. and Van Wagenen, R.W. (1957) *Political Community and the North Atlantic Area. International Organization in the Light of Historical Experience*, Princeton, NJ: Princeton University Press.

Dewey, J. (1927) *The Public and Its Problems*, Athens, OH: Swallow Press.

Diez, T. (2005) 'Constructing the self and changing others: reconsidering "normative power Europe"', *Millennium: Journal of International Studies*, 33(3): 613–636.

Dimitrova, D.V. and Strömbäck, J. (2005) 'Mission accomplished? Framing of the Iraq war in the elite newspapers in Sweden and the United States', *Gazette*, 67(5): 399–417.

Dörr, N. (2008) 'Deliberative discussion, language, and efficiency in the World Social Forum process', *Mobilization: An International Quarterly*, 13(4): 395–410.

Dörr, N. (2009) 'Language and democracy in movement. Multilingualism and the case of the European Social Forum process', *Social Movement Studies: Journal of Social, Cultural and Political Protest*, 8(2): 149–165.

Dörr, N. (2012) 'Translating democracy: how activists in the European Social Forum practice multilingual deliberation', *European Political Science Review*, 4(3): 361–384.

Downs, A. (1972) 'Up and down with the ecology: the "issue attention cycle"', *The Public Interest*, (28): 38–50.

Dreger, C. and Kholodilin, K. (2007) 'Preiskonvergenz in der erweiterten Europäischen Union', *Wochenbericht des DIW*, 74(38): 557–561.

Dryzek, J.S. (1999) 'Transnational democracy', *Journal of Political Philosophy*, 7(1): 30–51.

Duchêne, F. (1972) 'Europe in world peace', in R. Mayne (ed.), *Europe Tomorrow*, London: Fontana-Collins, pp. 32–49.

Duchêne, F. (1973) 'The European Community and the uncertainties of interdependence', in M. Kohnstamm and W. Hager (eds), *A Nation Writ Large? Foreign-Policy Problems before the European Community*, London: Macmillan, pp. 1–21.

Duffield, J. (2007) 'What are international institutions?', *International Studies Review*, 9(1): 1–22.

Durkheim, E. (1950[1895]) *The Rules of Sociological Method*, New York: Free Press.

Eckstein, P.P. (2006 [1997]) *Angewandte Statistik mit SPSS. Praktische Einführung für Wirtschaftswissenschaftler*, 5, Wiesbaden: Gabler.

Eder, K. and Kantner, C. (2000) 'Transnationale Resonanzstrukturen in Europa. Eine Kritik der Rede vom Öffentlichkeitsdefizit', in M. Bach (ed.), *Die Europäisierung nationaler Gesellschaften*, Wiesbaden: Westdeutscher Verlag, pp. 306–331.

References 169

Eder, K. and Kantner, C. (2002) 'Interdiskursivität in der europäischen Öffentlichkeit', *Berliner Debatte Initial*, 13(5/6): 79–88.

Eilders, C. (2006) 'News factors and news decisions. Theoretical and methodological advances in Germany', *Communications*, 31(1): 5–24.

Eilders, C. and Lüter, A. (2000) 'Research note: Germany at war: competing framing strategies in German public discourse', *European Journal of Communication*, 15(3): 415–428.

Eisenstadt, S.N. and Giesen, B. (1995) 'The construction of collective identity', *European Journal of Sociology*, 36(1): 72–102.

Eliassen, K.A. (ed.) (1998) *Foreign and Security Policy in the European Union*, London: Sage.

Elsie, R. (2004) *Historical Dictionary of Kosova*, Lanham, MD: Scarecrow Press.

Elster, J. (2004) *Closing the Books. Transitional Justice in Historical Perspective*, New York: Cambridge University Press.

Eriksen, E.O. (2005) 'An emerging European public sphere', *European Journal of Social Theory*, 8(3): 341–363.

Eriksen, E.O. and Fossum, J.E. (2004) 'Europe in search of its legitimacy: strategies of legitimation assessed', *International Political Science Review*, 25(4): 435–459.

Eriksen, E.O. and Weigård, J. (2003) *Understanding Habermas. Communicative Action and Deliberative Democracy*, London: Continuum.

Etzioni, A. (2007) 'The community deficit', *Journal of Common Market Studies*, 45(1): 23–42.

European Union (2003) *A Secure Europe in a Better World. European Security Strategy*. Brussels: European Council.

Evans, G. (2008) *The Responsibility to Protect: Ending Mass Atrocity Crimes Once and For All*, Washington, DC: Brookings Institution.

Fearon, J. and Wendt, A. (2002) 'Rationalism v. constructivism: a sceptical view', in W. Carlsnaes, T. Risse and B.A. Simmons (eds), *Handbook of International Relations*, London: Sage, pp. 52–72.

Finnemore, M. (2004) *The Purpose of Intervention: Changing Beliefs about the Use of Force*, Ithaca, NY: Cornell University Press.

Finnemore, M. and Sikkink, K. (1998) 'International norm dynamics and political change', *International Organization*, 52(4): 887–917.

Finnemore, M. and Sikkink, K. (2001) 'Taking stock: The constructivist research program in International Relations and Comparative Politics', *Annual Review of Political Science*, 4(1): 391–416.

Fleischhacker, H. (1996) 'Chronik der Europäischen Union', in D. Nohlen (ed.), *Lexikon der Politik*, München: C. H. Beck, pp. 303–313.

Føllesdal, A. and Hix, S. (2006) 'Why there is a democratic deficit in the EU: a response to Majone and Moravcsik', *Journal of Common Market Studies*, 44(3): 533–562.

Fossum, J.E. (2004) 'Still a Union of deep diversity? The convention and the Constitution for Europe', in E.O. Eriksen, J.E. Fossum and A.J. Menéndez (eds), *Developing a Constitution for Europe*, London: Routledge, pp. 226–247.

Fossum, J.E. and Trenz, H.-J. (2005) *The EU's Fledgling Society: From Deafening Silence to Critical Voice in European Constitution Making*, ARENA Working Paper 19, Oslo: ARENA, www.sv.uio.no/arena/english/research/publications/arena-publications/workingpapers/working-papers2005/wp05_19.pdf (accessed 28/01/2015).

Franzosi, R. (1987) 'The press as a source of socio-historical data: issues in the methodology of data collection from newspapers', *Historical Methods*, 20: 5–15.
Franzosi, R. (1990) 'Computer-assisted coding of textual data using semantic text grammars', *Sociological Methods and Research*, 19(2): 224–256.
Franzosi, R. (1994) 'From words to numbers: a set theory framework for the collection, organization, and analysis of narrative data', *Sociological Methodology*, 24(1): 105–136.
Franzosi, R. (2004) *From Words to Numbers: Narrative, Data, and Social Science*, New York: Cambridge University Press.
Fraser, N. (1992) 'Rethinking the public sphere. A contribution to the critique of actually existing democracy', in C.J. Calhoun (ed.), *Habermas and the Public Sphere*, Cambridge, MA: MIT Press, pp. 109–142.
Fuchs, D. (2011) 'European identity and support for European integration', in S. Lucarelli, F. Cerutti and V.A. Schmidt (eds), *Debating Political Identity and Legitimacy in the European Union*, London: Routledge, pp. 55–75.
Fuchs, D. (2013) 'What kind of community and how much community does the European Union require?', in R. McMahon (ed.), *Post-Identity? Culture and European Integration*, London: Routledge, pp. 87–104.
Fyle, C.M. (2006) *Historical Dictionary of Sierra Leone*, Lanham, MD: Scarecrow Press.
Gabrielatos, C. and Baker, P. (2006) 'Representation of refugees and asylum seekers in UK newspapers: towards a corpus-based analysis', Joint Annual Meeting of the British Association for Applied Linguistics and the Irish Association for Applied Linguistics (BAAL/IRAAL 2006): From Applied Linguistics to Linguistics Applied: Issues, Practices, Trends, 7–9 September, Cork: University College.
Gabrielatos, C. and Baker, P. (2008) 'Fleeing, sneaking, flooding: a corpus analysis of discursive constructions of refugees and asylum seekers in the UK press, 1996–2005', *Journal of English Linguistics*, 36(1): 5–38.
Galtung, J. and Holmboe Ruge, M. (1965) 'The structure of foreign news. The presentation of Congo, Cuba and Cyprus crises in four Norwegian newspapers', *Journal of Peace Research*, 2(1): 64–91.
Gerhards, J. (2000) 'Europäisierung von Ökonomie und Politik und die Trägheit der Entstehung einer europäischen Öffentlichkeit', in M. Bach (ed.), *Die Europäisierung nationaler Gesellschaften*, Wiesbaden: Westdeutscher Verlag, pp. 277–305.
Gerhards, J. (2001) 'Missing a European public sphere', in M. Kohli and M. Novak (eds), *Will Europe Work? Integration, Employment and the Social Order*, London: Routledge, pp. 145–158.
Gerhards, J. and Neidhardt, F. (1991) 'Strukturen und Funktionen moderner Öffentlichkeit. Fragestellungen und Ansätze', in S. Müller-Doohm and K. Neumann-Braun (eds), *Öffentlichkeit, Kultur, Massenkommunikation: Beiträge zur Medien- und Kommunikationssoziologie*, Oldenburg: Bibliotheks-u. Informationssystem d. Univ. Oldenburg, pp. 31–89.
Ghareeb, E. and Dougherty, B.K. (2004) *Historical Dictionary of Iraq*, Lanham, MD: Scarecrow Press.
Giesen, B. (2004) *Triumph and Trauma*, Boulder, CO: Paradigm.
Giesen, B. and Eder, K. (2000) 'Introduction. European citizenship. An avenue for the social integration of Europe', in K. Eder and B. Giesen (eds), *European Citizenship Between National Legacies and Postnational Projects*, Oxford: Oxford University Press, pp. 1–13.

References

Gilboa, E. (2002) 'Global communication and foreign policy', *Journal of Communication*, 52(4): 731–748.

Gilboa, E. (2005) 'The CNN effect: the search for a communication theory of international relations', *Political Communication*, 22(1): 27–44.

Glarbo, K. (2001) 'Reconstructing a common European foreign policy', in T. Christiansen, K.E. Jørgensen and A. Wiener (eds), *The Social Construction of Europe*, London: Sage, pp. 140–157.

Gleissner, M. and De Vreese, C.H. (2005) 'News about the EU Constitution: journalistic challenges and media portrayal of the European Union Constitution', *Journalism*, 6(2): 221–242.

Grabowsky, J.-K. (2010) 'Srebrenica als Bruch – Trauma und Identität', *Dissertation*. Berlin: Freie Universität Berlin.

Graf von Kielmansegg, P. (1996) 'Integration und Demokratie', in M. Jachtenfuchs and B. Kohler-Koch (eds), *Europäische Integration*, Opladen: Leske + Budrich, pp. 47–71.

Greven, M.T. (2000) 'Can the European Union finally become a democracy? The challenge of creating a democratic political community', in M.T. Greven and L.W. Pauly (eds), *Democracy Beyond the State? The European Dilemma and the Emerging Global Order*, Lanham, MD: Rowman & Littlefield, pp. 35–61.

Grimm, D. (1995) 'Does Europe need a constitution?', *European Law Journal*, 1(3): 282–302.

Grundmann, R., Smith, D. and Wright, S. (2000) 'National elites and transnational discourses in the Balkan war. A comparison between the French, German and British establishment press', *European Journal of Communication*, 15(3): 299–320.

Habermas, J. (1984) *The Theory of Communicative Action. Vol. 1, Reason and the Rationalization of Society*, Boston, MA: Beacon Press.

Habermas, J. (1987) *The Theory of Communicative Action. Vol. 2, Lifeworld and System: A Critique of Functionalist Reason*, Boston, MA: Beacon Press.

Habermas, J. (1989) *The Structural Transformation of the Public Shpere: An Inquiry into a Category of Bourgeois Society*, Cambridge, MA: MIT Press.

Habermas, J. (1995) 'Comment on the paper by Dieter Grimm "Does Europe need a constitution?"', *European Law Journal*, 1(3): 303–308.

Habermas, J. (1996a) *Between Facts and Norms. Contributions to a Discourse Theory of Law and Democracy*, Cambridge, MA: MIT Press.

Habermas, J. (1996b) 'Three normative models of democracy', in S. Benhabib (ed.), *Democracy and Difference: Contesting the Boundaries of the Political*, Princeton, NJ: Princeton University Press, pp. 21–30.

Habermas, J. (1998a) 'Does Europe need a constitution? Response to Dieter Grimm', in *The Inclusion of the Other*, Cambridge, MA: MIT Press, pp. 155–161.

Habermas, J. (1998b) *The Inclusion of the Other*, Cambridge, MA: MIT Press.

Habermas, J. (2001a) 'Braucht Europa eine Verfassung?', in *Zeit der Übergänge. Kleine Politische Schriften IX*, Frankfurt: Suhrkamp, pp. 104–132.

Habermas, J. (2001b) *The Postnational Constellation. Political Essays*, Cambridge, MA: Polity Press.

Habermas, J. (2004) 'Why Europe needs a constitution', in E.O. Eriksen, J.E. Fossum and A.J. Menéndez (eds), *Developing a Constitution for Europe*, London: Routledge

Habermas, J. (2006) *The Divided West*, Cambridge: Polity.

Habermas, J. and Derrida, J. (2003) 'February 15, or what binds Europeans together: a plea for a common foreign policy, beginning in the core of Europe', *Constellations*, 10(3): 291–297.

References

Herrmann, R.K. (2002) 'Linking theory to evidence in International Relations', in W. Carlsnaes, T. Risse and B.A. Simmons (eds), *Handbook of International Relations*, London: Sage, pp. 119–136.

Herrmann, R.K. and Brewer, M.B. (2004) 'Identities and institutions: becoming European in the EU', in R.K. Herrmann, T. Risse and M.B. Brewer (eds), *Transnational Identities. Becoming European in the EU*, Lanham, MD: Rowman & Littlefield, pp. 1–22.

Herrmann, R.K., Risse, T. and Brewer, M.B. (eds) (2004) *Transnational Identities. Becoming European in the EU*, Lanham, MD: Rowman & Littlefield.

Higgins, M., Levy, D. and Young, A. (2003) 'Sigma convergence versus beta convergence: evidence from US county-level data', Department of Economics, Emory University, Atlanta, http://economics.emory.edu/home/assets/workingpapers/higgins_03_16_paper.pdf (accessed 28/01/2015).

Hilgartner, S. and Bosk, C.L. (1988) 'The rise and fall of social problems: a public arenas model', *American Journal of Sociology*, 94(1): 53–78.

Hill, C. (ed.) (1996) *The Actors in Europe's Foreign Policy*, London: Routledge.

Holm, H.-H. (2002) 'Failing failed states: who forgets the forgotten?', *Security Dialogue*, 33(4): 457–471.

Hooghe, L., Marks, G. and Wilson, C.J. (2002) 'Does left/right structure party positions on European integration?', *Comparative Political Studies*, 35(8): 965–989.

Howorth, J. (2000) *European Integration and Defence: The Ultimate Challenge?*, Chaillot Paper 43, Paris: Western European Union, Institute for Security Studies, www.iss.europa.eu/uploads/media/cp043e.pdf (accessed 28/01/2015).

Howorth, J. (2007) *Security and Defence Policy in the European Union*, London: Palgrave Macmillan.

Iyengar, S. and Kinder, D.R. (1987) *News That Matters: Television and American Opinion*, Chicago, IL: University of Chicago Press.

Jacobs, R.H. (1991) 'A chronology of the Gulf War', *Arab Studies Quarterly*, 13(1/2): 143–166.

James, W.M. (2004) *Historical Dictionary of Angola*, new edn, Lanham, MD: Scarecrow Press.

Jopp, M., Brock, L. and Schlotter, P. (1991) 'Getrennt oder gemeinsam? Die sicherheitspolitische Zusammenarbeit in Westeuropa und die USA', in B.W. Kubbig (ed.), *Transatlantische Unsicherheit. Die amerikanisch-europäischen Beziehungen im Umbruch*, Frankfurt: Fischer, pp. 216–232.

Jopp, M. and Regelsberger, E. (1998) 'Die Stärkung der Handlungsfähigkeit in der Gemeinsamen Außen- und Sicherheitspolitik', in M. Jopp, A. Maurer and O. Schmuck (eds), *Die Europäische Union nach Amsterdam. Analysen und Stellungnahmen zum neuen EU-Vertrag*, Bonn: Europa Union Verlag, pp. 155–170.

Jopp, M. and Sandawi, S. (2003) 'Europäische Sicherheits- und Verteidigungspolitik', in W. Weidenfeld and W. Wessels (eds), *Jahrbuch der Europäischen Integration 2002/2003*, Bonn: Europa Union Verlag, pp. 241–250.

Jørgensen, K.E. (1997) 'PoCo. The diplomatic republic of Europe', in K.E. Jørgensen (ed.), *Reflective Approaches to European Governance*, Basingstoke: Macmillan, pp. 167–180.

Kagan, R. (2003) *Of Paradise and Power: America and Europe in the New World Order*, New York: Alfred A. Knopf.

References

Kaldor, M., Martin, M. and Selchow, S. (2008) 'Human Security: A European Strategic Narrative', Berlin: Friedrich-Ebert-Stiftung, http://library.fes.de/pdf-files/id/ipa/05172.pdf (accessed: 28/01/2015).

Kantner, C. (1995) 'Blockierte Potentiale. Meinungsbildungsprozesse in der DDR der achtziger Jahre', in G.-J. Glaeßner (ed.), *German Monitor. Germany After Unification*, Amsterdam: Rodopi, pp. 39–65.

Kantner, C. (1997) 'Deweys pragmatistischer Begriff der Öffentlichkeit und seine Renaissance in aktuellen Debatten', *Berliner Debatte Initial*, 8(6): 119–129.

Kantner, C. (2003) 'Öffentliche politische Kommunikation in der Europäischen Union. Eine hermeneutisch-pragmatistische Perspektive', in A. Klein, R. Koopmans, L. Klein, C. Lahusen, E. Richter, D. Rucht and H.-J. Trenz (eds), *Bürgerschaft, Öffentlichkeit und Demokratie in Europa*, Opladen: Leske + Budrich, pp. 215–229.

Kantner, C. (2004a) 'Gemeinsam geteilte normative Grundüberzeugungen und die Entstehung einer supranationalen europäischen Identität', *Berliner Debatte Initial*, 15(4): 85–91.

Kantner, C. (2004b) *Kein modernes Babel. Kommunikative Voraussetzungen europäischer Öffentlichkeit*, Wiesbaden: VS Verlag für Sozialwissenschaften.

Kantner, C. (2006a) 'Collective identity as shared ethical self-understanding: the case of the emerging European identity', *European Journal of Social Theory*, 9(4): 501–523.

Kantner, C. (2006b) 'Die thematische Verschränkung nationaler Öffentlichkeiten in Europa und die Qualität transnationaler politischer Kommunikation', in K. Imhof, R. Blum, H. Bonfadelli and O. Jarren (eds), *Demokratie in der Mediengesellschaft*, Wiesbaden: VS Verlag für Sozialwissenschaften, pp. 145–160.

Kantner, C. (2006c) *What is a European Identity? The Emergence of a Shared Ethical Self-Understanding in the European Union*, EUI Working Paper RSCAS 28, Florence: European University Institute, Robert Schuman Centre for Advanced Studies, http://cadmus.eui.eu/bitstream/handle/1814/6226/RSCAS_2006_28.pdf?sequence=1 (accessed 02/07/2015).

Kantner, C. (2010) 'L'identité européenne entre *commercium* et *communio*', in L. Kaufmann and D. Trom (eds), *Qu'est-ce qu'un collectif? Du commun à la politique*, Paris: Éditions de l'École des Hautes Ètudes en Sciences Sociales (EHESS), pp. 221–247.

Kantner, C. (2014) 'The European public sphere and the debate about humanitarian military interventions', *European Security*, 23(4): 409–429.

Kantner, C. (2015) 'National media as transnational discourse arenas: the case of humanitarian military interventions', in T. Risse (ed.), *European Public Spheres: Politics Is Back*, Cambridge: Cambridge University Press, pp. 84–107.

Kantner, C., Kutter, A. and Renfordt, S. (2008) *The Perception of the EU as an Emerging Security Actor in Media Debates on Humanitarian and Military interventions (1990–2006)*, RECON Online Working Paper 2008/19, Oslo: ARENA, www.reconproject.eu/main.php/RECON_wp_0819.pdf?fileitem=50511963 (accessed 28/01/2015).

Kantner, C. and Liberatore, A. (2006) 'Security and democracy in the European Union: an introductory framework', *European Security*, 15(4): 363–383.

Kantner, C. and Tietz, U. (2013) 'Identitäten und multiple Identitäten. Über die wertrationale Integration der Gemeinschaften unter den Bedingungen der Moderne', in E. Crome and U. Tietz (eds), *Dialektik – Arbeit – Gesellschaft. Festschrift für Peter Ruben*, Potsdam: WeltTrends, pp. 47–63.

Katzenstein, P.J. (ed.) (1996) *The Culture of National Security: Norms and Identity in World Politics*, New York: Columbia University Press.

174   References

Kennedy, G. (1998) *An Introduction to Corpus Lingustics*, London and New York: Longman.

Kevin, D. (2003) *Europe in the Media: A Comparison of Reporting, Representation and Rhetoric in National Media Systems in Europe*, London: Lawrence Erlbaum.

King, G., Keohane, R.O. and Verba, S. (1994) *Designing Social Inquiry. Scientific Inference in Qualitative Research*, Princeton, NJ: Princeton University Press.

Kluver, H. (2009) 'Measuring interest group influence using quantitative text analysis', *European Union Politics*, 10(4): 535–549.

Knorr, A. (2006) 'Europäische Öffentlichkeit und transnationale Kommunikation im sicherheitspolitischen Bereich: Eine Medienanalyse des Golf-, Kosovo- und Irak-Krieges', thesis, Berlin: Otto-Suhr-Institut für Politikwissenschaft der Freien Universität Berlin.

Kohler-Koch, B. (2000) 'Die GASP im kommenden Jahrzehnt – Gewappnet für Krisen?', in R. Hierzinger and J. Pollak (eds), *Europäische Leitbilder. Festschrift für Heinrich Schneider*, Baden-Baden: Nomos, pp. 155–170.

Kolb, P. (2008) 'DISCO: a multilingual database of distributionally similar words', in A. Storrer, A. Geyken, A. Siebert and K.-M. Würzner (eds), *Proceedings of KONVENS 2008 – Ergänzungsband: Textressourcen und lexikalisches Wissen*, Berlin: De Gruyter Mouton, pp. 5–12.

König, T. (2006) 'Compounding mixed-methods problems in frame analysis through comparative research', *Qualitative Research*, 6(1): 61–76.

Koopmans, R. (2004) *Integrated Report WP 2: Cross-National, Cross-Issue, Cross-Time*, EUROPUB.COM: FP5 Project Report, Berlin: WZB, http://europub.wzb.eu/Data/reports/WP2/D2-4%20WP2%20Integrated%20Report.pdf (accessed 28/01/2015).

Koopmans, R. (2007) 'Who inhabits the European public sphere? Winners and losers, supporters and opponents in Europeanised political debates', *European Journal of Political Research*, 46(2): 183–210.

Koopmans, R. and Erbe, J. (2004) 'Towards a European public sphere? Vertical and horizontal dimensions of Europeanized political communication', *Innovation: The European Journal of Social Science Research*, 17(2): 97–118.

Koopmans, R. and Statham, P. (1999) 'Political claims analysis: integrating protest event and political discourse approaches', *Mobilisation: An International Journal*, 4(2): 203–221.

Koopmans, R. and Statham, P. (eds) (2010) *The Making of a European Public Sphere. Media Discourse and Political Contention*, New York: Cambridge University Press.

Kriesi, H., Höglinger, D. and Wüest, B. (2005) Debattenanalyse. Auswahlverfahren und Codebuch. Version 5.1. Zürich: Institut für Politikwissenschaft.

Krippendorff, K. (2004) *Content Analysis: An Introduction to Its Methodology*, 2nd edn, London: Sage.

Kubbig, B.W. (ed.) (2003) *Brandherd Irak. US-Hegemonieanspruch, die UNO und die Rolle Europas*, Frankfurt: Campus.

Kutter, A. (2009) 'Polity-building and transnational dialogue in French and Polish media debates on the EU Constitution', PhD thesis, Berlin: Freie Universität Berlin.

Kutter, A. and Kantner, C. (2012) *Corpus-Based Content Analysis: A Method for Investigating News Coverage on War and Intervention*, International Relations Online Working Paper 2012/01, Stuttgart: Stuttgart University, www.uni-stuttgart.de/soz/ib/forschung/IRWorkingPapers/IROWP_Series_2012_1_Kutter_Kantner_Corpus-Based_Content_Analysis.pdf (accessed 28/01/2015).

Lacroix, J. (2003) *Communautarisme versus libéralisme. Quel modèle d'intégration politique ?*, Bruxelles: Editions de l'Université de Bruxelles.
Lacroix, J. (2006) 'Pertinence du paradigme libéral pour penser l'intégration politique de l'Europe', *Politique Européenne*, (19): 21–43.
Larsen, H. (1997) *Foreign Policy and Discourse Analysis: Britain, France and Europe*, London: Routledge.
Larsen, H. (1998) 'Explaining the common foreign and security policy – the new research agenda', in A. Wivel (ed.), *Explaining European Integration*, Copenhagen: Copenhagen Political Studies Press, pp. 237–255.
Larsen, H. (1999) *New Approaches to the Common Foreign and Security Policy of the EU (CFSP): The Constructivist Research Agenda*, paper presented to the 1999 ISA Annual Convention, 16–20 February, Washington, DC.
Larsen, H. (2000) 'Europe's role in the world: the discourse', in B. Hansen and B. Heurlin (eds), *The New World Order: Contrasting Theories*, Basingstoke: Macmillan, pp. 283–302.
Larsen, H. (2014) 'The EU as a normative power and the research on external perceptions: the missing link', *Journal of Common Market Studies*, 52(4): 896–910.
Laursen, F. (ed.) (2006). *The Treaty of Nice. Actor Preferences, Bargaining and Institutional Choice*, Herndon, VA: Brill.
Lenz, S. (2000). *Korpuslinguistik*, Tübingen: Julius Groos Verlag.
Levy, D. and Sznaider, N. (2002) 'Memory unbound: the Holocaust and the formation of cosmopolitan memory', *European Journal of Social Theory*, 5(1): 87–106.
Levy, D., Torpey, J. and Pensky, M. (eds) (2005) *Old Europe, New Europe, Core Europe: Transatlantic Relations After the Iraq War*, London: Verso.
Levy, J.S. (2001) 'War and peace', in W. Carlsnaes, T. Risse and B. Simmons (eds), *Handbook of International Relations*, London: Sage, pp. 350–368.
Lippmann, W. (1922) *Public Opinion*, New York: Harcourt Brace.
Livingston, S. (1997) 'Beyond the "CNN effect": the media-foreign policy dynamic', in P. Norris (ed.), *Politics and the Press: The News Media and their Influence*, Boulder, CO: Lynne Rienner, pp. 290–318.
Lucarelli, S. and Fioramonti, L. (eds) (2011) *External Perceptions of the European Union as a Global Actor*, New York: Routledge.
Luhmann, N. (1990) 'Gesellschaftliche Komplexität und öffentliche Meinung', in N. Luhmann (ed.), *Soziologische Aufklärung*, Opladen: Westdeutscher Verlag, pp. 170–182.
Machill, M., Beiler, M. and Fischer, C. (2006) 'Europe-topics in Europe's media. The debate about the European public sphere: a meta-analysis of media content analyses', *European Journal of Communication*, 21(1): 57–88.
Mackey, W.F. (1965) *Language Teaching Analysis*, Bloomington, IN: Indiana University Press.
Malmborg, M. and Stråth, B. (eds) (2002) *The Meaning of Europe. Varieties and Contention Within and Across Nations*, Oxford: Berg.
Manners, I. (2002) 'Normative power Europe: a contradiction in terms?', *Journal of Common Market Studies*, 40(2): 235–258.
Manners, I. and Whitman, R.G. (2003) 'The "difference engine": constructing and representing the international identity of the European Union', *Journal of European Public Policy*, 10(4): 380–404.
Mansbridge, J., Bohman, J., Chambers, S., Christiano, T., Fung, A., Parkinson, J., Thompson, D.F. and Warren, M.E. (2012) 'A systemic approach to deliberative

176   References

democracy', in J. Parkinson and J. Mansbridge (eds), *Deliberative Systems: Deliberative Democracy at the Large Scale*, Cambridge: Cambridge University Press.

March, J.G. and Olsen, J.P. (2004) *The Logic of Appropriateness*, ARENA Online Working Paper 2004/09, Oslo: ARENA, www.sv.uio.no/arena/english/research/publications/arena-publications/workingpapers/working-papers2004/wp04_9.pdf (accessed 28/01/2015).

Martin, I. (1999) 'Haiti: international force or national compromise?', *Journal of Latin American Studies*, 31(3): 711–734.

Maull, H.W. (2002) 'Die "Zivilmacht Europa" bleibt Projekt. Zur Debatte um Kagan, Asmus/Pollack und das Strategiedokument NSS 2002', *Blätter für deutsche und internationale Politik*, (12): 1467–1478.

Mays, T.M. (2004) *Historical Dictionary of Multinational Peacekeeping*, Lanham, MD: Scarecrow Press.

McCourt, D.M. (2014) *Britain and World Power Since 1945: Constructing a Nation's Role in International Politics*, Ann Arbor, MI: University of Michigan Press.

McQuail, D. (1992) *Media Performance. Mass Communication and the Public Interest*, London: Sage.

Mead, W.R. (2001) *Special Providence. American Foreign Policy and How it Changed the World*, New York: Alfred A. Knopf.

Menon, A. (2003) 'Why ESDP is misguided and dangerous for the Alliance', in J. Howorth and J.T.S. Keeler (eds), *Defending Europe: The EU, NATO and the Quest for European Autonomy*, New York: Palgrave Macmillan, pp. 203–217.

Menon, A. (2004) 'From crisis to catharsis: ESDP after Iraq', *International Affairs*, 80(4): 631–648.

Mérand, F. (2003) 'Dying for the Union? Military officers and the creation of a European defence force', *European Societies*, 5(3): 253–282.

Mérand, F. (2006) 'Social representations in the European Security and Defence Policy', *Cooperation and Conflict*, 41(2): 131–152.

Mérand, F. (2008) *European Defence Policy: Beyond the Nation State*, Oxford: Oxford University Press.

Merton, R.K. (1957) 'The role-set: problems in sociological theory', *British Journal of Sociology*, 8(2): 106–120.

Meyer, C.O. (2006) *The Quest for a European Strategic Culture: Changing Norms on Security and Defence in the European Union*, Basingstoke: Palgrave Macmillan.

Meyer, C.O. and Zdrada, A. (2006) 'Unpacking the "coalition of the willing": a comparative analysis of norms in British and Polish press debates on the Iraq invasion', *European Security*, 15(1): 23–45.

Miall, H. (ed.) (1994) *Redefining Europe. New Patterns of Conflict and Cooperation*, New York: St Martin's Press.

Mitzen, J. (2006) 'Anchoring Europe's civilizing identity: habits, capabilities and ontological security', *Journal of European Public Policy*, 13(2): 270–285.

Moravcsik, A. (2006) 'What can we learn from the collapse of the European constitutional project?', *Politische Vierteljahresschrift*, 47(2): 219–241.

Mukhtar, M.H. (2003) *Historical Dictionary of Somalia*, new edn, Lanham, MD: Scarecrow Press.

Münkler, H. (1996) *Reich, Nation, Europa. Modelle politischer Ordnung*, Weinheim: Athenäum.

Münkler, H. (2003a) *Clausewitz' Theorie des Krieges*, Baden-Baden: Nomos.

Münkler, H. (2003b) *Über den Krieg: Stationen der Kriegsgeschichte im Spiegel ihrer theoretischen Reflexion*, Weilerswist: Velbrück Wissenschaft.
Münkler, H. and Malowitz, K. (2008) 'Humanitäre Interventionen: Bedeutung, Entwicklung und Perspektiven eines umstrittenen Konzepts – Ein Überblick', in H. Münkler and K. Malowitz (eds), *Humanitäre Intervention. Ein Instrument außenpolitischer Konfliktbearbeitung. Grundlagen und Diskussion*, Wiesbaden: VS Verlag für Sozialwissenschaften, pp. 7–27.
NATO Public Diplomacy Division (2006) *NATO Handbook*, Brussels: NATO, www.nato.int/docu/handbook/2006/hb-en-2006.pdf (accessed 29/01/2015).
Neidhardt, F. (1994) 'Öffentlichkeit, öffentliche Meinung, soziale Bewegungen', in F. Neidhardt (ed.), *Öffentlichkeit, öffentliche Meinung, soziale Bewegungen*, Opladen: Westdeutscher Verlag, pp. 7–41.
Neidhardt, F. (2006) 'Europäische Öffentlichkeit als Prozess. Anmerkungen zum Forschungsstand', in W.R. Langenbucher and M. Latzer (eds), *Europäische Öffentlichkeit und medialer Wandel. Eine transdisziplinäre Perspektive*, Wiesbaden: VS Verlag für Sozialwissenschaften, pp. 46–61.
Nerlich, B. and Clarke, D.D. (2000) 'Semantic fields and frames: historical explorations of the interface between language, action, and cognition', *Journal of Pragmatics*, 32(2): 125–150.
Neuman, W.R., Just, M.R. and Crigler, A.N. (1992) *Common Knowledge: News and the Construction of Political Meaning*, Chicago, IL: University of Chicago Press.
Niethammer, L. (2000) *'Kollektive Identität'. Heimliche Quellen einer unheimlichen Konjunktur*, Reinbek bei Hamburg: Rowohlt.
Nussbaum, M. (2001) *Upheavals of Thought. The Intelligence of Emotions*, Cambridge: Cambridge University Press.
Nuttall, S. (2000) *European Foreign Policy*, Oxford: Oxford University Press.
O'Connell, M.E. (2000) 'The UN, NATO, and International Law after Kosovo', *Human Rights Quarterly*, 22(1): 57–89.
Olsen, J.P. (2005) *Unity and Diversity – European Style*, ARENA Working Paper 24/2005, Oslo: University of Oslo, www.sv.uio.no/arena/english/research/publications/arena-publications/workingpapers/working-papers2005/wp05_24.pdf (accessed 02/07/2015).
Orpin, D. (2005) 'Corpus linguistics and critical discourse analysis: examining the ideology of sleaze', *International Journal of Corpus Linguistics*, 10(1): 37–61.
Östgaard, E. (1965) 'Factors influencing the flow of news', *Journal of Peace Research*, 2(1): 39–63.
Overbeck, M. (2014) 'European debates during the Libya crisis of 2011: shared identity, divergent action', *European Security*, 23(4): 583–600.
Parsons, T. and Bales, R.F. (1956) *Family, Socialization and Interaction Process*, London: Routledge & Kegan Paul.
Peter, J. and de Vreese, C.H. (2003) 'Agenda-rich, agenda-poor: a cross-national comparative investigation of nominal and thematic public agenda diversity', *International Journal of Public Opinion Research*, 15(1): 44–64.
Peter, J., Semetko, H.A. and de Vreese, C.H. (2003) 'EU politics on television news: a cross-national comparative study', *European Union Politics*, 4(3): 305–327.
Peters, D., Wagner, W. and Glahn, C. (2014) 'Parliamentary control of CSDP: the case of the EU's fight against piracy off the Somali coast', *European Security*, 23(4): 430–448.

Peterson, J. and Sjursen, H. (eds) (1998) *A Common Foreign Policy for Europe? Competing Visions of the CFSP*, London: Routledge.

Pfetsch, B. (2004) *Integrated Report WP 3: The Voice of the Media in European Public Sphere*, EUROPUB.COM: FP5 Project Report, Berlin: WZB, http://europub.wzb.eu/Data/reports/WP3/D3-4%20WP3%20Integrated%20Report.pdf (accessed 28/01/2015).

Pond, E. (2005) 'The dynamics of the feud over Iraq', in D.M. Andrews (ed.), *The Atlantic Alliance Under Stress: US–European Relations after Iraq*, Cambridge: Cambridge University Press, pp. 30–55.

della Porta, D. and Caiani, M. (2006) 'The Europeanization of public discourse in Italy. A top-down process?', *European Union Politics*, 7(1): 77–112.

Przeworski, A. and Teune, H. (1970) *The Logic of Comparative Social Inquiry*, New York: Wiley-Interscience.

Pütter, U. and Wiener, A. (2007) 'Accommodating normative divergence in European foreign policy co-ordination: the example of the Iraq crisis', *Journal of Common Market Studies*, 45(5): 1065–1088.

Quine, W.V.O. (1981) *Theories and Things*, Cambridge, MA: Harvard University Press.

Rabinder, J.M. (1999) 'Tribal sovereignty and the intercultural public sphere', *Philosophy Social Criticism*, 25(5): 57–86.

Rayson, P. (2008) 'From key words to key semantic domains', *International Journal of Corpus Linguistics*, 13(4): 519–549.

Regelsberger, E. (ed.) (1993) *Die gemeinsame Außen- und Sicherheitspolitik der Europäischen Union. Profilsuche mit Hindernissen*, Bonn: Europa Union Verlag.

Regelsberger, E., Tervarent de Schoutheete, P. and Wessels, W. (eds) (1997) *Foreign Policy of the European Union. From EPC to CFSP and Beyond*, Boulder, CO: Lynne Rienner.

Reif, K. (1993) 'Cultural convergence and cultural diversity as factors in European identity', in S. Garcia (ed.), *European Identity and the Search for Legitimacy*, London: Pinter, pp. 131–154.

Renfordt, S. (2007a) *Auf dem Weg zu einer europäischen Öffentlichkeit? – Eine Mediananalyse europäischer und amerikanischer Debatten über den Irak-Krieg 2003*, Saarbrücken: VDM Verlag.

Renfordt, S. (2007b) *Do Europeans Speak with One Another in Time of War? Results of a Media Analysis on the 2003 Iraq War*, RECON Online Working Paper 2007/17, Oslo: ARENA, www.reconproject.eu/main.php/RECON_wp_0717.pdf?fileitem=50511942 (accessed 28/01/2015).

Renfordt, S. (2009) 'The emerging international law script in the media: evidence from a longitudinal, cross-national analysis of western mass debates about military interventions, 1990 to 2005', PhD thesis, Berlin: Freie Universität Berlin.

Renfordt, S. (2011) *Framing the Use of Force: An International Rule of Law in Media Reporting. A Comparative Analysis of Western Debates about Military interventions, 1990–2005*, Baden-Baden: Nomos.

Riffe, D., Aust, C.F. and Lacy, S.R. (1993) 'The effectiveness of random, consecutive day and constructed week sampling in newspaper content analysis', *Journalism Quarterly*, 70(1): 133–139.

Ringsmose, J. and Børgesen, B.K. (2011) 'Shaping public attitudes towards the deployment of military power: NATO, Afghanistan and the use of strategic narratives', *European Security*, 20(4): 505–528.

Risse, T. (2000) '"Let's argue!" Communicative action in International Relations', *International Organization*, 54(1): 1–39.
Risse, T. (2001) 'A European identity? Europeanization and the evolution of nation-state identities', in M.G. Cowles, J.A. Caporaso and T. Risse (eds), *Transforming Europe. Europeanization and Domestic Change*, Ithaca, NY: Cornell University Press, pp. 198–216.
Risse, T. (2002a) 'How do we know a European public sphere when we see one? Theoretical clarifications and empirical indicators', paper prepared for the IDNET Workshop 'Europeanization and the Public Sphere', 20–21 February, Florence: European University Institute.
Risse, T. (2002b) 'Zur Debatte um die (Nicht-) Existenz einer europäischen Öffentlichkeit. Was wir wissen, und wie es zu interpretieren ist', *Berliner Debatte Initial*, 13(5/6): 15–23.
Risse, T. (2003) 'Social constructivism and European integration', in T. Diez and A. Wiener (eds), *European Integration Theory*, Oxford: Oxford University Press, pp. 159–176.
Risse, T. (2004) 'European institutions and identity change: what have we learned?', in R.K. Herrmann, T. Risse and M.B. Brewer (eds), *Transnational Identities. Becoming European in the EU*, Lanham, MD: Rowman & Littlefield, pp. 247–271.
Risse, T. (2010) *A Community of Europeans? Transnational Identities and Public Spheres*, Ithaca, NY: Cornell University Press.
Risse, T. (ed.) (2015) *European Public Spheres: Politics Is Back*, Cambridge: Cambridge University Press.
Risse, T. and Grabowsky, J.-K. (2008) *European Identity Formation in the Public Sphere and in Foreign Policy*, RECON Online Working Paper 2008/04, Oslo: ARENA, www.reconproject.eu/main.php/RECON_wp_0804.pdf?fileitem=50511948 (accessed 28/01/2015).
Risse, T. and Kantner, C. (2003) *Auf der Suche nach einer Rolle in der Weltpolitik. Die gemeinsame Außen- und Sicherheitspolitik der Europäischen Union (GASP/ESVP) im Lichte massenmedial ausgetragener kollektiver Selbstverständigungsdiskurse*, Berlin: Freie Universität Berlin.
Risse-Kappen, T. (1991) 'Public opinion, domestic structure, and foreign policy in liberal democracies', *World Politics*, 43(4): 479–512.
Roberts, C.W. (1989) 'Other than counting words: a linguistic approach to content analysis', *Social Forces*, 68(1): 147–177.
Robinson, P. (2000a) 'The news media and intervention – triggering the use of air power during humanitarian crises', *European Journal of Communication*, 15(3): 405–414.
Robinson, P. (2000b) 'The policy-media interaction model: Measuring media power during humanitarian crisis', *Journal of Peace Research*, 37(5): 613–633.
Rorty, R. (1986) 'Solidarity or objectivity?', in J. Rajchman and C. West (eds), *Post-Analytic Philosophy*, New York: Columbia University Press, pp. 3–19.
Rosengren, K.E. (1970) 'International news: intra and extra media data', *Acta Sociologica*, 13(2): 96–109.
Rosengren, K.E. (1974) 'International news: methods, data and theory', *Journal of Peace Research*, 11(2): 145–156.
Rytter, J.E. (2001) 'Humanitarian intervention without the Security Council: from San Francisco to Kosovo – and beyond', *Nordic Journal of International Law*, 70: 121–160.
Salomon, R.C. (1993) *The Passions. Emotions and the Meaning of Life*, 2nd edn, Indianapolis, IL: Hackett.

Schenk, M. and Rössler, P. (1994) 'Das unterschätzte Publikum. Wie Themenbewußtsein und politische Meinungsbildung im Alltag von Massenmedien und interpersonaler Kommunikation beeinflußt werden', in F. Neidhardt (ed.), *Öffentlichkeit, öffentliche Meinung, soziale Bewegungen*, Opladen: Westdeutscher Verlag, pp. 261–295.

Schlesinger, P.R. (1999) 'Changing spaces of political communication: the case of the European Union', *Political Communication*, 16(3): 263–279.

Schlesinger, P.R. (2007) 'A fragile cosmopolitanism: on the unresolved ambiguities of the European public sphere', in J.E. Fossum and P. Schlesinger (eds), *The European Union and the Public Sphere*, London: Routledge, pp. 65–83.

Schlesinger, P.R. and Kevin, D. (2000) 'Can the European Union become a sphere of publics?', in E.O. Eriksen and J.E. Fossum (eds), *Democracy in the European Union. Integration Through Deliberation*, London: Routledge, pp. 206–229.

Schmidt, P. (1996) 'Zum Verhältnis von GASP, NATO und WEU. Perspektiven der weiteren Entwicklung', *Österreichische Zeitschrift für Politikwissenschaft*, 25(4): 403–412.

Schmidt, V.A. (2010) 'Taking ideas and discourse seriously: explaining change through discursive institutionalism as the fourth "new institutionalism"', *European Political Science Review*, 2(1): 1–25.

Schmitt, C. (1996 [1932]) *The Concept of the Political*, Chicago, IL: University of Chicago Press.

Schulz, W. (1976) *Die Konstruktion von Realität in den Nachrichtenmedien. Analyse der aktuellen Berichterstattung*, Freiburg im Breisgau: Albert-Ludwigs-Universität.

Schüßler, C. and Heng, Y.-K. (2013) 'The Bundeswehr and the Kunduz air strike 4 September 2009: Germany's post-heroic moment?', *European Security*, 22(3): 355–375.

Searle, J.R. (1978[1969]) *Speech Acts. An Essay in the Philosophy of Language*, Cambridge, MA: Cambridge University Press.

Searle, J.R. (2010) *Making the Social World: The Structure of Human Civilization*, New York: Oxford University Press.

Sedelmeier, U. (2004) 'Collective identity', in W. Carlsnaes, H. Sjursen and B. White (eds), *Contemporary European Foreign Policy*, London: Sage, pp. 123–140.

Semetko, H.A., de Vreese, C.H. and Peter, J. (2000) 'Europeanised politics – Europeanised media? European integration and political communication', *West European Politics*, 23(4): 121–141.

Silber, L. and Little, A. (1997) *Yugoslavia: Death of a Nation*, revised and updated edn, New York: Penguin.

Sjursen, H. (2006) 'The EU as a "normative" power: How can this be?', *Journal of European Public Policy* 13(2): 235–251.

Sjursen, H. (2007) *Enlargement in Perspective. The EU's Quest for Identity*, RECON Online Working Paper 2007/15. Oslo: ARENA, www.reconproject.eu/main.php/RECON_wp_0715.pdf?fileitem=50511940 (accessed 28/01/2015).

Staab, J.F. (1990) 'The role of news factors in news selection: a theoretical reconsideration', *European Journal of Communication*, 5(4): 423–443.

Stahl, B., Boekle, H., Nadoll, J. and Jóhannesdóttir, A. (2004) 'Understanding the Atlanticist-Europeanist divide in the CFSP: comparing Denmark, France, Germany and the Netherlands', *European Foreign Affairs Review*, 9(3): 417–441.

Stahl, B. and Harnisch, S., (eds) (2009) *Vergleichende Außenpolitikforschung und nationale Identitäten. Die Europäische Union im Kosovo-Konflikt 1996–2008*, Baden-Baden: Nomos.

References 181

Stavridis, S. (2001) *Why the "Militarising" of the European Union is Strengthening the Concept of a "Civilian Power Europe"*, EUI Working Paper 17/2001, Florence: European University Institute, Robert Schuman Centre for Advanced Studies, http://cadmus.eui.eu/bitstream/handle/1814/1726/01_17.pdf?sequence=1 (accessed 28/01/2015).

van de Steeg, M. (2000) 'An analysis of the Dutch and Spanish newspaper debates on EU enlargement with Central and Eastern European countries: suggestions for a transnational public sphere', in B. Baerns and J. Raupp (eds), *Information und Kommunikation in Europa*, Berlin: Vistas, pp. 61–87.

van de Steeg, M. (2002a) 'Eine europäische Öffentlichkeit? Die Diskussion um die Osterweiterung der EU', *Berliner Debatte Initial*, 13(5/6): 57–66.

van de Steeg, M. (2002b) 'Rethinking the conditions for a public sphere in the European Union', *European Journal of Social Theory*, 5(4): 499–519.

van de Steeg, M. (2004) *Does a Public Sphere Exist in the EU? An Analysis of the Content of the Debate on the Haider-case*, EUI Working Paper SPS 05, Florence: European University Institute, Department of Political and Social Studies, http://cadmus.eui.eu/bitstream/handle/1814/1910/sps2004-05.pdf?sequence=1 (accessed 28/01/2015).

van de Steeg, M. (2006) 'Does a public sphere exist in the European Union? An analysis of the content of the debate on the Haider case', *European Journal of Political Research*, 45(4): 609–634.

van de Steeg, M., Rauer, V., Rivet, S. and Risse, T. (2003) 'The EU as a political community. a media analysis of the "Haider debate" in the European Union', Annual Meeting of the European Union Studies Association (EUSA), Nashville, TN.

Stichweh, R. (2003) 'The genesis of a global public sphere', *Development*, 46(1): 26–29.

Stråth, B. (ed.) (2000) *Europe and the Other and Europe as the Other*, 3, Brussels: P.I.E.-Peter Lang.

Stråth, B. (2005) 'Methodological and substantive remarks on myth, memory and history in the construction of a European community', *German Law Journal*, 6(2): 255–271.

Stubbs, M. (2001) *Words and Phrases. Corpus Studies of Lexical Semantics*, Oxford: Blackwell.

Stubbs, M. (2003) 'Two quantitative methods of studying phraseology in English', *International Journal of Corpus Linguistics*, 7(2): 215–244.

Taylor, C. (1995) 'Liberal politics and the public sphere', in A. Etzioni (ed.), *New Communitarian Thinking. Persons, Virtues, Institutions, and Communities*, Charlottesville, VA: University Press of Virginia, pp. 183–217.

Thome, H. (2005) *Zeitreihenanalyse. Eine Einführung für Sozialwissenschaftler und Historiker*, München: Oldenbourg.

Tietz, U. (2001) 'Verstehen versus Mißverstehen. Re- und Dekonstruktion des hermeneutischen Negativismus', *Dialektik: Zeitschrift für Kulturphilosophie*, 2/200145–59.

Tietz, U. (2002) *Die Grenzen des 'Wir'. Eine Theorie der Gemeinschaft*, Frankfurt: Suhrkamp.

Tobler, S. (2002) 'Transnationale Kommunikationsverdichtungen im Streit um die internationale Steuerpolitik', *Berliner Debatte Initial*, 13(5/6): 67–78.

Tönnies, F. (2001[1935]) *Community and Civil Society*, Cambridge: Cambridge University Press. (Based on 8th edn 1935; originally published 1887.)

References

Trenz, H.-J. (2004) 'Media coverage on European governance. Exploring the European public sphere in national quality newspapers', *European Journal of Communication*, 19(3): 291–319.

Trenz, H.-J. (2005) *Europa in den Medien. Die europäische Integration im Spiegel nationaler Öffentlichkeit*, Frankfurt: Campus.

Twagilimana, A. (2007) *Historical Dictionary of Rwanda*, new edn, Lanham, MD: Scarecrow Press.

Ullmann, S. (1951) *The Principles of Semantics*, Glasgow: Jackson, Son & Co.

Varwick, J. (2008) *Die NATO. Vom Verteidigungsbündnis zur Weltpolizei?*, München: C.H. Beck.

Vasquez, J.A. (1993) *The War Puzzle*, New York: Columbia University Press.

Vobruba, G. (1999) 'Währungsunion, Sozialpolitik und das Problem einer umverteilungsfesten europäischen Identität', *Leviathan*, 27(1): 78–94.

Volkmer, I. (2003) 'The global network society and the global public sphere', *Development*, 46(1): 9–16.

Wagner, W. (2002) *Die Konstruktion einer europäischen Außenpolitik: Deutsche, französische und britische Ansätze im Vergleich*, Frankfurt: Campus.

Wagner, W. (2003) 'Why the EU's common foreign and security policy will remain intergovernmental: a rationalist institutional choice analysis of European crisis management policy', *Journal of European Public Policy*, 10(4): 576–595.

Wagner, W. (2006) 'The democratic control of military power Europe', *Journal of European Public Policy* 13(2): 200–216.

Wagner, W. (2007) *The Democratic Deficit in the EU's Security and Defense Policy – Why Bother?*, RECON Online Working Paper 2007/10, Oslo: ARENA, www.reconproject.eu/main.php/RECON_wp_0710.pdf?fileitem=50511935 (accessed 28/01/2015).

Wallace, H. (1985) *Europe: The Challenge of Diversity*, London: Royal Institute of International Affairs.

Wallace, W. (2005) 'Foreign and security policy. The painful path from shadow to substance', in H. Wallace, W. Wallace and M.A. Pollack (eds), *Policy-Making in the European Union*, 5th edn, Oxford: Oxford University Press, pp. 429–456.

Walzer, M. (1983) *Spheres of Justice. A Defence of Pluralism and Equality*, Oxford: Martin Robertson.

Walzer, M. (1992[1977]) *Just and Unjust Wars. A Moral Argument with Historical Illustrations*, New York: HarperCollins.

Walzer, M. (1994) *Thick and Thin: Moral Argument at Home and Abroad*, Notre Dame, IN: University of Notre Dame Press.

Weber, M. (1978[1922]) *Economy and Society. An Outline of Interpretive Sociology*, Berkeley, CA: University of California Press.

Wendt, A. (1999) *Social Theory of International Politics*, Cambridge: Cambridge University Press.

Wessels, W. and Jantz, B. (1997) 'Flexibilisierung: Die Europäische Union vor einer neuen Grundsatzdebatte? Grundmodelle unter der Lupe', in R. Hrbek (ed.), *Die Reform der Europäischen Union. Positionen und Perspektiven anläßlich der Regierungskonferenz*, Baden-Baden: Nomos, pp. 345–368.

Wessler, H., Peters, B., Brüggemann, M., Kleinen-von Königslöw, K. and Sifft, S. (2008) 'Together we fight? Europe's debate over the legitimacy of military interventions', in *Transnationalization of Public Spheres*, Basingstoke: Palgrave Macmillan, pp. 95–130.

White, B. (1999) 'The European challenge to foreign policy analysis', *European Journal of International Relations*, 5(1): 37–66.
Whitman, R.G. (1998) *From Civilian Power to Superpower? The International Identity of the European Union*, New York: St Martin's Press.
Whitman, R.G. (ed.) (2011) *Normative Power Europe: Empirical and Theoretical Perspectives*, Basingstoke: Palgrave Macmillan.
Wilson, A. (1993) 'Towards an integration of content analysis and discourse analysis: the automatic linkage of key relations in text', Lancaster: Lancaster University.
Zangl, B. and Zürn, M. (2003) *Frieden und Krieg*, Frankfurt: Suhrkamp.
Zielonka, J. and Mair, P. (2002) 'Introduction: Diversity and adaptation in the enlarged European Union', *West European Politics*, 25(2): 1–18.
Zürn, M. (1998) *Regieren jenseits des Nationalstaates. Globalisierung und Denationalisierung als Chance*, Frankfurt: Suhrkamp.
Zürn, M., Binder, M., Ecker-Ehrhardt, M. and Radtke, K. (2007) 'Politische ordnungsbildung wider willen', *Zeitschrift für Internationale Beziehungen*, 14(1): 129–164.

Index

9/11 11, 53, 97, 120, 148

A Secure Europe in a Better World (*see* European Security Strategy)
Action-oriented community (*see* Commercium)
Additive outlier (*see* Pulse event)
Additivity hypothesis 43, 150
Afghanistan, intervention in 11, 85, 148
Analytic philosophy 28–29
Angolan Civil War 97
Appropriateness, logic of 33
ARIMA model 93–95
Attentive public 60
Austria 40, 44
Automatic character string comparison 64, 70

Balkans (*see* Yugoslavia)
Bosnia 53, 108–110, 140

CNN effect (*see* Media agenda setting)
Collective identity 6, 9, 16–17, 23–25, 28–29, 117; Formation 9; Transnational 10, 22–24
Collective problem-solving 2, 44
Collective sense-making 1–3 14
Collective violence 18–19
Collocation 67, 73, 75–76
Cologne-Declaration 86
Commercium 2, 6, 30, 45–46, 117–119, 134–135
Common Foreign and Security Policy (CFSP) 10–11, 18
Common language 15
Communio 2, 6, 31, 33–34, 44–46, 117–119, 134–135
Communitarianism 14, 24

Community membership 25–29; Hermeneutic dimension 27; Ontological dimension 27
Community of values (*see* Communio)
Concept-ontology (*see* Semantic field)
Corpus-linguistic analysis 70
Counter-public 58–59
Crisis event 18, 43

Democracy; identity as a precondition of 14–16
Discourse 58–59; Elite 58–59; Ethical 6, 32, 44; Pragmatic 6, 44

Elite nations 43–44
Ethical community (*see* Communio)
Ethical convictions 17–18; Thick 24–25
Ethical self-understanding 9, 28, 32
Euro-optimism 15
European foreign policy (*see* Common Foreign and Security Policy (CFSP))
European Security and Defence Policy (ESDP) 13, 17–18
European Security Strategy 53, 125
European strategy, lack thereof 12
European values 16
Euro-pessimism 14
Event 40; Dramatic crisis 43, 150; Institutional 43–44, 100, 133–134
Expert community 13

First Gulf War 52, 99
France; Country Selection 44, 54–55; Results 87, 90, 97, 101–106, 120–140

Germany; Country Selection 44, 54–55; Results 87, 90, 101–107, 120–140
Globalisation 35

Index

Haiti, military coup in 97
Hermeneutic circle 37
Historical experiences (as a source of identity) 14
Human rights 21
Humanitarian military intervention 21–22

Interdependence 148–149
International law 20, 22
Interpretative framing 149
Iraq/Kuwait crisis 85
Ireland; Country Selection 44, 54–55; Results 86, 90–92, 101–107, 120–140
Issue 40; framing thereof 39, 45
Issue attention cycle (*see Issue cycle*)
Issue cycle 40; simultaneity of 85, 99–103, 147–148

Just war theory 20
Jus ad bellum 22
Jus in bello 22

Kosovo crisis 59, 85–86, 99, 110, 123, 132–134, 148

Legitimate governance, collective identity as a precondition for 15
Letter of the Eight 124
Level shift 94
Linguistic sense 29–30, 37

Maastricht Treaty 10–11
Mass media 13, 58; National 40
Media agenda setting 36
Media content analysis 56–57
Media debates 36
Middle East 90, 92, 106–107, 129, 154
Military intervention (*see* Humanitarian military intervention)
Moral dialogue (*see* Discourse, ethical)
Multilateral missions 50, 55, 104

Netherlands, the; Country selection 44, 54–55; Results 87–90, 101–108, 113–141
New Europe 124
News value 41–44, 113, 151
Normative corridor 35, 155
Normative framing 100–101
Normative power 115
Normative-affective community building 16

Old Europe 124
Operation Desert Shield 97
Opération Retour 123, 144
Other, the 129

Peace-keeping (-enforcing), (-making) 47
Perspective; Observer 25; Participant 25, 28
Policy integration 16
Political community 27, 31
Political integration 10–11
Post-problem stage 41
Pre-problem stage 41
Problem perception 30, 83–100
Problem-solving community (*see Commercium*)
Problem-solving debates (*see* Discourse, pragmatic)
Process-generated data 57
Public, strong 48
Public, weak 48
Public sphere 35–36, 39–40
Pulse event (*see Additive outlier*)

Qualitative identity 26–33

Role conflict 24
Rwanda 1, 103, 110, 123, 144, 151

Security community 47
Security identity 55, 83
Semantic field 66–70
Sense-making 14
Sigma-convergence 143
Similarity measure 65
Social constructivism 13, 78
Somalia 1, 87
Srebrenica 1, 99, 108
Supra-nationalisation 39

Time series analysis 92–93
Transatlantic gap 100, 110
Transnational public sphere (*see* Public sphere, transnational)

UCDP/PRIO Armed Conflict Dataset 80
United Kingdom (UK); Country selection 44, 54–55; Results 91–92, 97–98, 101–108, 113–141
United Nations (UN) 11; Security Council 54, 85, 124–125, 142–143
United States of America (USA); Country selection 44, 54–55; Results 88–92, 97–108, 113–141

Universalist community (*see* We$_1$)
Universalist principle 32, 155
Use of force; without UN mandate 86, 88–89, 104–105, 128–129

Value-oriented (*see Communio*)
Vergemeinschaftung 35
Vergesellschaftung 35

we$_1$ 28–30
we$_2$ 30
we$_2$/commercium (*see Commercium*)
we$_2$/communio (*see Communio*)

Yugoslavia 4, 10, 45, 52, 86, 98–99, 123, 140–141